Tragic Humanity and Hope

Tragic Humanity and Hope

*Understanding Our Struggle to
Be Scientific, Sapiential, and Moral*

Pius Ojara, SJ

TRAGIC HUMANITY AND HOPE
Understanding Our Struggle to be Scientific, Sapiential, and Moral

Copyright © 2007 Pius Ojara, SJ. All rights reserved. Except for brief quotations in critical publications or reviews, no part of this book may be reproduced in any manner without prior written permission from the publisher. Write: Permissions, Wipf and Stock, 199 W. 8th Ave., Eugene, OR 97401.

ISBN 13: 978-1-55635-149-5

Manufactured in the U.S.A.

Dedication

I dedicate this work to Caroline Mbonu, HHCJ, James F. Duffy, SJ, Howland T. Sanks, SJ, and Donald L. Gelpi, SJ.

Contents

Preface / ix
Acknowledgements / xvii

1
Pessimism, Nihilism, Optimism, and Hope / 1

2
Hope and Despair in Life / 21

3
The Priority of Mystery over Problem / 43

4
Precincts of the Scientific and the Sapiential in Existence / 105

5
Communion and Transcendence / 143

6
Human Existentiality / 189

7
The Meaning of Commitment / 235

Conclusion / 259
Bibliography / 265
Subject Index / 269

Preface

In our contemporary contexts, scientific knowing is becoming an increasingly dominant form of knowledge. Interests in a wide variety of scientific knowing expand our understanding of the world in performance. It seems as though the leadership, influence, growth and center of gravity of the human existence depend on scientific thinking. As a result of the development of scientific knowing, we live in an information age which prizes production and immediate satisfaction, and devalues the cultivation of wisdom. Noticeably, "emphasis is systematically diverted from the subject as a subject and laid exclusively on a job to be done, a return to be produced, a bill to be paid."[1] In other words, in our contemporary times, we risk diminishing the significance of sapiential knowing in dealing with the immensely complex and intricate domains of human relationality. For, a process of instrumentally dominating existence, which scientific thinking fosters, assents easily to increasing fragmentation and domination of human beings. These existential attenuations easily lead to the vagaries of a manipulative, callous and cruel commodity culture.

Furthermore, inquiry into the methods for moral discernment is increasingly expanding and becoming diverse; yet, scholarly conversations that engage the vital exigencies founding moral sensibility seem conspicuously insufficient. In addition to striving to overcome this lack, this work also seeks to expand narratives and fountains of ethical discourse that exceed the language of pragmatic utility and aesthetic preference. Foundations of morality cannot exclude questions of the common good and shared moral obligations which free people to reach out to one another with hopes and memories that endow life with shared meaning. Through the continuity and cohesion that the interlacing of scientific, sapiential and moral knowing bring, life assumes a beautiful expression of light, joy and fervor. This integral beauty, something which shines forth, is what people palpably aspire towards. Of course, that human existence remains incongruent is something of which we must not lose sight.

---

1. Gabriel Marcel, *The Mystery of Being Vol.II: Faith and Reality* (Lanham: The University Press of America, 1984), 55.

Preface

Gabriel Marcel's thought offers the mainstream or basic thrust of the discussions and perspectives of *Tragic Humanity and Hope*. *Tragic Humanity and Hope* strives to give an honest insight into the practice of effective living in a pluralistic world that, at one and the same time, is able to build and shatter people's lives and expectations. The goal of *Tragic Humanity and Hope* is to offer luminous perspectives on the authority, partnership and interdependence of scientific,[2] sapiential,[3] and moral responses, living and understanding. This is also to say it is important that the plural dimensions of life are guided and lived with an attitude of positive and complementary realizations that energize and enliven people even in the midst of much challenge, complexity and difficulty. It is important that people not caricature what they live and how they live their lives so that they live authentic and open, meaningful and purposeful lives.

The human demand, purpose and striving to be scientific, sapiential and moral particularly typify different trajectories of living. Often enough, we can confuse distinctions. In positive terms, the scientific, sapiential and moral dimensions of life continually fuel people's pride and passion for life, learning and human growth. In this way, scientific, sapiential and moral perspectives on life help people discover, communicate and apply knowledge, truth and freedom in ways that foster and expand life, relationships and the sense of purpose. Understanding and appropriately

---

2. The scientific refers to being methodic, systematic, exact, verifiable and specialized. In this regard, we can speak of the positive and human sciences.

3. Sapiential in this work refers to being characterized by understanding, discernment and consciousness of goodness, value, harmony, fraternity and unity. In short, sapiential refers to being characterized by wisdom that expands people's perceptions of themselves, others and the world. And wisdom implies good judgments about what is true, right, creative, sensible or insightful in human existence. At the heart of wisdom, then, lies the preservation of life, promotion of peaceful and fruitful relationships and coping with life's demands meaningfully. In enabling people to live well together wisdom helps them to recognize what fosters the good life and to develop their abilities to cultivate prudently their humanity. An added *proviso* here is that wisdom is internally resonant, multi-layered, wholesome and, ultimately, simple and unitive. Wisdom draws persons and human relations into the value of humanity; wisdom attracts, corrects and elevates humanity. Because wisdom is about right and living relationships among people, it has both moral and aesthetic dimensions to it. Wisdom initiates, instructs and exercises a fascinating grip on the human sense of care and virtuous living. As cultivated yet never fully possessed, wisdom points toward the gift, task and responsibility which involve the entire orientations of individuals and communities in existence. In this sense, the social settings of wisdom include households, villages, neighborhoods, growth points, trading centers, workplaces, marketplaces, towns, cities, tribes, regions and religious communities and institutions. In the end, the sapiential imagination liberates and re-creates concrete situations and realities of life. It directs daily human experiences of needs, work, speech, basics of life and relationships to wholesomeness.

linking these important dimensions of life provide tremendous awareness and opportunities that support liberative[4] existence. What is more, human life and relations consistent with or vectored towards pluralistic wholeness leaven, enlighten and catalyze the human sense of availability and freshness. In the negotiations and incorporation of these perspectives and dimensions of life, the singularity of the human subject and the tensions and demands of human relations direct and evolve in existence.

In its task, *Tragic Humanity and Hope* illuminates and serves three goals. First, it seeks to discern the nature of scientific, sapiential and moral demands or exigencies within the drama of ambivalent life, illuminating indwelling tensions and dynamics and articulating a liberative understanding of the *élan* that marks the different forms of human striving. The conviction is that expanding such awareness enables people to redefine and understand their lives according to different circumstances. Of course, diverse nuances and subtleties typify how people live in different and several respects. Further, the strivings of scientific, sapiential and moral life ground themselves in the intrinsic significance of life and human relations. In this sense, this work grants that people bear greatness and significance within themselves and in their living ties with one another.

Also, a rightful claim of *Tragic Humanity and Hope* is that fundamental attitudes, moral character, norms, particularities of situations and appeals to human experience and demands of existence touch on values by which people live, the kinds of persons they strive to become and their perceptions of the world around them. Yet, people always live life with and for others. In order that interpersonal relationships and questions of meaning may be truly liberating, they need depth to them. The pragmatic dimensions of human life always require solid grounding. Unless people have depth in their lives and their relationships, they cannot have depth in their scientific, sapiential and moral living and understanding. Individuating the reality and sense of depth in different sets of circumstances will always call for clarity or bring forth fresh thought for vivacious, free and personal lives. What is more, experience and existence do not interpret themselves; they require insight into the contexts and imaginations of particular cultures. A community interprets, inhabits and expresses different trajectories of understanding and a vision of the full life.

---

4. When experiences or events, actions or behaviors, understanding and life are liberative it means that they unburden and lighten, honor and exalt, refresh and restore, enliven and energize, and enhance and expand the humanity of persons, individually, relationally and communally.

Preface

Subsequently, *Tragic Humanity and Hope* seeks to inspire, nurture and enable people to continually re-constitute contexts and a sense of human togetherness that act as, lift up and identify liberative ways of living in this exigently pluralistic world. Knowing how to live in freeing ways presupposes knowing life's dimensions and their demands, clarifying values and their sources, and honoring rights and responsibilities that ought to be recognized in personal, cooperative and collaborative living. All these begin with a deep respect and sensitivity to the unconditional worth and lovableness of persons and the diversity of people, personal lives and human relationships.

In speaking about particular sciences, *Tragic Humanity and Hope* makes the point that scientific experiences need to exist always in dialogue with the lifeworld, together with its compelling and passionate anguish and hopes. The lifeworld is the cultural and contextual world of lived, dynamic and flexible experience. The scientific and lifeworld need the moral and sapiential life in order to sustain human kinship, enlivenment and the sense of life's plenitude. The interconnection between the scientific, sapiential and moral world can be intellectual, emotional, cultural or physical. In addition, these interconnections need to be lived in a spirit that encourages and fosters human openness, growth in positive respect and inviting communication among people of different persuasions or ideologies.

What is more, questions of freedom, evil and commitment remain pertinent in scientific, sapiential and moral life. In this regard, this life always remains deeply ambivalent. We participate in human greatness and misery, creative and destructive works as well as in love and in struggle. Yet, it is with hope that the process of living can continue to go on within an ambivalent existence with focus, steadfastness, serenity and openness. Ambivalence of existence implies that the meanings of personal and shared experiences will always fall under different aspects of life's demands. These demands always call for some clarifying through active communication, conversations, affective listening, sharing, insight and interpretation. These species of human connections work well when situated within the contexts of life-fostering understanding of human exigencies, reconciliation and expansive freedom, of which communion and transcendence become unmistakable manifestations or expressions. Pursuit of human flourishing and liberative welfare of human togetherness affect the making and carrying out of practical judgments scientifically, sapientially and morally. In the end, living this life well requires an ongoing re-imagination and a continual relevant interpretation and redefinition of issues according to insight, circumstance, time and place.

Preface

Since life is lived as a unity, not excepting the multiplicity of its aspects, there exists the human need and demand to correlate and integrate the scientific, sapiential and moral exigencies or dimensions of living. Creating awareness and understanding of these human demands, as this work does, helps foster human appreciation of the complementarities of different aspects of life. In the absence of such appraisal, people may face conceptual and pragmatic difficulties and fail to work out their life's itinerary in coherent and liberative ways. And as they fail to balance their lives people may also become self-preoccupied, which preoccupation will not enable them to experience and appropriate their sense of intrinsic worth as persons. The consequence is that life itself may become overwhelmed by confusion, frustration, anger and disenchantment. All these difficult experiences can blind people to the living resonances of their scientific, sapiential and moral life. There is a broad spectrum of perceptions and beliefs about what it means to be a human being, each of which will always bring its emotional tides, storms, riptides and delights, peace and joy which motivate or influence people.

People are more than titles on their doors, the empirical conditions of their bodies, the money or wealth that they have, or the kind of house or neighborhood in which they live. These extrinsic realities do not ultimately resolve the issue of who people deeply are with all their unexpressed gifts and blessings as well as unconfessed mistakes and liabilities. In fact, many people live or rather struggle with distorted self-images and self-perceptions that tend to lead to self-doubt and low self-regard which they may try to anesthetize or sanitize or deny altogether. In short, gnawing anxiety besets the lives of many people.

Gnawing anxiety manifests itself in the experience of deconstitution; it consists in the felt awareness and discovery that one's existence has no secure foundation or answer to it. Such anxiety reveals a lack of personal grounding in a given context of life. In this sense, it participates in the experience of groundlessness. The search inherent in the experience of anxiety calls for an explanation of one's very being and freedom. Paradoxically, anxiety discloses people's own capacities and longings for aliveness that come with the disclosure of the value of persons and kinship ties. When this disclosure comes about, it urges people to find the living root and center that change and pacify their consciousnesses.

People can always become vivacious agents or vortices of hope. This further implies that people can always redefine themselves from the perspectives of dignity and responsibility, resourcefulness and fair resolution of tensions, expansive freedom and joy. The preceding affirmations also mean that hope nourishes positive self-respect, sensitivity and affection that replenish the common life and liberating existence.

People long for more than roles and jobs in their lives, as these can easily mark them with frustrations and misunderstanding, miscommunication and bumps or diversions in facing life's real challenges. Affirmative and appreciative identities and ontologies from occupations and accomplishments are important but they are not enough. People need a liberative and affirming relationships and the sense of purpose and meaning that embalm them emotionally, vivify them spiritually and nourish them imaginatively.

In many respects, responsible human existence is a highly differentiated and yet also interdependent reality woven into the sense and worth of individual and relational wellbeing. In existence, a conjunction of scientific, sapiential and moral approaches to life remain vital, as together they seek intelligibility and fullness of experience in its multiple aspects. Of course, it must also be added that human beings can be impetuously self-centered and selfish. People can self-referentially mold the world and imagination. Such a life is, at best, tenuous and, at worst, tragic.

Of course, the intuition of being is at the heart of a liberative experience of wholesomeness that connects science, wisdom and morality with freedom, joy and, ultimately, plenitude. Yet, human participation in being is never exhausted. It is never-ending. It remains a startlingly new and an ever-deepening experience.

As it happens, human beings' pre-linguistic abilities, dispositions, desires and beliefs as well as their abilities to reflect upon their existential experiences, practices and possibilities inform personal choices. The choices people make influence the experience of human kinship and common wellbeing. Within the plural dimensions of life's strivings, the differentiation of the scientific, sapiential and moral takes place. When cultivated and nurtured with insight, this differentiation shapes families, customs and common life according to beliefs and interpretation of existence. The full scope of human cognitive and affective heritages influences the way people act scientifically, sapientially or morally. As people recognize, come to terms with and reflect on the demands of their lives, they also appropriate the insights of scientific, sapiential and moral understandings, insights and interpretations.

The integration of scientific, sapiential and moral perspectives of understanding roots and fosters a healthy sense of human heritage. While scientific exigencies are fundamentally concerned with the problematic character of the world, sapiential considerations and demands relate to the sense of human kinship, responsible care and compassion. The medium of sapiential consideration is positive presence. On the other hand, moral exigency touches on the intrinsic desirability, attractiveness and lovableness of people that instruct, comfort, relieve and nestle with people's conduct. Subsequently, the exercise of living communication and care become vital for the interdependence of the scientific, sapiential and moral impulses in existence. While the scientific aspect of life is rooted in problems, the sapiential internalizes and reflects on personal responsibility for human kinship through the prism of positive presence. The moral aspect of life evaluates the concrete expressions of people's sense of intrinsic significance and plenitude as experienced and expressed in conduct.

Scientific, sapiential and moral insights expand through engagement with concrete experiences. Particular experiences help develop the human shades and capacities of perception, discretion and judgments. In fostering and cultivating dialectical, local or topical reflection particular scientific, sapiential and moral cases come to offer models or frameworks from which people can understand existence analogically. After all, to reason is to intuit some reality, to abstract and conceptualize it and to be able to assume responsibility for one's own understanding and anticipated or probable actions. In this light, it is through particular engagement with concrete experiences that people identify, clarify and hone tangible skills and concrete dispositions. These aptitudes and capacities enhance people's interpretations, communication, self-expressions and practices of concrete living.

Coming to grips with particular cultural and contextual experiences constitute the theater, crucible and fount, which concretize and hone scientific, sapiential and moral credibility, legitimacy and authority. Only within the perspective of this outlook and approach do human efforts truly revitalize, renew, develop and serve the course of human harmony and become forward-looking. In other words, the liberative goals of scientific, sapiential and moral exigencies are best achieved through the honest dialectical and historical coordination of interests, needs and demands. Further, the different languages and viewpoints about life distinguish scientific, sapiential and moral approaches to reality.

Last but not least, an assumption that pervades this work is the experience of human inter-communication as rooted in a felt unity and commonalities of the human race even amidst diverse cultural experiences.

Acknowledgements

IN THIS work, I would like to thank my friends to whom I have dedicated this book. You have all been a supportive and illuminating presence to me. I also thank my Jesuit Province of Eastern Africa, AOR, which always supported me through the Provincial, Fr Valerian Shirima, SJ, and the Delegate for formation, Fr Gaspar Sunhwa, SJ.

I am grateful to Patrick and Maureen Doherty for their personal friendship and honest belief in me. Their financial support facilitated the publication of this book.

I also would like to thank Fr Stephen Msele, SJ. My encounter with him was very instrumental in sharpening my thoughts in important respects. Fr Stephen, my encounter with you particularly renewed and refined my understanding and appreciation of the divine mystery that always remain contemporaneous with us and vice-versa. I also would like to particularly thank Mr. Omada S. Esibo, SJ, for a fruitful time that I had with him regarding the question of commitment. The result of that encounter plays out particularly in the last chapter.

I am also personally thankful to my friends Marie Thomas, Amanda Stempson, Erin Palermo, Bobbi Dykema, Debra Paullin, Sean Dempsey, SJ, and Donald L. Gelpi, SJ, for reading through parts of this manuscript and drawing my attention to details which I would have missed.

I must also thank my professors, Howland T. Sanks, SJ, William O'Neill, SJ, and Prof. Alejandro Garcia-Rivera whose thinking and perspectives have flavored my articulation of the various topics in this work. The scholarly environment at the Jesuit School of Theology has been very conducive to my scholarly enterprise, I must add.

My thanks go to the students and faculty members at the Jesuit School of Theology at Berkeley as well as the students at the University of California at Berkeley that I worked with at SEEKERS at Newman Hall, Holy Spirit Catholic Church, in Berkeley. My encounters with you over the last three years have been inspiring, enlightening and stimulating. Thank you all for positive and questioning presence. Of course, I must add that I have met many people who have shaped my thinking, experiences and attitudes that have crystallized in the pages of this book. I am heartily

Acknowledgements

grateful to all with whom I had meaningful encounters that have molded me in small yet real significant ways. You are simply too many to name individually. Thank you for enriching my life so much. Blessings and peace!

1

Pessimism, Nihilism, Optimism, and Hope

Preamble

THERE EXISTS no community or society apart from culture with its many disparate and incomparable claims and interests that present themselves to feelings, imagination and visions of prestige and wellbeing. Within this context, each human being is born and initiated in a particular cultural and historical milieu where courses of human conduct tend to happen in fairly established patterns or trajectories in light of some organic vision of life. We grow up as members of some historic ethnic grouping with associated loyalties based on common background and interactions.

The basis of human sociality is normally constituted by language, beliefs, heritages, expectations and control, neighborhood and village or nation. Regulating assumptions, meanings, customs, constraints, codes of behavior, social heritage and human imagination mark common life. Just as a person is born into a family on which he or she depends absolutely for life, sustenance, protection and promotion, so one's understanding develops in community in terms of relations to other persons and habits. Community and society not only bring forth the human personality and character, they also maintain them and, at times, decree their forms of death. As we grow up and live in a rich context of locally inherited wisdom and the self-image of humanity we appropriate, transmute and transmit the values, judgments and attitudes of our environing community. Communal expression and self-understanding connect and shape horizons of individual and shared human consciousness, work patterns, living conditions, self-expressions and social organizations.

Social life coincides with cultural life. Culture and social life hang together: They realize and evidence purposeful human efforts. As we experience, explore, communicate, receive and transmit values in specific social situations, we come to the recognition that the human reality, at the deepest level, consists of a "we" attuned in the quest for concrete forms, rhythms, meanings and symbols of the good, aesthetic satisfaction and social harmony. The sense of a "we" maintains and advances human life and human wellbeing. And in so being, the "we" also embodies some experience and expressions of implicit human choices, questioning, renewal, transcendence and freedom. Where we live, the way we live and work shapes our sensibility and symbolisms which, in turn, define how we think, feel and picture possibilities within the world. In other words, the historical and cultural contexts of our existence lead to a series of surprises and awakenings in terms of assumptions, values and lifestyles. They also shape our sense of identity, expectations, words, modes of meaning and perception, practices, beliefs and typical ways of interpreting our lives and existence.

The human social reality consists of people in constant interrelationship with one another. Of course, it must be borne in mind that this reality includes denials and affirmations, reconstructions and compromises, advantages and distinctions. In the quest to live a coherent life, people usually enter into the rapport of encounter, compassion, freedom and interactions with others through layers of significance that restructure human consciousness in ongoing ways. People also enter into the rapport of disharmony, disconnection, conflict, distrust, aversion and distance. Human experience reveals itself as deeply ambiguous. Accordingly, the human social reality discloses positive and negative dimensions, not always in balance, that provoke some basic human responses, of one kind or another, from every human being. Accordingly, it is appropriate to consider case examples of each dimension.

The Positive Dimensions of the Human Social Reality

Here, positive means whatever may be genuinely regarded as an expression of the experience of goodness, beauty and truth, or a realization of the ideals of justice, liberty, equality and true human kinship. These experiences are rooted in an appreciation and respect for our human dignity in ways that free human energies for constructive relations and purposes. Cases of prudence, fortitude and temperance which have strong personal overtones express some such experiences.

As we grow and live with others, we discover the positive side of life, which may seek to combine peace with prosperity, justice with order, welfare with freedom and practical wisdom with scientific life. Many people are instruments of peace and do offer friendships and understanding and seek reconciliation with others from whom they have been estranged. Some even live with others in communities based on these criteria and visions. Cases in point are: the *L'arche* community for the mentally handicapped in Waterfalls, Harare; the Mother of Peace home at Mutemwa in Mutoko for AIDS (Acquired Immune Deficiency Syndrome) orphans and children infected with HIV (Human Immunodeficiency Virus), the virus that causes AIDS; and the Mutemwa home for lepers, also in Mutoko. All these places are found in Zimbabwe and are functioning well. The people who administer these places do so on a, basically, voluntary basis. In socialization, it does happen that we frequently know, choose and realize what can truly be conducive to not only our personal well-being but also that of others.

Experiences of love beautify many people's lives. In the concrete, love consists in transcending oneself or surpassing self-concern and extending the self to share with others about whom one cares or whom one serves. In the act of love one tends to identify new purposes and goals for oneself and others for whose sake one makes choices. Living in a variety of situations love can be very enriching. For example, every now and then, we experience and discover in our lives and that of others that when people link their sense of duty with love they breed consistency and effective work. We see that people who couple their sense of responsibility with love build a spirit of concern and patience for the less gifted. It is not uncommon that we know that friendly and loving people in our lives elicit responses of good will and understanding. We do speak of people in authority who exercise their power with love, thereby generating a sense of loyalty, trust and appreciation from us. Further, we see that people who integrate honor with love expand the human sense of graciousness and admiration. In these case examples, we see people living in ways that foster the experience of genuineness, warm-heartedness and liberating existence. Often encounters with positive experiences promote human cooperation and inspire people with a sense of meaning and enlivening life-directions. Even in a world dominated by the capitalist market, we know of generous people who give of their time, resources and themselves to help others.

Furthermore, advances in human communication and transportation, experimental sciences, human medicine and material prosperity can make the human social reality quite promising and invest it with an enduring sense of promise and value. As a result of these material developments, human contacts have been made easier, some diseases are easy to treat, clothing is cheaper to buy and convenient means of transportation are made more accessible than ever before. On the whole, however, we also have to admit that human beings have not been brought closer nor their relations strengthened or enhanced by technological achievements that at times remind us more of our distance from one another, of our division and discord than anything else. In addition, technological achievements have also been sources of manipulation, trivialization, consumerism, permissiveness and commercial superficiality divorced from living relationships among people. This is also to say, sometimes technological advancement has made its darker possibilities felt in palpable ways. Technological developments have not always been put at the service of human values like truth and respect, freedom and love. Sometimes, even the esteem, dignity and fundamental rights of people are violated through the abuse of technological advantage or tools. This is not to deny that there are many people who encourage and live in noble ways because of technological refinement.

The Negative Dimensions of the Human Social Reality

The human social reality is also characterized by precarious and negative, divisive and degrading experiences. Again and again we experience, sometimes from people who endow our lives with positive experiences and at other times from others who do not, weariness and unconcern, rigidity and defiance, rifts and ugly pettiness, dogmatism and violence, arrogance and greed, bigotry and fanaticism. Conditions that facilitate these negative aspects may include a social environment where illiteracy is coupled with rashness; or war situations in which people are displaced or forced to hack their parents and relatives to death; or a political set up in which blackmail and intimidation are used to create, win and retain coercive power; or a sociopolitical set up where preferential treatment of a minority section of a society makes the majority wallow in misery or vice versa.

There are many people who find self-acceptance a colossal difficulty. Such persons can neither speak with authority nor act with confidence, a sense of dignity and worth. Modesty and deference tend to mark such people's efforts to accommodate themselves to others' feelings, sense of superiority or wellbeing. Examples could be the slow-learner in a class or the "black sheep" of the family whose ideas or contributions, because of his or her special situation, are repeatedly rejected and looked down upon. Such a person easily ends up with a broken self-image because he or she has not been appreciated, valued, welcomed or loved very much. Such a person fails to be himself or herself as he or she imitates or wants to be like others. In such a circumstance, a person does not wake up to and appreciate his or her own value and goodness. Self-acceptance becomes a serious difficulty. Here and there, we encounter the burning of witches, a thug hopelessly lynched, a drug addict in need of a job or home, a single parent family in which the bread-winner is crippled by a terminal illness, a man or woman out of prison in search of a job, a child or an immigrant on the run. Also, we repeatedly meet the school drop-outs and deviants and the socially displaced that have become prostitutes or criminals. There are so many families in which not only material misery and filth humiliate, wound and batter the members, but also in which children and women suffer abuse and beating.

In political life, for instance, the police, army and customs' checkpoints have been known to arrest petty offenders and treat them severely. Treatment of the offenders may imply sadistic beating which they might not survive with life or limb intact. Ironically, these same authorities would bow and defer to the spouses and friends of political heavy-weights, who seem immune to scrutiny or regular procedures. Indeed, contexts that breed fear and contempt adversely affect the possibilities and opportunities for harmonious relations among people. Still, in wars, there are frequent cases of half-starved teenaged soldiers. In the struggle to eke out a living it is commonly the fittest, which often means the greediest and the most powerful, who survive and prosper. The culture of greed, indulgence and complacency peppers and entrenches a value system based on personal satisfaction and acquisition of wealth by all means and at all costs. The accumulated effect of greed and selfishness burdens, constrains, fragments and shatters people's shared perspectives and hope for a better life of care, joy, and peace.

Moreover, in the medical sphere, not all is rosy. Good affordable medical treatment is beyond the reach of many people. In many countries and places, nurses may have to be bribed in hospitals to administer treatment to a patient prescribed by the doctor, who himself or herself may as well have been bribed before examining the patient. Many patients are not only condemned to long hours of waiting but also negligent care if they do not grease the palms of the doctors and nurses. Already, in the educational sphere, many schools in different places lack very basic equipment and good professional teachers. The cost of running schools is not only soaring astronomically but even adequate food supply is becoming difficult to obtain for an increasing number of school children. Besides, in many schools discipline is breaking down and discontent with the profession of teaching is becoming widespread. Further, it is not uncommon in many places that schools seem improperly planned, overcrowded, under-staffed, under-resourced or neglected.

Even as the world becomes increasingly interdependent, rural hunger and poverty, disease and ignorance still hold many people hostage. Illegal immigration, cross border crimes, outbreaks of pandemics such as

HIV/AIDS and bird-flue are not uncommon. There is growth in financial crimes driven by greed. Besides, sophisticated and blatant human rights abuses, killings and tortures are increasingly being committed out of blind pursuit of resources, profit and dominating power. Politics remains less than transparent while many governments are largely inefficient and regrettably, sometimes, corrupt.

The negative experiences within the human social reality can make one wonder what life holds for many people living in the depths of insecurity and anxiety, squalor and fear. The very prospect of human dignity, in fact, seems lost to many as life itself assumes a negligible value.

The Ambiguity of Life

Ambiguity characterizes human life and experience. This ambiguity points to the stark beauty and refreshing skepticism which coexist with haunting imagery and preoccupation with death. Our lively and colorful life has ambivalence about it. Life contains sources of unity, solidarity, healing and wholeness. It also contains sources of separation, conflict, division and violence. Unsettling aspects of everyday life evoke a sense of human precariousness, vulnerability, helplessness and uncertainty. That is also to say, a moral hero today, for instance, can become a victim of extortion and deceit from his supporters or yield to a bribery of some sort tomorrow. Besides, bewilderment and confusion can unsettle human endeavors. Of course, an initial impression about a person's life can belie a dense, complex and multi-layered existence filled with joys and sorrows. The ambivalence of life challenges any air of certainty or self-assurance one may have about existence.

Paradoxically, an unquenchable thirst for life points to a staggering presupposition of a drama that accompanies our lives. As a result, bleak dismal experiences that pull or yank us out of comfortable and stagnant lives can reveal our deep longing for the unity of human life. When we cut through the façade of shallow and perverted life, we can discover that it truly belies the sense that life is ultimately fake or absurd.

Without doubt, the social human reality reveals itself as profoundly uncertain with successes and failures, struggle and appeasement, joys and disappointments, fortune and misfortune, weal and woe, victory and reconciliation. Further, the human social reality may be marked with sense and nonsense, doubts and anxieties, beauty and ugliness. One could also add to these the understanding of right and wrong, good and evil, presence and absence, character and fate, kindliness and anger, virtues and vices.

Life is profoundly characterized by a mixture of difficulties and potentialities, negative experiences and experiences of promises, obstacles and alternatives, viciousness and big-heartedness, revenge and forgiveness.

Life brings with it lights and shadows, success and limitations. This ambivalence calls forth an interpretative reading of the world in order to distinguish the varying elements in it. At the same time, it is important that elements of experiences do not become overly isolated and contradictory to one another by making them absolutes and at odds with one another. In fact, what lie hidden in various kinds of experiences are demands for authentic values like truth, freedom and justice. As we struggle with uncertainty we also long for liberation, harmony and order and the voyage of life.

In our apparently interdependent world, then, there is the "scarcity paradox" according to which there is an unprecedented abundance coexisting with unparalleled dearth; the "poverty paradox" according to which tremendous affluence coexists with frightful poverty; the "care paradox" according to which extensive availability of medical resources and expertise exist side by side with deteriorating care for the environment and the health of the human majority; and there is the "labor paradox" in which increased need for workers coexists with prevalent unemployment. In the last analysis, the human social reality is no more an idyll and good will than it is a confusion or dangerous savagery.

The ambivalence of human life provides the starting points for different attitudes towards human existence. The selective picture of life that people draw for themselves and others means that they do not sing the same tune towards life. Different people confront the deep riddles or ambiguity of life differently. The ambiguous and multivalent life provokes different responses in people since it can overturn expectations and upset accepted attitudes and notions of existence. From life's discordance arise four basic free human responses as overriding stances to the positive and negative experiences of human social reality. In each response, the human being always remains free in the sense of self-definition and self-determination within the limits of innate disposition and the set of circumstances in which he or she lives or acts in existence. These responses to the ambivalent human social reality are pessimism, nihilism, optimism and hope.

The Case of Pessimism

Pessimism is the basic attitude to the human social reality in which the negative experiences are considered dominant over the positive ones. Mortality controls, limits and diminishes life with a negative vision. Besides, life loses all fascinating sense of mystery. For the pessimist, the world is ordered for the worst; essentially the world is considered to be evil and shall remain so despite human efforts.[1] Gloom, grief, pain, and death constitute the basic and enduring components of life. Pessimism arises from the reality of so much horror, injustice and scorn or pain that people suffer. Worth noting is the fact that the metaphysical origins of pessimism coincide with the basis of non-disposability or unavailability.[2] In this regard, it may be set forth that obsession with having or possessing or ownership itself is a sort of signpost of possible non-disposability. Indeed, a dead person becomes one who no longer has anything.[3] It is human openness and availability which constitute the thrust and spark that rekindle and lift up human dignity and human living ties.

A pessimist like Eduard Von Hartmann,[4] for example, maintains that "this is the best possible world; yet evil necessarily outweighs good in it, and it would be better if there were no world at all."[5] He is convinced of the finiteness and ultimate failure of all the values of human life, particularly the ethical, religious and aesthetic values. Furthermore, he maintains that most pleasure is merely the negative kind that results from the cessation of positive unpleasantness; and so, cannot equal in any way the unpleasantness it terminates. He also contends that history shows that the overbalance of suffering increases proportionately with every advancement human beings make.[6] Within this framework, the human social reality provides more pain than pleasure, more sorrow than joy, more dissatisfaction than satisfaction, more destruction than conservation of life, more decay than progress of cultural and political institutions, more experiences of bondage than human freedom. But even in modern liberal democracy scores of churches, religious institutions and charitable organizations like the International Committee of the Red Cross continue to deliver and proclaim the values of respect for life, sharing and solidarity with the needy, equality in moral and legal standing of every human being and

---

1. Peter A. Angeles, *The Harper Collins Dictionary of Philosophy* (London: HarperPerenial, 1992), 225.

2. Gabriel Marcel, *Being and Having: An Existentialist Diary* (New York: Harper and Row Publishers, Inc., 1965), 73.

3. Ibid., 84.

4. L. E. Loemker, "Pessimism and Optimism," in *Encyclopedia of Philosophy*, Vol.6 (1967), 118.

5. Ibid., 114.

6. Ibid., 119.

tolerance of the differences in belief systems. There are individuals and institutes, like the Graduate Theological Union, in Berkeley, California, that strive to promote sensitivity and a caring attitude that pays due regard to the rights and well-being of others. In the light of these experiences, it is notable that pessimism does not honor the wholeness and complexity of the human social experience.

As a result, pessimism disparages human efforts and the liberating significance of human connections and companionship. After all, the world abounds in oppression and inexplicable suffering. Anything we do does not have a lasting positive value. Life is transitory and wearisome. Indeed, when jaded and surfeited by negative experiences, we can lose the capacity for surprise and wonder. In other words, life experiences can generate so much skepticism in us that we can truly wonder if anything of meaning, value and lasting significance really exists.

It always remains the case that within the framework of pessimism many sad situations make the overall balance of good in the human social reality negative. Out of deep wounds of rejection or hatred, a person may come to see no value in striving to be creative and affirmative. Of course, pessimists are right to acknowledge the vicious course of life and the fact of violence and murder, hatred and resentment or experiences of pain and superficiality, pretentiousness and egoism in the human social reality. Sure, it is important to take account of the tragic element in human existence, particularly so in a world fraught with instances or cases of injustice, levity, brutality, suffering and death. The slightest intellectual probity demands that we face squarely these facts, even if it takes more courage to do so than to indulge in the illusion of destiny or fantasy.

The pessimist, however, goes too far to maintain that negative experiences are dominant in the human experience as a whole. The pessimist is merely partial in his or her appreciation of the human social reality. Can we simply maintain that the positive experiences of friendliness and benevolence, celebrations and excitements, esteem and affection, forgiveness and respect are outweighed by the negative ones? Perhaps, the critical problem with the pessimist lies in the narrative construction the pessimist gets into as he or she perceives and interprets his or her own experiences. But the contrary experience of others that in turn molds their narrative constructions cannot simply be dismissed or ignored. These experiences cannot be discounted in appraising the human reality in its multiplicity of aspects. Herein, too, lies the inability of pessimism to explain the tragic sense of human life. The rich complexity of human experiences needs to be taken into account, for this richness calls attention to the continuity and significance of the great motifs that appear and shape existence. Putting focus and emphasis mainly on limitations, shortcomings and the negativities of human existence tends to misdefine and distort the ambivalent unity, mosaic picture and complexus of lived experience. While pessimism takes seriously the issue of bodily and mental pain and suffering in its appraisal of human existence, it must also be pointed out that pessimism remains inadequate. In fact, pessimistic judgment itself presupposes attitudes of responsible engagement of human suffering. Mundane existence constantly makes use of difficult and painful contexts of life.

The Case of Nihilism

Nihilism is an extreme form of pessimism best represented by Nietzsche. According to Nietzsche, nihilism denotes the meaninglessness of existence and the tawdriness of all values that persons and society esteem. Nihilism asserts the basic nullity, inherent contradiction, futility and worthlessness of all reality. In this light, Nietzsche contends that "underneath all becoming there is no grand unity; any comprehensive unity in the plurality of events is lacking."[7] Still, the overall character of existence cannot be interpreted by the notion of truth nor, ultimately, may the comprehensive character of being be interpreted by means of the notion of purpose or the exigency of the full life, which symbolizes and reveals the vital nexus of positive relations, deliverance and reconciliation.

In this contemporary time, it might be contended that Nietzsche articulates the interpretative logic of narcissistic individualism and neo-liberal thinking which atomize the human subject and understand freedom merely in terms of radical individual autonomy. Yet even the subjective individualism of the neo-liberal morality is informed by the sense of truth and some sense of objective goodness. But who says that neo-liberal thinking is the measure of an orderly social life for all people? The limitations of neo-liberal thinking paradoxically authenticate the need for a greater experience of intentional sociality and expansive human freedom. After all, to undermine is not to delete or cancel altogether.

According to the viewpoint of nihilism, the overall atmosphere of life evokes a sense of decay, collapse and ruin. Haunting devastation, suffering and death cancel all achievements and the results of any human endeavors or any sense in life. Attainments of life do not truly fulfill. Nothing ever satisfies us ultimately. We are condemned to frustrating experiences which offer no fulfillment. Immediate gain and positive advantage offer no per-

7. Ibid.

manent value. As human toil becomes meaningless, life becomes hateful because its fruits do not last. Basic powerlessness and contradiction of existence trap us. We remain caught in a circle of limitation and destined for incompleteness. The futility of life and the emptiness of human labor only confront us with despair.

Enthusiasm, pleasure and enjoyment of life yield no enduring satisfaction. They only turn out to be concessions to the circumstances of life. They only disclose, in the end, the futility of experiences. The grim perspective of death always haunts us. Death has the final and annihilating power which casts a threatening shadow over all human life. Despair and death negate all. Futility and arbitrariness lurk in the background of life. We cannot access the meaning of life. Emptiness diminishes and destroys all human effort. Frustrations and waste make up our pointless destiny. Ultimately, nihilistic nullity implies the destruction of the structure of being.

In any case, for nihilism, "everything is meaningless. The world is being swept along by a storm which nobody controls, simply because there is nobody who could control it."[8] Unreasoning chance, unyielding anarchic necessity forms the basic elements of the world's foundations.[9] Nihilism negates all positive appreciation of the human social reality. The menacing realities of the breakdown of cooperation and compassion and realities of human dividedness and decay assume supremacy so that the human social reality appears void, aimless and counterfeit. In this sense, the human social milieu becomes a placeholder of waste, collapse, nullity and faithlessness. Values and ideals have significance only from the perspectives of utility. Experiences of harmony and union can be only fleeting because they eventually dissolve themselves in abiding disorder and contradictions. Within this perspective, Nietzsche, for example, says, "every Greek statue can teach us that the beautiful is only a negation."[10] Nihilism declares the dogma that vacuity prevails ultimately in the world. Yet might not such a statement in itself imply a meaning? Additionally, for nihilism time becomes a sum of discontinuous moments which must be endured here and now. No goal or sense of significance or purpose endures in time. The human being cannot escape the creeping process of disintegration and dissolution in time. In effect, all appeals to reason and conscience lose their meaning.[11]

---

8. Helmut Thielicke, *Nihilism: Its Origin and Nature—with a Christian Answer* (New York: Schoken Books, 1969), 30.

9. Ibid.

10. Ibid., 127.

11. Ibid.

The nihilist always keeps his or her vision open to the nothingness that chips away at the realm of goals. The nihilistic lawyer, for instance, may defend the falsely accused but he or she has no reason why he or she does so. He or she may know the reason but he or she detests it because ultimately it is futile. With the accused in the dock, the nihilist lawyer exercises a breed of double standards. He or she does not harp on the nihilistic hopelessness of the world to which he or she defends the accused so as not to paralyze the accused's will to find joy in living. The nihilist may talk of restoring interests and joy in his or her own task, although he or she deems that all work is ultimately useless and meaningless. The nihilist lawyer may indicate to the accused that the accused is being defended for the sake of his or her family, though it would be in keeping with the nihilist's attitude to reprimand the accused for having a family.

Now, how can it be meaningful to appreciate individual steps if the whole of the human reality is absurd? If the human social reality or human existence were *a priori* absurd, the nihilist would not need to deny it or keep on denying it. Indeed, one is freed from nihilistic despair whenever one is faced with a genuine human task, responsibility or relationship that engages one's loyalty, attention and enduring sense of significance. The constant quest for meaning in life frees many men and women from triviality and fleetingness. People fulfill this quest when they find some task that engages their efforts, fidelity and the sense of meaning.[12] Nihilism, however, refuses to acknowledge the question of meaning. Rather, it becomes an expressed assent to the instant activity, the straightforward duty and the immediate pleasure. Since life bears no inherent meaning neither can individuals create their own meanings. No sense of positive purpose in life truly exists.

In practice, however, nihilism gets caught up in contradiction and inconsistency. Consistent nihilism is goallessness in itself, that is, the untenability of values, ideals, worth and meaningfulness of human existence. This option is untenable for humans incessantly remain purposeful agents. Thus, even Nietzsche can say, "nihilism represents a pathological interim state."[13] Nihilism cannot be an absolute; otherwise it would not have an ethos of its own. Since the basic human values of life, friendship, security, health and striving for good over evil are not eliminable from the human realm as a whole, pure nihilism is impossible. An intermittent sense

---

12. William H. Halverson, *A Concise Introduction to Philosophy* (New York: Random House, 1981), 467.

13. Thielicke, 166.

Pessimism, Nihilism, Optimism, and Hope

of meaninglessness serves rather to indicate that only fractured nihilism remains possible.[14]

Accordingly, the major weakness of nihilism is its spectator situatedness. This stance in life can only be consistent with the artificial disconnectedness from other people, social arrangements and intraworldly affairs that enrich human existence and supply human life and relationships with the sense and interpretative framework of lived significance. Subsequently, nihilism implies a false relation to things and people.[15] The moment one becomes a spectator and detaches himself or herself from life's involvements, all human values and relationships become confused and sucked into the engulfing stream of pointless events.

The Case of Optimism

In contrast to pessimism and nihilism, optimism simply emphasizes the positive or enthusiastic aspects of human life more than the negative ones. In optimism, no matter the context, the good constantly prevails over evil in the sparks of life.[16] The optimist has a firm conviction, or, in certain cases, just a vague feeling that difficulties, conflicts or contradictions will turn out for the best.[17] Optimism is easy: it simply consists in supposing that everything will work out automatically in the end. Its understanding of evil is one of a transitional dislocation, or a disturbance which will rectify itself. Optimism affirms life from its friendly, attractive, admirable and assuring perspectives. The optimist fails to be integral in his or her vision of the human reality. Optimism does not duly reckon with the tragic sense of life. As an attitude, optimism primarily views things from the most promising viewpoints. The optimist perceives everything as ordered for the best.[18] Yet experiences of pain and tragedy are real and continue to disrupt many people's lives. Of course, difficulties, hardships and struggles cannot resolve themselves automatically. Human efforts need to be part of the resolution.

A typical example of an optimist is Mary Baker Eddy, the founder of Christian Science Church.[19] She denies the reality of sin, fear, sickness

---

14. Ibid.

15. Ibid.

16. Ibid., 114.

17. Gabriel Marcel, *Homo Viator: An Introduction to a Metaphysics of Hope* (Chicago: Henry Regnery Company, 1951), 33.

18. Angeles, 16.

19. E. D. Canhan, "Christian Science Church of Christ, Scientist," in *The New Catho-*

and death. In fact, she regards the experience of death as an illusion. Pain and stress are reduced to states of consciousness experienced by individuals according to their own spiritual growth or lack of it.

Leibniz is also known for his optimism, put more precisely, his metaphysical optimism. His optimistic viewpoint would imply that despite evident evils, the world of human social reality is the best of all possible worlds. Its creation involves the fullest possible realization of divine attributes. In the world thus prevails a certain divine harmony that requires evil. This is not only for the full manifestation of the infinite greatness of the world's creator but also in order that this evil may contribute to a greater good than would otherwise be possible.[20] However, this optimism needs to be situated within the larger metaphysics of Leibniz. "Leibniz's metaphysical optimism is based on his rationalistic theology. From the ontological argument, he knows that God, the most perfect being exists; and such a being must have created the best of all possible worlds; hence this must be that world."[21] But the moment Leibniz's optimism is understood as part of his metaphysics, which is a theodicy, it becomes clear that he is not one-sided. Of course, the view that this is the best of all possible worlds remains an open question, especially in the light of all the evils that occur like tsunamis, earthquakes, diseases and wars and, ultimately, death that interfere with and destroy human purposes and hopes. Accordingly, the metaphysics of Leibniz was profound not insofar as it is optimistic, rather, insofar as it is presented as a theodicy.[22] Leibniz's theodicy, and not his optimism, involves human efforts in achieving the human good. Leibniz's theodicy is integrative in its character. From this perspective, Leibniz is an example of a hopeful person.

Essentially, thus, the attitude of an optimist hinges upon an experience which is not inferred from the most intimate part of the self and relational life. The optimist regards life from a sufficient remoteness to let certain contradictions blend into a general consonance. The optimist does not labor to influence events. The optimist only desires and looks to the good outcome from the ambivalent human experiences. In the end, no such thing as deep optimism exists.

---

lic Encyclopedia, Vol.3 (1967), 654.

20. Loemker, 117.

21. D. Ber, "Pessimism and Optimism," in *The Oxford Companion to Philosophy*, Ted Honberich (ed.), (Oxford: Oxford University Press, 1995), 656.

22. Marcel, *Homo* Viator, 34.

The Case of Hope

Some examples of people generally acknowledged to be signs and concrete embodiments of hope include Nelson Mandela, Martin Luther King, Mother Theresa and Mahatma Gandhi. Their individual responses have been attentive to creating a world for every human being to live a fully human life. Martin Luther King captures this understanding thus:

> As long as there is poverty in the world I can never be rich, even if I have a billion dollars. As long as diseases are rampant and millions of people in this world cannot expect to live more than twenty-eight or thirty years, I can never be totally healthy even if I just got a good checkup at the Mayo Clinic. I can never be what I ought to be until you are what you ought to be. This is the way our world is made. No individual or nation can stand out boasting of being independent. We are interdependent.[23]

Martin Luther King, Jr., here articulates a vision of hope. This is a vision of the world where people, regardless of race, gender, creed or place of origin, can live in dignity, delivered from servitude enjoined by others or natural forces. This vision manifestly accords with the deep-felt human need, demand and aspiration for a certain fullness of life. In hope, a concrete human being or human relation maintains that, ultimately, compassion and universal love, fraternity and peace will triumph and reign in this ambivalent world. This promise, however, does not mean that the exploitation and the sufferings of so many people in hospitals, prisons and ghettos, despairing and lonely, hungry and thirsty, can be remedied without much struggle.

Planted in the experience of the present and the past, hope looks with engagements and creativity towards a fuller future in the experience of the present. Hope's distinctive quality is nonresignation to servitude. Hope does not surrender expectations of a fuller life. In hope:

> ... the ultimate measure of a man[24] is not where he stands in moments of comfort and convenience, but where he stands at times of challenge and controversy. The true neighbor will risk his position, his prestige, and even his life for the welfare of others. In danger-

---

23. Coretta Scott King, *The Words of Martin Luther King, Jr.* (New York: Newmarket Press, 1983), 21.

24. In this work, "man" when used in citations is frequently a generic term for both men and women. All quotations are preserved in fidelity to the original works of the authors, who for the most part wrote according to the customs of their time. In reading these quotations, appropriate inclusions may be added or adopted.

ous valleys and hazardous pathways, he will lift some bruised and beaten brother and more noble life.[25]

Unlike pessimism, hope does not underestimate the fact of the human being's ability to improve his or her lot. To hope truly entails a free will that has already touched the limits of its own activity.[26] It further entails faith as a vital vehicle and force of invisible truths. Faith refers to the relation of being grasped by the recognition and experience of intrinsic value and plenitude, perhaps conceived as power or transcendence. In this regard:

> A will without intelligence would be a mere impulse, and an intelligence which lacked will would be devitalized. But we shall only make it possible for ourselves . . . to discover some of [faith's] essential characteristics, if we establish ourselves at the ideal point of conjunction of these wrongly dissociated faculties; and we could . . . add to this analogous statements concerning affectivity in its relation with intelligence and will.[27]

Hope is not easy. Hope should not be confused with a contemplation or conviction that not everything deserves to perish. Hope demands praxis: in hope one helps to construct, build and create with a sense of sublimity. "As regards hope, nothing could be more mistaken than to see it as a kind of inactive hovering over an event which is expected to come to pass by itself. It is indeed true that hope or patience can sink to the level where a sense of ease becomes mere slackening."[28] The life-giving praxis of hope critiques, illuminates and liberates existence. Within its framework, people decide on their acts in light of how they can bring about a vision of what life can and should be. Hope gives a vision of a transformed world that affects our decisions and efforts. The light of this vision creates an ethical mandate in us. This also means that the future comes to depend on us in a certain sense.

In hope, people actively seek to build a new alternative world. This world of a gracious order is envisaged as contrary to obtaining inadequacy, fragmentation and dissatisfaction of life. People become subjects of moral agency. They cultivate self-understanding, perception and capacity to imagine alternative ways that re-create the world and human relations. All this hinges on the liberative vibrancy which hope brings to understanding

25. King, 24.
26. Marcel, *Homo Viator*, 67.
27. Marcel, *The Mystery of Being Vol.II: Faith and Reality*, 178.
28. Gabriel Marcel, *The Existential Background of Human Dignity* (Cambridge: Harvard University Press, 1963), 143.

the mechanisms of particular contexts. The process of re-imagining, transforming and reshaping the world in new ways implies that much of what happens to us does not wholly lie beyond our control or our ability to mold our contexts. In many ways, the shape of the future lies in our own hands as we strive for the experience and expression of abundant and wondrous life. The dignity of human agency and responsibility shape and define our very foundations of being in the world. People can always bring expectations and ambitions, sense of rights and responsibilities, individuated and shared identities, lived freedom, thought, language and creativity to their world.

As such, then, hope acknowledges that evils exist and proposes process-possibilities for the human being and the human community to realize some concrete and yet a fuller experience and expression of human life and existence in the forms of some orderedness, harmony and justice. This realization requires a perception of and sensitivity to existing evils that need to be overcome or minimized. Hope affirms that from a state of human difficulty, confusion, or a sense of relational inadequacy, human beings can advance to greater clarity, sharper distinctness, a more expansive adequacy and achieve a greater experience and expression of human flourishing. One who hopes, if his or her hope is real and not just a platonic wish, is engaged and involved in some kind of a process; and it is only from this viewpoint that it is possible to realize what is specific in hope.[29]

As someone who participates in its experience, hope, then, implies that I do not give up. I do not consent to pointlessness and meaninglessness of conditions and situations, however negative they may seem. Hope achieves this through a felt and persistent urge for liberative plenitude. Here, then, steadfastness and creativity justify and verify hope in life. This spirit of hope was particularly embodied by Nelson Mandela during his trial in 1964 for opposing apartheid. In defiance of the social evils wrought by apartheid, Mandela echoed:

> I have fought against white domination and I have fought against black domination. I cherished the ideal of a democratic and free society in which all persons live together and with equal opportunities. It is an ideal which I hope to live for and to achieve. But if need be, it is an ideal for which I am prepared to die.[30]

---

29. Marcel, *Homo Viator*, 35.

30. Sheridan Johns and R. Hunt Davis, Jr. (eds.), *Mandela, Tambo and the African National Congress* (New York: Oxford University Press, 1991), 228.

These statements of Mandela echo nonacceptance of the uncertain reality as having the last say on the individual and social experiences. Hope accepts struggle as a component of the self in the human experiences yet with a demand and aspiration for a creative process of growth and development that enable people to live together in kinship.

In hope, one concedes that any form of disintegration or separation ushers in pain which maims human vitality and that, through a creative process, communion and collaboration, no matter the cost to realize them, carry with them tones of healthy living. Again, Mandela reflected and manifested this grounding attitude when he wrote to the people of Soweto:

> I cherish my own freedom dearly, but I care even more for your freedom. Too many have died since I went to prison. Too many have suffered for the love of freedom. I owe it to their widows, to their orphans, to their mothers and to their fathers who have grieved and wept for them. Not only I have suffered during these long, lonely wasted years. I am not less life loving than you are. But I cannot sell my birthright, nor am I prepared to sell the birthright of the people to be free . . . I cannot and will not give any undertaking at a time when I and you, the people, are not free.[31]

As a vision and creative attitude which confronts problematic life, hope strives to put sense into human tensions, apparent contradictions and paradoxes. In the nerve center of hope lies the wisdom of balance. This balance implies understanding the world as encompassing activity and passivity, joy and pain, talking and listening, searching and trusting, living and dying, constantly in tension and, perhaps, moving towards an ever-greater fullness. The process dimension of hope, that may involve battling in pain and/or loneliness in charting a way forward, is absent in optimism. At the same time, hope implies depth and expansive responsibility that do not claim outright self-righteousness: therein lies humility which typifies hope. Hope also remains inseparable from patience and chastity. As a form of creative love, patience has to do with persistence in time: it gives space for existence and for the unfolding of being. A person learns and grows as one commits himself or herself to the wellbeing of human existence. Hope asserts that life in the human reality is ultimately noncontradictory, meaningful and worthwhile. Of course, this is not to deny the concrete riches and ambiguities of existence.

---

31. Ibid., 215.

Pessimism, Nihilism, Optimism, and Hope

In the light of ambiguous human existence, hope becomes a more realistic response to life than pessimism, nihilism and optimism. These other interpretative responses embrace life only nonintegrally, embracing and, perhaps, exaggerating the pleasant or unpleasant dimensions of life. The realism of hope lies in its ardent embrace of ambivalence that characterizes human existence and transmuting that ambivalence into a liberative vivacity. It is a fact that the human reality has both the positive and negative dimensions. An interpretative response to it that emphasizes only one dimension does a disservice to the experiences, growth and well-being of the human individual and the human communities and societies. The overlooked dimension would repeatedly contradict and undermine such an attitude and, hence, undermine its credibility. An interpretative attitude that duly considers both dimensions is not only truly realistic but also sustainable in the long run. Accordingly, pessimism, nihilism and optimism cannot be maintained consistently in practice. Even one who trusts the least trusts sometimes and one who trusts the most does doubt seriously at times.

Hope invests sense into the human realities of death and life, confusion and meaning, weakness and strength, darkness and light. In hope, in spite of one's rags, pain or rotten teeth, as it were, one still lays claim to one's aspirations for human plenitude. The sense of assurance and positive outcome through positive involvement in life makes a person who hopes persist amidst attendant obstructions. The exigency of hope marks itself by the demand for other human beings, relationships, dialogue and liberative sense of significance. Hope makes a human being an active subject of his or her own life: one always remains a partial architect of one's own destiny which also shapes the destiny of others. This is not to say that success is assured in hope. Success is not assured but counted on through patience, humility, a diligent steadfastness and a creative spirit. In part, one's destiny depends on what one is able to do and accomplish with others. One shapes one's destiny through the assertion and exercise of one's freedom.

Hope releases physical and psychological energy by aspiring with the sense of unconditional assurance. What results is that one not only realizes this assurance in one's conception but one also inserts oneself into a tenacious course of action with the belief that one shall realize some plenitude. Wish that characterizes hope is something one represents to oneself and acts upon wisely, progressively and creatively.[32]

Consequently, in hope's enterprise we encounter liberation that surpasses a simple return to the status quo; it is a creative advancement. Hope

32. Marcel, *Homo Viator*, 44.

constantly signifies both restoration and a new creation. Hope relates to and proclaims the indestructibility of human communion and transcendence. Hope involves a steady, trustful outreach of a person who has depth of communion experience so as to be able to effect and expand acts of self-transcendence in existence. Nelson Mandela again typified this on the occasion of his release from prison thus:

> My friends, comrades and fellow South Africans, I greet you all in the name of peace, democracy, and freedom for all. I stand here before you not as a prophet but as a humble servant of you, the people . . . We call on our people to seize this moment so that the process toward democracy is rapid and uninterrupted. We have waited too long for our freedom . . . We call on our white compatriots to join us in the shaping of a new South Africa. The freedom is a political home for you, too.[33]

Hope is vitality and an existential assurance whose transcendence exceeds the will to simply remain physically alive. Hope connects deeply with the experience and recognition of some intrinsic value and plenitude for which no price is too high to pay.

Conclusion

Human life and existence are profoundly ambivalent. The complex mesh and tapestry of life cannot be denied. This complexity elicits the human responses of pessimism, nihilism, optimism and hope. Each of these insightful responses, which are fundamental attitudes that people adopt in real life, have interpretative grounding in concrete experiences that justify, support and continuously verify them, one way or the other.

At the same time, as this chapter has demonstrated, unlike pessimism, nihilism and optimism which tend to lift up only certain dimensions of lived experience, hope is a more realistic attitude to our existence since it does not discount any aspect of it. In this way, hope as a true-to-life response serves the course of personal and shared living in this world. And in seeking to expand, deepen and articulate further dimensions and aspects of hope, the next chapter deals with the questions and perspectives of hope as experienced and expressed in the thought of Gabriel Marcel. Marcel's thoughts and reflections inform and guide the basic thrusts and tenor of this entire work. In fact, this work strives to render relevant, contemporaneous and current the touchstone of Marcel's thoughts and reflections on hope.

33. Johns and Davis, 225.

2

Hope and Despair in Life

Preamble

ONE THINKER whose life was imbued with hope was Gabriel Marcel, for whom life implied being with others and reflection about others, personal relationships and intersubjectivity.[1] Additionally, it must be set forth that Marcel's insights offer the mainstream or basic thrust of the discussions and perspectives of this work. Within this perspective, the forthcoming considerations of the centrality of hope in his life become needful and appropriate.

The Centrality of Hope in Marcel's Life

Hope was not only an important part of Marcel's personal life; it was a feature and a notion that dominated his philosophical works. Marcel points out that the reflections he made on hope are in reality at the heart of his entire work.[2] The notion of hope gave coherence to the ambivalent history of Marcel. For Marcel, hope enables all preventable and unpreventable misery, pain and death to point beyond themselves. Hope focuses on salvation as a restoration of life that participates in an order of supreme integrity and fullness. Salvation delivers us from death and it is less a state than a pathway. Marcel says:

> I have apprehended the nature of hope . . . It always has to do with the restoration of a certain living order in its integrity. But it also carries with it the affirmation of eternity and eternal goods . . . Even the integrity of the organism—when I hope for the recovery of an invalid—is, as it were, the prefiguring or symbolic expression

---

1. Gabriel Marcel, *Tragic Wisdom and Beyond* (Evanston: Northwestern University Press, 1973), 234.

2. Gabriel Marcel, *Presence and Immortality* (Pittsburgh: Duquesne University Press, 1967), 231.

of a supreme integrity. In this sense . . . hope is hope of salvation, and that it is quite impossible to think of the one without treating the other.³

Without a doubt, when a person suffers evil he or she experiences a split and hurt in his or her unity and integrity respectively. When engulfed by suffering, dithering, naivety and lassitude can damage a blossoming life. Amidst pain people easily misinterpret, misrepresent and distort their realities. But even amidst much pain and suffering, hope can remain completely healthy and even gain strength. Hope gives invincible assurance that the tragedies of current life do not have the final say on life. Using some other concrete categories, Marcel relates the urge towards salvation that characterizes hope thus:

> The "I hope" in all its strength is directed towards salvation. It really is a matter of my coming out of a darkness in which I am at present plunged, and which may be the darkness of illness, of separation, exile or slavery. It is obviously impossible in such cases to separate the "I hope" from a certain type of situation of which it is really a part.⁴

To further underscore the centrality of hope in his thought and life, Marcel made the following declaration on the occasion when he was presented with a Peace Prize from the Börsenverein des Deutschen Buchhandels at Frankfurt am Main:

> If there is a notion in my work dominating all others, it is without doubt that of hope, understood as *mysterium*, a notion as I have previously stated, that is enlivened as though from within through ardent anticipation, "I hope for us of You." I have written and that is still today the only formulation that satisfies me.⁵

In the same work he asserts, "We can still say more accurately, I hope for You, Who are the living peace, and for us, who are still fighting with ourselves and each other, that one day it will be granted us to enter You and share your completeness."⁶ Hope is thus a mystery and founded on the intimacy of communion which refers to communal being in which one person encounters and participates in the life of another.

3. Marcel, *Being and Having*, 75.
4. Marcel, *Homo Viator*, 30.
5. Gabriel Marcel, *Philosophical Fragments 1909–1914 and The Philosopher and Peace* (Notre Dame, Indiana: University of Notre Dame Press, 1965), 19.
6. Ibid.

The centrality of hope in Marcel's thought is further recognized in a conversation between him and Paul Ricoeur:

> PAUL RICOEUR: Yes. We have come to see that hope and journeying are not two different things, but that hope is what makes the passage something more than just simple wandering. I like very much one of your expressions, the one where you say, "being is being underway." That's hope. It is hope that gives all your research a tempo, a groping and yet confident rhythm. The unity of your concrete philosophy is the conjunction of two ideas, the labyrinth of existence and the rays of hope that cross it. I am thinking also of another of your formulations: "I hope in you for us." Hope is always coming back, but beneath our experience and not above it, if I may put it that way.
>
> GABRIEL MARCEL: Perhaps we could add that hope is connected with *disponibilité* [unconditional availability] just as it is connected with patience. Here too are values which all great spiritual masters have recognized but which the philosophers, particularly contemporary philosophers are not sufficiently concerned with.[7]

Thus far, it may be stated that when persons hope they participate in an experience that harmonizes being-on-the-way with availability. Hope signifies an active state of the will and action in adventure and availability.

But hope was also central to Marcel's thought and life because of the experience of despair. In this regard, he says:

> The fact that despair is possible is a central datum here. Man is capable of despair, capable of hugging death, of hugging his own death. A central datum for metaphysic, but such definitions of man as that proposed by Thomism cover it up and disguise it. The essential merit of Kierkegaard and his school, to my mind, is their having brought this datum to full view. And metaphysic ought to take up its position just there, face to face with despair. The ontological problem cannot be separated from that of despair.[8]

He adds:

> The fact that suicide is possible is, in this sense, an essential point of reference for all genuine metaphysical thought. And not only suicide: despair *in all its forms*, betrayal *in all its aspects*, in so far as they appear to us as active denials of being, and in so far as the soul which despairs shuts itself up against the central and mysteri-

---

7. Marcel, *Tragic Wisdom and Beyond*, 255.
8. Marcel, *Being and Having*, 104.

ous assurance in which we believe we have found the principle of positivity.[9]

The principle of positivity is being, the encounter with which is implied in the above quotation. The experience validates awareness of the divine filiation within oneself and in one's presence to another.

Hope and Despair

According to Marcel, thus, an inquiry into hope must take into account the questions that despair raises. This is because despair can be the springboard to the loftiest affirmation, that is, a groundswell for an affirmation of the principle of all positivity.[10] "The truth is that there can strictly speaking be no hope except when the temptation to despair exists. Hoping takes place amidst chaos and much turbulence. Hope is the act by which this temptation is actively or victoriously overcome."[11] Hope does not give up on value, awe and respect for life. This also means that the center of human reality is not empty. Human efforts may be incomplete but they do not amount to vaporous and unyielding futility. At the same time, it needs to be recognized that, in despair, actual devaluation of persons takes place on account of the fact that their worth comes to be premised and validated only extrinsically. Or again, one could ask, what does it mean to despair? What is the essence of despair? It seems as though it were always a capitulation before some *fatum* (outcome) laid down by our judgment.[12] This *fatum* refers to judgments people frequently make in relation to worth of persons as dependent on or determined by extrinsic validation. Of course, a certain mass-prejudice constantly threatens the integrity of people's judgments of who they are or who other people are.

When it comes to understanding despair, it may be noted that it fundamentally consists in the experience of closing in on oneself. The experience of *one's time being plugged up* coincides with the dynamics of despair. The man or woman in despair is *affected* in the strongest sense of the word by that absence of exit. Or again, it is really as if the despairer kept hitting against a faceless and hostile wall, as it were. The result of this shock or impact is that a person's very being starts to disintegrate. The man or woman who despairs is one whose situation appears to be without

9. Ibid., 119.
10. Gabriel Marcel, *The Philosophy of Existentialism* (Secaucus, N.J.: The Citadel Press, 1967), 29.
11. Marcel, *Homo Viator*, 36.
12. Ibid., 36–37.

exit. Despair then reflects and expresses the shock felt by consciousness when it meets with an experience which may be expressed thus: "enough, there is no more." The place of despair is where we make an inventory or extrinsic validation.[13] Quantification tends to encrust human existence with impoverishment.

As a person gives up in despair, he or she fails to make any effort to *hold* up. Experience such as this expresses itself in a total collapse of the human organism, which is what capitulation is about. Capitulation expresses itself, at the level of relations to other persons, by an impoverishment of communication. The resulting derisive consciousness discloses itself in gossip, pettiness, swearing, sarcasm and obscenity.[14] Moreover, the possibility of despair is bound up with freedom which can exercise and exert itself in self-betrayal. In this sense, nothing outside ourselves can shut the door to despair. After all, things are constantly happening around us which counsel us to drown ourselves in despair, which means that life cannot be lived meaningfully without stakes.[15] We cannot live life fruitfully without some form of risk.[16] In effect, to live, for the human being, implies accepting ambivalent life. This is what it means to say "yes" to life; or else the opposite, to avow oneself to a state of internal war even if one may act as if one accepts that one is living for something worthwhile. The resulting state of internal war means that a person can be alive while actually refusing to live for anything of enduring worth.[17]

Of course, incarnation or bodiliness is the point at which despair touches and affects concrete human existence. The precarious human pilgrim condition in the world reveals itself bodily or incarnationally. Incarnate life offers the concrete possibilities for living the experience and expression of despair. Incarnate existence exposes persons to physical vulnerability, the experience of loss, or the radical fears of nonacceptance, weakness, rejection or failure. In effect:

> . . . the possibility of suicide which is engraved in our nature of incarnate beings is nothing but the expression of another much more profound and more hidden possibility, the possibility of a spiritual denial of the self or, what comes to the same thing, of an impious

---

13. Marcel, *Being and Having*, 102.
14. Gabriel Marcel, "Desire and Hope," in *Readings in Existential Phenomenology*, Nathaniel Lawrence and Daniel O'Connor, eds. (Englewood Cliffs: Prentice-Hall, Inc., 1967), 281.
15. Marcel, *Being and Having*, 95–96.
16. Ibid., 70.
17. Ibid., 95.

> . . . affirmation of self which amounts to a radical rejection of being. There is a sense in which that rejection is the final falsehood and absurdity; for it can exist only . . . as it becomes embodied . . . into perverted being.[18]

Suicide simply implies, if not the wish for annihilation, then at least the overpowering need to escape from a set of restraints which one feels that one can no longer endure. A person who wants to commit suicide normally tends towards the perception that he or she cannot irrevocably disengage himself or herself from a network of elements in which he or she is enmeshed.[19] Such a person closes in on himself or herself. In contrast, a person who is inhabited by hope remains open to others; he or she is able to establish communication with them.[20] In hope, the one tempted to give up will be upheld by the thought of another, perhaps conceived as a friend, for whom discouragement would be considered contagious and sacrilegious. This dimension of hope coincides with that of love.[21] Herein lies the spiritual economy of intersubjectivity or genuine human kinship. If it is shifted to the level of intersubjectivity or the experience of genuine human kinship, then, the problem of despair changes its character and tenor. In a framework of intersubjectivity or genuine human kinship a man or a woman is established in his or her condition as a subject. He or she is also integrated into a living relation with the world of all men and women from which he or she had cut himself or herself off.[22] The élan and experience of *all in all* expresses truly a culminating experience of hope. In its élan hope locates itself in a dimension of perpetual novelty that fosters and celebrates life with others; it is not fatigued.[23]

What also cannot be denied is the fact that as long as disease, famine, war, glaring injustices and repression define and characterize the human condition, suffering, loss and pain will always diminish human inner resources, possibilities and positive potentials. As a consequence, life becomes visibly unattractive; it may also become imbued with a certain sense of meaninglessness. Yet precarious human conditions will not diminish until basic human existential insecurity is acknowledged and transcended by wakefulness to the realm of intrinsic value and plenitude. Of course,

---

18. Marcel, *The Mystery of Being Vol.II: Faith and Reality*, 173.
19. Marcel, "Desire and Hope," 282.
20. Ibid.
21. Ibid., 283.
22. Ibid., 285.
23. Ibid., 278.

to transcend is not to remove. Fundamental existential insecurity, which characterizes stifling dependence on extrinsic validation for one's own sense of attractiveness, desirability and worth or lovableness, constitutes the basic captivity in the human condition. This existential captivity cripples the human being by devitalizing him or her. And here we may note that the fragile state of dependence on extrinsic validation for one's own sense of worth may be exacerbated by experiences of illness, loss or injury. Under such circumstances:

> The despairing man not only contemplates and sets before himself the dismal repetition, the eternalisation of a situation in which he is caught like a ship in a sea of ice . . . he anticipates this repetition . . . simultaneously he has the bitter certainty that this anticipation will not spare him from living through the same trial day by day until . . . extinction . . . seeing it . . . as a supreme outrage.[24]

In other words, if I were the despairing person, I would feel that I am condemned to death. Yet paradoxically, if I reflect more profoundly on this situation of being condemned to death and the temptation to absolute despair which it exposes me to, I must recognize that this temptation is addressed to my freedom—a freedom which can of course take the form of suicide.[25]

Anyhow, the experience of a despairing man or woman portrays what disappointment (i.e., the breach of confidence) and giving up are about. Whenever and wherever people give up despair becomes a reality. A person then truly becomes a prisoner to the *conditional sense of the self, the ego.*[26] "In all suffering, I risk becoming self-centered and thus locking myself up in despair."[27] Yet, by definition, the truth is that no hope is possible without the temptation to despair. Hope springs to life against a backdrop of some threat to human excellence or the experience and expression of human integrity. Or again, true hope surrounds itself by a sort of halo or fringe of possible despair.[28] Hope looks far out above this wrinkled

24. Marcel, *Homo Viator*, 42.

25. Marcel, "Desire and Hope," 283.

26. The notion of ego for Marcel designates the emphasis we give to a certain portion of our experiences that we functionally identify with. The ego, in the final analysis, then refers to my conditional self or value of my person as premised on external circumstances with which I identify.

27. Gabriel Marcel, "Reply to Otto Friedrich Bollnow," in *The Library of Living Philosophers Vol. XVII: The Philosophy of Gabriel Marcel*, Paul Arthur Schilpp and Lewis Edwin Hahn, eds. (La Salle, Illinois: Open Court, 1991), 201.

28. Ibid.

world of ours and precisely therein lies the secret, or even the proof, of its transcendence.[29] Such transcendence takes place on the condition that we wake up to, appropriate and live from a certain sense of intrinsic value and plenitude of our own persons, relationships and life itself. We cannot speak meaningfully of any hope except in a context of surviving and triumphing over life's struggle whose stake is ultimately salvation or perdition.[30] In a word, a comprehending sense of significance sponsors hope inasmuch as it directs itself towards eternity.[31] Hope does not attach final significance to the dismal repetition of a trial, some captivity or test and the subsequent repugnance of disgrace which become attached to the particular unpleasant and painful experience.

Hope and Its Unconditional Character

Hope as a counterweight to despair offsets the existential devaluation that takes place in despair with a valuation that is alert to worth of persons as unconditional. Such a valuation furnishes persons with inexhaustible inward resourcefulness amidst trials. So, an indissoluble connection binds together hope and love. The nearer hope approaches to true charity, the more the meaning of its declarations is inflected and tends to become full of an unconditional quality which is the very sign of its presence.[32] True charity can be thought of as presence in the sense of absolute availability. At the heart of charity lies presence in the sense of the absolute gift of one's self, a gift which, by no means, implies no impoverishment to the giver. Therefore, through charity we reach the realm where categories of the valid in the world of things entirely become inapplicable. In effect, the whole spiritual life may be seen as the sum of activities by which persons try to reduce in themselves the part played by lack of availability to others. Spiritual life expands people's capacity for presence.[33]

---

29. Gabriel Marcel, *Searchings* (New York: Newman Press, 1967), 66.

30. Ibid., 23.

31. As Pannenberg recognizes, eternity achieves an inner possessing of the totality of life. The simultaneity of past, present and future culminates in eternity. In this sense, eternity includes time and what happens in time. Eternity has to do precisely with being the source, epitome and basis of time. Of course, we take hold of the totality of our life only inasmuch as we reach out to the past and future, even though this can only be fragmentary and incomplete. See, Wolfhart Pannenberg, *Systematic Theology, Volume 3* (Grand Rapids, Michigan: William B. Eerdmans Publishing Company, 1998), 595–98.

32. Marcel, *Homo Viator*, 66.

33. Marcel, *Being and Having*, 69.

The unconditional quality that is a sign of presence also enfolds and touches on inwardness or interiority as the favorite abode of dignity and the sacral.[34] The sacred dignity of persons refers to the integrity of their being which transcends any opposition between the static and dynamic. Dignity constitutes the living centers of men and women and their relationships. When persons wake up to their sacred centers and to the intrinsic significance of living ties among themselves, they hope, that is, they begin to live in hope.[35] Hope actuates itself in the experience and recognition of the unconditional value and presence. The freedom that this experience bequeaths makes possible the grasp of human light-heartedness which opens persons up to others and to life itself. In the experience, persons come to ground themselves in being and in who they most deeply are. The more we are able to know the individual being, the more we shall be oriented and, as it were, directed towards, a grasp of being as such.[36] In the light of being, hope means that human existence transcends quantification and mechanization.

Being refers to or touches on the ground of who *we are*; my being refers to my *I am*. My being is also inexhaustibly concrete. My being is a reality given to the self; it belongs to the very nature of self. It is as immediate as beyond the self. It is truly the self in its self-transcending quality. The experience of being returns people to themselves and to one another. In this experience, people awaken to the truth[37] of their persons and to ties of human kinship. Connection with being empowers people with joy which consists in recognizing that they veritably stand in right relation to their humanity. In being we find not only the explanation of hope but also the font of joy understood as warm-heartedness. It is a mirroring of personal placement in a liberating light. Joy arises when people awaken to the light of who they deeply are. In being, persons stand in awe of who they are and, perhaps, how they luminously bear their existence.

---

34. Marcel, *Searchings*, 52.

35. Marcel, *Homo Viator*, 49.

36. Gabriel Marcel, *Creative Fidelity* (New York: The Crossroad Publishing Company, 1982), 148.

37. Here it may be pointed out that truth precedes subjective insight, otherwise it could not be missed always. Our insight into truth does not control it. Actual truth arises from epistemological decision and assessment. In principle, the plausibility of binding truth cannot be mine alone: openness of truth demands declaration to all. Admittedly, too, complete clarity often lacks about actual truth. Besides, truth is reliable and lasting. As a result, ongoing process of experience clarifies and confirms the binding truth of persons accessible to the relativity of human thought and reflection.

In its essence inwardness, as an encounter with being as intrinsic value and plenitude, does not tantamount to restriction. It would be gravely deceptive to think so. The profound stillness of contemplation or mindfulness that facilitates the encounter with being reflects some honesty of the human spirit and kinship with plenitude. In inwardness, persons open themselves up: they do not close in on themselves.[38] The implication is also that:

> We can . . . conceive, at least theoretically, of the inner disposition of one who, setting no condition or limit and abandoning himself in absolute confidence, would thus transcend all possible disappointment and would experience a security in his being, or in being . . . This is what determines the ontological position of hope—absolute hope, inseparable from a faith which is likewise absolute, transcending the laying down of conditions, and for this very reason every kind of representation whatever it might be.[39]

Participation in being refers to a connectedness with plenitude that transcends the laying down of conditions or the fulfillment of conditions in order to validate the self. The ensuing security actuates vibrancy and self-possessed openness and availability of persons which oppose the inertia of contraction and rigidity. The resulting transcendence initiates, establishes and expresses hope. Indeed, hope belongs to a transcendent order of presence, a connectedness with a felt sense of plenitude. Hope has a supernatural or transcendent foundation in being and, ultimately, in the absolute Thou. As a result, human existence unilluminated by hope can only appear to us to be the scene of a sort of an immense and inexorable book-keeping.[40] This means that to despair of myself, or to despair of us, is essentially to despair of the Thou.[41] In the last analysis, hope belongs to heaven, as the symbol of plenitude, as the only place where it will find its fulfillment. In the experience of hope the soul goes beyond the visible world so that the visible world becomes interior to it. The visible world

---

38. Marcel, *Searchings*, 53.

39. Marcel, *Homo Viator*, 46. We may note that Marcel uses "being" and "Being" interchangeably. I follow a similar usage in this book.

40. Marcel, *Being and Having*, 79. Book-keeping in the quotation referred to here is about the conditional value of persons; it also refers to quantifiable aspects of human existence.

41. Marcel, *Homo Viator*, 61.

itself becomes a symbol of hope.[42] The estuaries of hope do not lie entirely within the bounds of the visible world.[43]

Hope is a resource vital to the sense of wellbeing that sustains persons and relationships through the crises and challenges of life. "The soul lives by hope alone; hope is perhaps the very stuff of which our souls are made."[44] Ironically, the conditions that make it possible to hope are strictly the same as those which make it possible to despair. Death constitutes the springboard of an absolute hope. A world in which death misses, hope only exists in the larval stage.[45] The human individual, with flesh and blood, with a name and in pain, needs inner resources to go on living amidst daily challenges of frustrations and failures that invite despair. Hope situates itself within a framework of trial, not only corresponding to it, but constituting our being's veritable *response*.[46] In this regard, hope constitutes a resource that the human being, as a wayfarer, may use as he or she faces his or her precarious pilgrim condition. Ultimately, hope grounds itself in a felt sense and experience of being as intrinsic value and plenitude of which persons and relationships partake:

> Hope seems to me, as it were, the prolongation into the unknown of an activity which is central—that is to say rooted in being. Hence it has affinities, not with desire but with the will. The will implies the same refusal to calculate possibilities, or at any rate it suspends this calculation. Could not hope therefore be defined as the will when it is made to bear on what does not depend on itself?[47]

Hope and Meaningfulness of the World

Hope implies that the world as a whole is not absurd. For, to say that the world as a whole is absurd signifies that:

> . . . either I am myself absurd in my ultimate nature—in which case so are my judgments absurd, they negate themselves, it cannot be conceded that they have any sort of validity—or, on the other hand, we have to admit that I have a double nature, that there is

---

42. Marcel, *Searchings*, 66.
43. Marcel, *Being and Having*, 76.
44. Ibid., 80.
45. Ibid., 93.
46. Marcel, *Homo Viator*, 30.
47. Marcel, *The Philosophy of Existentialism*, 33.

a part of me which is not absurd and which can make valid judgments about absurdity . . .[48]

Or again, the assertion that the universe is absurd can only be meaningful if I refer this universe to some order or rationality of which the universe does not represent an instance nor to which it does not conform. Accordingly, the universe as a whole cannot be absurd after all. The whole human endeavor is worthwhile; to participate in it is to share in its worth as well. There is intelligibility of significance in the world. Hope denies absurdity, anguish and despair as the final elements of the universe. It denies that negative elements of life have the decisive say on a person in a painful or problematic situation. In this way, hope can survive an almost total ruin of the human organism.[49]

The far-reaching significance of the idea that this life is without meaning is that it originates from the spectator of life. The idea derives from someone who merely contemplates life and not from someone who is fully involved in the actual living of life. To live is to commit oneself to life itself. It also implies being caught up in the world of values that well up from the depths of life. These values thrust themselves upon our everyday interests, skills and circumstances. They present themselves as directly deserving our commitments in the concrete details of our lives.[50]

Hope reveals the assurance of life's intrinsic significance. Hope is, above all, hope for liberation from the existential tyranny of extrinsic validation.[51] This liberation could be from despondency, which people have when they look at their lives and, ultimately, despair of themselves and die. Hope involves a deliverance from inner insecurity and fear, anxieties and sadness in it ascendancy over the limitations that come with the conditional sense of self or the premising of worth of persons and relationships extrinsically. Much as troubling situations may invite us to despair they also suggest hope as a possibility or option. Indeed:

> At the root of hope is the consciousness of a state of things which invite us to despair (illness, damnation, etc.). To hope is to put one's trust in reality, to assert that it contains the means of triumphing over this danger . . . all hope is hope of salvation, and that it is quite impossible to treat of the one without treating of the

---

48. Gabriel Marcel, *Man Against Mass Society* (Chicago: Henry Regnery Company, 1971), 118.
49. Marcel, *Homo Viator*, 36.
50. Halverson, 466.
51. Marcel, *Presence and Immortality*, 231.

other . . . There is no place for salvation except in a universe which *admits of real injustices.*[52]

So, the conflict between love and death poses the only essential problem in this world. A world deserted by love can only be swallowed up by death. But where love persists, where it triumphs over whatever tends to degrade it, death cannot but be definitively vanquished.[53] The difference between despair and hope lies in the fact that, while despair consists in a certain consciousness of time as closed and as a prison, hope appears as a piercing through time because hope infuses circumstances with the light of its openness and unconditional character.[54] Hope relates to the core of a person's being and brings to light an expansive and liberative freedom even amidst much experience of trial or captivity.

Hope and Communion

Importantly, hope cannot be separated from a certain sense of communion or from a more or less explicit dependence on the power of being as intrinsic value and plenitude which guarantees this communion itself.[55] An intimate and essential link exists between hope and communion:

> Hope is generative of action . . . it creates or implies a communion . . . a "we" is constituted, which is not simply the functional we of the crew, but rather an interiorized, spiritualized expression of it . . . Hope has almost the quality of choral song, and furthermore it is by singing that it expresses itself most freely.[56]

An authentic formula of hope is: "I hope in thee for us."[57] This also means that qualitative human experience, characteristic of hope, goes beyond quantified calculations. Or rather, quantitative calculations remain insufficient in regard to it. Hope involves the intimacy of personal freedom and communion with others; it is ultimately founded in wakeful participation in being as the font of intrinsic value and plenitude. Hope truly takes place in a real community where the sense of *us* opens people up in love and freedom. Intersubjectivity constitutes the fact and the experience of being together with others in the light of liberative living. Real

52. Marcel, *Being and Having*, 74–75.
53. Marcel, *Presence and Immortality*, 231.
54. Marcel, *The Mystery of Being Vol. II: Faith and Reality*, 162.
55. Marcel, *Homo Viator*, 93.
56. Marcel, "Desire and Hope," 282–83.
57. Marcel, *Homo Viator*, 60.

communion encompasses being known and knowing, being saved and saving, being loved and loving.[58] Every human being desires someone to recognize, accept, appreciate and ratify who he or she is. People appreciate having others enter into their experience and become genuine companions and fellow travelers in the human pilgrimage. This is the meaning of encounter, inseparable from the notion of co-presence.[59] Encounter can only be accomplished at level of presence. There is true encounter only if there is a being *with*.[60] In this light, hope does not remain centered on the subject himself or herself.[61] A dimension of *being with* is essential to and defines hope. In existential terms, openness and connectedness with others through presence sets a person free from a threatened experience of insignificance, oblivion or nonbeing. The mediated sense of personal significance embraces awareness of one's vulnerability but through the deeper consciousness of one's own unconditional attractiveness, desirability and lovableness as a person.

An available person connects with others and refuses the right to dispose of himself or herself through suicide. The decisive point is that suicide renders a person inaccessible to others. At any rate, the person who commits suicide acts, at least, like someone who does not care whether or not he or she remains available to others. The man or woman dedicated to others remains the most available; he or she wills to be an efficacious instrument of availability. When a person commits suicide, he or she denies himself or herself the condition and possibility of becoming available to others.

In the end, hope expresses itself in the availability to participate—despite the specters of captivity and trial, despair and death—in the experience of communion which, in present life, is an act of adventure, often precarious, aimed at a better life for the community of "us." The *us* is a community of individuals given positive value by their own dignity and having personal and interpersonal interaction with their existential situ-

---

58. In *The Existential Background of Human Dignity*, 40 and in *Creative Fidelity*, 54–57, Marcel discusses, using examples from human relations, what real communion consists in, i.e., in bonding between persons.

59. Gabriel Marcel, *The Mystery of Being Vol.I: Reflection and Mystery* (Lanham: University Press of America, 1984), 137–38.

60. Gabriel Marcel, "Reply to Gene Reeves," in *The Library of Living Philosophers Vol. XVII: The Philosophy of Gabriel Marcel*, Paul Arthur Schilpp and Lewis Edwin Hahn, eds. (La Salle, Illinois: Open Court, 1991), 273–74.

61. Marcel, *Homo Viator*, 66.

ations.⁶² The *us* here is not any ordering of automatons or a collection of individuals considered as objects but living individuals endowed with the value of human dignity and having kinship with others through presence, openness, creativity, rights and responsibilities. Furthermore, "love and hope must not be separated. For a person without love, hope is not possible, only lust and ambition; every ambition seeks to acquire some satisfaction for itself."⁶³ Ambition as a species of obsession fixates a person on the self and on goals that tend to blind and undercut positive attitude towards other people. Or again:

> . . . hope is only possible at the level of the *us*, or we might say of the *agape*, and that it does not exist on the level of the solitary *ego*, self-hypnotised and concentrating exclusively on individual aims. Thus it also implies that we must not confuse hope and ambition, for they are not of the same spiritual dimension.⁶⁴

In light of communion where love in-forms relationships it becomes clear that the subject of "I hope" cannot refer back to the ego, the conditional sense of the self. The ego, which stands in relation to individual moments experienced as centers of life, can only be the subject of desire whose object is never integrity as such but a mode of enjoying. In this sense, the ego is constantly self-seeking. But the subject of "I hope" excludes all claims for *myself*.⁶⁵ Communion as a context of hope means that a person adapts his or her freedom, confirms his or her uniqueness and fits his or her gifts and talents to the conditions of his or her neighbors. This further implies that in a cohesive community, as far as is possible and reasonable, people meet one another with respect. Hope, even of a low order, always confirms the reality not merely of togetherness of bodies, but of kinship and communion, the experience of *being with* others. We can only speak of hope where the interaction exists between him or her who gives and him or her who receives, namely, where the exchange which marks all spiritual life exists.⁶⁶ The relations that people have with themselves are existentially and functionally mediated by the presence of others who are for them and for whom they matter.⁶⁷ So, the essential connection between hope and communion implies that hope, in its concrete

---

62. Ibid., 67.
63. Marcel, *Searchings*, 65–66.
64. Marcel, *Homo Viator*, 10.
65. Marcel, *The Existential Background of Human Dignity*, 142.
66. Marcel, *Homo Viator*, 50.
67. Marcel, "Desire and Hope," 283.

manifestation, alludes to and embraces the notion of the common destiny as a universal good.

Hope and Time

Hope connects closely to the human being's temporality. The perceived objective of hope lies often in some anticipated future. The person who lives in hope pays attention to the future that can unfold from the present in terms of its renewal and re-creation. The anticipated future may imply restyling and reorganizing *modus operandi* and *modus vivendi* of particular contexts of existence. In this sense, hope directs itself futuristically. In hope always exists a tacit or implicit need for transforming obtaining problematic situations. The goal is to triumph over and transcend wrongs, perversions, woundings and failures by relativizing and fulfilling them. However, hope becomes misrepresented if it leads to excessive concerns with the future. Concern with only the future can pass on distaste and insensitivity to the present. In such a case, the future alone is seen as claiming genuine truth and value so that all that is in the present or past can become expendable.

A person engrossed solely in the future loses touch with concrete realities and begins to live in a world of fantasy. One who lingers only in the past reduces life to routine and habits which resist change and novelty. The attendant fear of change also comes to constitute a mode of suffering. Also, one who focuses only on the present subjects himself or herself to fleeting conditions. Accordingly, not to link the future to the past and present can lead to the sense of the insignificance of the present and past situations, escapism and, at worst, callousness. "Hope has its being in the tension of future and present, driving us out of the present, yet seeing the future from the present situation."[68] A sense of hope that relates *only* to an imagined future is false and alienating. The bonds of hope with the present and past set the criterion for distinguishing it as either genuine or fanciful. Unavoidably, the human being always remains a historical and interactive being.

Fostering Hope

At the pragmatic and operational level of understanding, there are four things to say about the evolution and the development of hope in human existence.

First, one who wishes to cultivate an attitude of hope needs to be a person who participates in life's affairs and develops or expands awareness

---

68. John Macquarrie, *Christian Hope* (New York: The Seabury, 1978), 28.

of the problems which arise in the world. This implies living from the heart and sharing in the experiences of the burdened and voiceless and of suffering the vulnerability, anguish and impotence of being human. The heart here symbolizes the whole of the human being as conscious, free, affective, compassionate and understanding. Living from the heart implies that a person lives inward facts of life and experience with all the compassion and achievements, loneliness and misgivings, even urgings of despair. Only then can one come to a realization that human life is greater than anything that can be realized in it or whatever dimension of it that may be called into question. All human life bears intrinsic value and significance even though it may not have an obvious face or voice that makes it recognizable as such. Who a particular human being is is more important than anything he or she has done, than the best possible robe or any amount of wealth or any issue that can be related to the person. Worth of persons and living ties among people surpasses any issue or question of faithful service, obedience to commands, propriety and righteousness, and proving oneself worthy of rewards or gains.

When people realize that all they are has been reduced to power, honor, glory and things that they have, they tend to experience delusion, disillusionment and emptiness that can, in turn, lead to addictive practices, indiscipline and a loss of the sense of responsibility and self-care. This experience arises from the fact that a person discovers at a deep level that nobody really loves him or her; what is loved is what he or she possesses. We find here an explanation of and background for a sad existence. In other words, quantified existence easily obscures and paralyzes the sense of personal significance and dignity.

Secondly, to foster an attitude of hope one needs insertion into the experiences of profound human interpersonal relationship of love and friendship or companionship. The intersubjective plane actuates the vibrancy of hope. Kinship ties dispose people to give of themselves to others who come into their lives. Kinship ties further imply that one can repeatedly yield to the destiny of others whom one serves by striving to answer for them and to share in their frailties and misfortunes as well as their delights and joys. As persons forge identities and aspirations through life with others they come to share their legacies and narrative languages.

Thirdly, for an attitude of hope to evolve and deepen, a person needs to be present to and for the well-being of others with a certain disposition of freshness. Spontaneity constitutes freshness in human relationality. With this spontaneity tends to come people's lived sense of responsibility, self-transcendence and composure which enriches and expands life. Nelson Mandela, when in Robben Island, truly exemplified this experience:

> Despite his prominent position within ANC, Mandela (and other ANC leaders) insisted that no distinctions be made between their prison routine and that of the others in the single-cell section. Mandela received the same clothes, ate the same food, and performed the same hard labor in the limestone quarries. He cleaned his chamber pot ("bowly") each morning and assisted his sick colleagues, when necessary, in cleaning theirs.[69]

In brief, the basic disposition in hope can be summed as: serenity[70] amidst toils, peace amidst agitation, creative responses amidst difficulties and an acceptance of one's limitations while maintaining constant and unlimited aspirations. Hope pursues a fuller and more liberative life by realistically accommodating the various elements of experience. To live in hope, then, places a person in a self-spending trajectory of life. The center of concern constantly shifts from oneself to others and common destiny which engenders unselfishness and self-giving. A person who lives in hope acknowledges and embraces others. He or she also accepts the grandeur of life itself.

Lastly, we foster an atmosphere of hope when we ground ourselves and endeavors in a certain love of life which truly consists in some unconditional affirmation and acceptance of life. When we pronounce love of life, nothing is excluded. Life in its totality is included. Here it is not simply a question of the desire for health, pleasure, honor, sport, career, money, property, or the need to consume. Love of life signifies the beauty and value of human life as well as the entire uncertainty of human praxis and history. It primarily implies the care for and joy in life that can be lived in all its tensions, ruptures and conflicts. It also encompasses the human life in all its color, warmth, togetherness, opportunities, losses, successes and defeats. In the contexts of exploitation, oppression, antagonism and domination, love of life further suggests protests and actions which foster and cherish cooperation, good will and tenderness in dealing with others persuasively, collaboratively and inspiringly. The spirit of solidarity and fraternity for a decent and shared living characterizes hope. We fulfill and work out the meaning of our lives in a context of kinship ties and human efforts.

---

69. Johns and Davis, 142.

70. Serenity is an affirmative, composed accepting frame of consciousness that witnesses to inward strength and openness before an experience.

Precisely because we love life we do not permit ourselves to be deprived of the aspiration that manifests some human fullness, lest we sink to futility. We are in this world to live a truly liberative human life. This means that we need to continually fortify ourselves against resignation, despair and cynicism. Every moment of our lives is not complete, however. The experience and expressions of our lives in a given moment is not the whole of our lives. Not only in suffering or frustration, but even in our most satisfying moments do we poignantly feel limitations in our experiences. Whenever we affirm this life, we also face the need for an ever-ongoing transcendence through the quest for an unambiguous existence.

Attitudes that contradict hope link closely with or constantly refer to petty egotism, bitterness, rash discretion, intolerance and insensitivity in individual and communal relationships. Loss of sensitivity leads to an inaptitude for admiration which deteriorates in proportion to how a particular world yield to the domain of having, covetousness and paralyzing fears. Such a life also includes disregard for the inner life of others. People who are not signs of hope stifle and hinder others from expressing who they most truly are.

Significance of Hope

Hope describes credibly positive human living. In hope, there exists some desirable, accessible and absent experience and expression of human fullness whose attainment is strenuous. That persons and human relations will always remain dissatisfied with some extrinsic or conditional value whose attainment was even arduous is in itself one of the greatest resourcefulness and surest riches of human hope. In other words, one of the wellsprings of hope is the fact that we have many expectations the fulfillment of which often bestirs new claims on us. The decisive point is that hope expresses itself in a multiplicity of aspects, from what seems the most trivial to what may appear the most profound. Hope always involves sensitivity, willingness and availability whose groundswell or mainspring is being itself. Where there is hope, there exists a vision that integrates through enthusiasm, passion and growth in freedom and warm-heartedness. If I can keep my hope alive, my sense of direction will be stable, open and fresh. In such a context I root myself in an inexhaustible source of inspiration and a channel of resourcefulness, integration and fulfillment which is being. In this sense, hope symbolizes and expresses the human exigency for a fuller and liberative life. Hope catalyzes human resourcefulness that re-creates the facticity, relational strata and planes of human experiences.

Wherever there is political repression, economic perversion, social bigotry and breach of fundamental human rights of subsistence, security and participatory liberties, the human being is hindered from going beyond himself or herself. The human subject fails to be free for transcendence necessary for genuine experiences of human kinship. The same case applies when the idol-making of a nation, race, church, state, job, business, class or an ideology leads to asserting its dominance over human existence itself. The idol-making of human creations stifles the ever-ongoing demand for fuller humanity which shall not be silenced. Furthermore, such idol-making frequently generates much sense of mistrust, hate, fears and misery which disfigure and destroy human capacities and striving for a liberating experience of togetherness.

Conclusion

Hope acknowledges the distorted human itineraries of wickedness and tragedies, battles and victories, crimes and follies. Strife, greed and cruelty as well as big-heartedness, kindness and compassion mark many people's lives. Human existence is practically and potentially ambiguous, paradoxical and discordant. Against the backdrop of this acknowledgment hope refuses to be romantic about life. Narratives of hope contain deliberate criticisms and corrections. They contain the positive development of human talents as well. Above all, hope recognizes the tremendous dignity and excellence of each man and woman and of kinship ties among people. In effect, man and woman can always start a new beginning, bring forth new creation and renew the historical process of existence. In this sense, hope establishes man and woman as creatures of intrinsic worth and as partial architects of their destiny.

Inbuilt in the narratives of hope are contrasting attitudes and emphasis with regard to the meaning and confidence in human existence. In hope, the human story cannot but be ultimately meaningful; it has meaning in unity and concord founded on human kinship and familyhood. Only when set against this background can individual or shared transcendence establish itself.

Hope implies that the world in which we live is frequently problematic. It also needs to be constantly re-created. From this perspective, hope looks forward with a sense of unyielding assurance. In hope exists a certain confident assurance in the human reality that precedes and pervades human awareness, questioning, inferences and considerations. Hope affirms that there is a way out of difficult issues and problems. The human subject can control and survive inner and external captivity. Hope perceives the possible, the new and the better. In this light, hope flows from the responsible and loving levels of human consciousness which seek to resolve or make sense of the ambiguities of experience, understanding and judgments.

To live in hope implies an imagination that sees things differently and in noble ways. Such imagination envisions a way forward and out of present predicaments. Such imagination also exists in some dialectical tension with rational criticism and perception. In this way, hope engages people with the belief and trust that there is a way out of felt difficulties. The present does not have the final say on one's life or existence. Accordingly, hope enables people to reflect, think and act according to their best and deepest resources. The inspiration and conviction of hope expresses itself particularly in the human quest to be scientific and sapiential in ways that make liberative morality possible and a reality. To speak this way is also to imply the intermesh of the problematic and mysterious spheres of life and freedom that play out in the scientific, sapiential and moral dimensions of human existence. In this light, the next chapter looks into the constructs of problem and mystery as capturing existential terrains and forms of human existence.

3

The Priority of Mystery over Problem

Precincts of Problem and Mystery

WE CANNOT understand human existence without addressing the issue of wisdom and freedom. And meaningful and attentive talk about wisdom and freedom needs to be set against the distinction between problem[1] and mystery[2] as one set of constructs for understanding experience. At times, freedom has been mistakenly reduced to freedom of choice which tends to set up a framework for superficiality, consumerism, pretentiousness and sensuality. An organic understanding of human wisdom and freedom places freedom beyond the right to freely choose. Freedom and wisdom hinge on the question of authentic self-expression, self-awareness and availability in living with others.

As realms of human experience, true freedom and wisdom expand self-understanding, heal human relationships, renew creative communication and forge responsible ways of living. In freedom and wisdom we find a convergence of deep human urges and cultural potentials for self-transcendence, self-giving and self-development according to circumstance, time and place. The foregoing affirmations set the stage for appreciating the distinction between problem and mystery as helpful constructs for conceiving and understanding the world well.

In this life when we meet people who primarily define and see themselves as, say, engineers, janitors, doctors, security guards, farmers or gardeners, professors or taxi-drivers, we face a functionalized world. In such a world a person tends to principally look at himself or herself as an agglomeration of functions. Indeed, the characteristic feature of our age seems to be specializations and division of labor in the form of functions (occupa-

---

1. A problem is something that you can fix through some technical means. Later sections in this chapter shall clarify further the meaning of a problem.

2. A mystery is something that cannot be simply fixed by technical means; fixing through technical means always remains inadequate. A mystery requires more than technical fixing. Further clarification of the meaning of mystery follows in the later sections of this chapter.

tions) or roles people play in existence. Subsequently, the individual tends to appear both to himself or herself and to others as an agglomeration or an assemblage of functions.³ People just become role players. They also become subject to all kinds of quantified mechanisms. At the same time, atomization and collectivization of human subjects tend to devitalize and de-spiritualize life. Life which generates the problematic world obstructs our acknowledgement of personal and significance and contentment. Fundamentally, a person becomes a *him* or *her*, namely, someone about whom one can speak in a detached way. As such, this problematic world harbors intolerance of those who are not able to do anything productive. This can make the problematic brutal.⁴ Also, human relationality and the sense of kinship among people become tenuous.

The world of mystery exists in contrast with the problematic world. The world of mystery refers to the domain of human presence of one person to one another and to life itself. The ambiance of presence touches on mystery. Mystery means that human existence cannot be wholly mathematized or quantified. The visible world is not the whole world. Furthermore, the domain of mystery transcends the localized sphere of problems which permit technical remedies. The domain of mystery cannot be separated from that of being, that is, from the experience and expression of *who we are and our living ties with one another*. Mystery and problem as fundamental constructs of experience inform one another. While the constructs of mystery and problem are connected, mystery goes beyond problem.

With the expansion of scientific thinking in our contemporary world, the forthcoming section will take particular interest in pointing out the limits, risks and dangers of the thinking that characterizes the problematic world. In our times, technical progress, materialistic focus and positivist tendencies increasingly impact people's lives. The pulses of this impact affect people's self-definitions together with their hesitations, limitations and sense of service and generosity as well as life's directions. Of course, it must at once be noted that problematic thinking does not always exists in its pure form. It frequently intermixes with thinking proper to the realm of mystery or presence. As many scientists and philosophers would note, natural science frequently confronts mysteries as well. With this preliminary acknowledgement, we next consider first what a problem is.

---

3. Gabriel Marcel, *The Philosophy of Existentialism* (Secaucus, N.J.: The Citadel Press, 1967), 10.

4. Ibid., 12.

Problem

What Is a Problem?

A problem is what I can objectively consider and study without bearing in mind or impacting on the realities of my inner life. My whole subjective and transubjective reality is not automatically involved when I study a problem. When faced with a problem, say, when my bicycle gets a flat tire or when I lose a particular recoverable document in my computer, I need not focus on or consider myself. In order to solve the problem of retrieving my recoverable document, I can either call an expert or follow a prescribed technical procedure to recover the document. Once I apply the relevant technique and recover my document I solve the problem. When faced with a problem I need not take into account the human subject who is at work—it is a factor which is presupposed and nothing more.[5] Therefore, a problem exists before me in its entirety. In this regard:

> . . . there can only be a problem for me where I have to deal with facts which are, or which I can at least cause to be, exterior to myself; facts presenting themselves to me in a certain disorder for which I struggle to substitute an orderliness capable of satisfying the requirements of thought. When this substitution has been effected the problem is solved. As for me, who devote myself to this operation, I am outside (above or below if you like) the facts with which it deals.[6]

A problem is something that bars one's path and against which one runs. In a problematic situation, I tend to be outside of the facts with which I deal.[7] The understanding gained in dealing with a problem is, in principle, universal, abstract, technical and verifiable. Again, taking the case of recovering my lost document in my computer I will only need to follow some laid out steps that would enable me to retrieve my document. If I cannot do this myself, I can call on an expert to carry out the operations for me. In fact, the world of natural tangible objects coincides with that of the problematic. Strictly speaking, the problematic is coextensive with my "body." The *percipio* as the quantifiable remains the field of problems. The *percipio* can be mathematized; in this sense it corresponds to the physical world. It signifies the sensible and perceptible presence of things

---

5. Ibid., 17.
6. Marcel, *Homo Viator*, 68.
7. Marcel, *Being and Having*, 100.

or entities as their most immediate manifestation. All problematizing implies concrete experience and a continuity of a "system for me."[8]

When people deal with a problem they try to discover a solution or technique that can become common property and which, consequently, can, at least in theory, be rediscovered by anybody at all. "A genuine problem is subject to an appropriate technique by the exercise of which it is defined."[9] Similar techniques address similar problems. Flat tires, for example, get dealt with in similar ways. A technique is comparable to a kind of manipulation of the physical objects or, at least, of mental elements comparable in some respects to physical objects. The validity of a technique for anybody and everybody grounds its truth. Every technical manipulation, even the simplest, implies the possession by the manipulator of certain minimal aptitudes, without which a technique cannot be practical.

As specialized and rationally elaborated form of knowledge, a technique concerns itself with skills and the transformation of the world.[10] When technicians apply techniques that they have mastered, they experience a joy which can be innocent and noble. This joy connects with a consciousness of power over inanimate things, that is, over reality subordinate and is, in a certain sense, meant to be controlled by human beings.[11] When properly understood, this joy cannot be separated from warm-heartedness. In the soundness or purity of their joy, technicians think not of themselves but of their tasks. In this regard, a personal advantage that comes with success becomes ancillary or a derived benefit.[12]

The superiority of one technical process to another depends on how it improves output or makes it possible to produce the same amount in less time with less cost and the least disadvantages.[13] The value of a technique lies in the precision or accuracy of its application and the corresponding intellectual honesty. In this way, technicians need to carry with them an incessant sense of responsibility which must not assume the form of an obsession. This responsibility constitutes the spirit with which the technician performs or carries out his or her task according to the virtue

---

8. Ibid., 127.
9. Ibid., 117.
10. Gabriel Marcel, *The Decline of Wisdom* (London: Harvill Press, 1954), 7.
11. Ibid., 8.
12. Ibid., 9.
13. Ibid., 8.

of accuracy. The very light of the technician is his or her sense of accuracy or precision.[14]

On account of bodiliness, the human being may be examined with instrumentalist techniques.[15] The human being is subject to technical control and measurement insofar as his or her body can be reduced to certain details.[16] A lot of medical assessments work this way. A completely problematic approach to human beings easily confuses the distinction between who we are and what we are. In the end, we can find ourselves in real danger of confusing our personalities with our formal and functional identities. The consequence of this confusion is that:

> . . . the human, all too human, powers that make up my life no longer sustain any practical distinction between myself and the abstract individual all of whose "particulars" can be contained on the few sheets of an official dossier, but . . . what is going to become of . . . inner life . . . ? What does a creature who is thus pushed about from pillar to post, ticketed, docketed, labelled, become, for himself and in himself? One might almost speak, in this connection, of a social nudity, a social stripping, and one might ask oneself what sort of shame this exposure is likely to excite among those who see themselves condemned to undergo it? . . . a man in his social nakedness—stripped, by society, of all his protections . . . .[17]

In other words, "man can become like a piece of machinery even in what we call a free country, and he becomes such where all creativity is removed from his environment, where he is no longer anything more than a cluster or a complex of functions."[18]

In the problematic milieu, the human being ceases to be a free being. The freedom of men and women depends on their being more than their bio-physical existence.[19] Personal and human existence becomes impoverished when chiefly looked at from the point of view of physical characteristics and measurements. The human being cannot be wholly reducible to his or her biological attributes and/or realities.[20] Human life goes beyond

---

14. Ibid., 9.
15. Marcel, *Being and Having*, 103.
16. Ibid., 101.
17. Marcel, *The Mystery of Being Vol.I: Mystery and Reflection*, 36–37.
18. Gabriel Marcel, "Truth and Freedom," *Philosophy Today*, Vol.9, No.4, 1965, 236–37.
19. Ibid.
20. Marcel, *The Mystery of Being Vol.I: Reflection and Mystery*, 81.

biological functioning; it hinges on spiritual life.[21] Human beings have dimensions of the sacred and depths to them. The human being transcends any attempt to reduce him or her to objective categories and details of a simple problem. In other words, I am more than my height, skin color or my fact of being a male or female. In fact, people grow in their humanity as they continually evaluate their lives and take stance with regard to these evaluations that they make. Here it must be stated clearly that people grow in their humanity gradually, interactively and reflectively.

The problematic milieu also easily nurtures social atomization through impersonal bureaucratization. In this light, the practice of collective registration and enrolment can end up serving anonymous bureaucracy. With this bureaucracy comes the general compartmentalization of life which can weaken the creative impulses of individuals. Furthermore, in a bureaucratized world a certain social equality prevails as a result of standardization and uniformity. This equality tends to annul the sense of individuality and the true feeling of fraternity.

In a conception of the human being that is predominantly problematic, an "exclusively human rhythm tends in fact to become that of a machine or an automaton, for it is a rhythm which is not super-organic but sub-organic."[22] As a technical world, the problematic world makes use of a variety of instruments of homogenization. These include thinking and behavioral patterns, armaments, advertising techniques, language hegemonies, body forms, clothing styles, food regimes and patterns which become absorbed into local and cultural ways of living. In this way, the human person also becomes subject to a gradual process of quantification, technicalization and standardization. This is also to say, "it is a matter of changing the individual into a simple instrument which cannot in any way present an obstacle to the oppressor's pursuit of his objectives."[23] The individual human being becomes depersonalized as he or she is reduced to an abstraction and a unit of utility or a cog in the wheel. This process of depersonalization sets the precedent for ceasing to treat a human being as a subject. What a person thinks and feels quickly lose their significance. People easily deny each other's humanity. This denial blurs the experience of the individual's intimate quality and basic impulses.[24]

---

21. Marcel, *Searchings*, 33.
22. Marcel, *Homo Viator*, 81.
23. Marcel, "Truth and Freedom," 229.
24. Marcel, *The Mystery of Being Vol.I: Reflection and Mystery*, 29.

Under the circumstances of functional categories, death changes its meaning. For, death becomes something like a scrapping of what has ceased to be of use and can be written off as total loss.[25] This perspective endows a growing prestige to youth and discredits old age, the latter being seen as a burden or a drain. The old increasingly come to symbolize burden or even good for nothing. This happens when productivity supplies a critical criterion or determinant of human value.[26] Life begins to define itself in strictly bio-sociological terms assumed as utterly objective.[27] When people become objects, we also see a world addicted to empty words of manipulation and political gamesmanship. We then confront depreciation of words and the failure of trust and of credibility:

> Our world is more and more given over to the power of words, and of words that have been in a great measure emptied of their authentic contents. Such words as *liberty, person, democracy,* are being more and more lavishly used, and are becoming slogans, in a world in which they are tending more and more to lose their authentic significance. It is even hard to resist the impression that just because the realities for which these words stand are dwindling away, the words themselves are suffering an inflation, which is just like the inflation of money when goods are scarce.[28]

In the interest of further clarity, however, we need to realize that the oath bears little significance in a world that does not honor the sense of the sacred. It is perhaps from this point of view that we should understand the whole phenomenon of empty words that prevail in many circumstances of living.

Subsequently, in the problematic world the human being tends less and less to be treated as a subject and is consequently less and less respected. As a result, we come to witness a constant and widespread violation of privacy.[29] Even the so-called free world becomes infected by the destructive consequences of the uncontrolled power of institutionalized greed. Social isolation and economic pressures of a competitive world tend to precipitate breakdown of families, interpersonal networks of support and mutual assistance. Kinship ties, human loyalty and compassion easily give

---

25. Marcel, *The Philosophy of Existentialism*, 11–12.

26. Marcel, *The Decline of Wisdom*, 22.

27. Ibid., 17.

28. Marcel, *The Mystery of Being Vol.I: Reflection and Mystery*, 33–34.

29. Gabriel Marcel, *The Existential Background of Human Dignity* (Cambridge: Harvard University Press, 1963), 165; Marcel, *The Decline of Wisdom*, 17.

way to the will to power and the pursuit of material gains. Consequently, the triumphant forces become hypocrisy and falsehood which sap the lives and energies of people.[30] Additionally, collective selfishness, disregard for others and dishonesty easily lead to the plundering of natural resources in ways which ignore the integrity and continuity of creation.

Of course, it must also be underscored that technical progress can go a long way in improving the material conditions of people. Technical progress can enable people meet their basic needs. Technical progress can help reduce ignorance, fight diseases and minimize material poverty. In fact, the improvements of agriculture, food security, the provision of clean water, good medical care and hygienic social environment have expanded as a result of technical advancement. A proper use of technological advantages makes it possible for some people to offer financial and material support to others. As a result of technical advancement, new communication possibilities, for example, bind together many countries in ways previously unimaginable. Personal computers, fiber optics, satellites, networks of faxes, e-mails and internet links make human multinational interdependence and integration more and more a reality. Further, technical progress makes it possible to move money and information across countries at incredible speeds and in unbelievable magnitudes. In spite of the advantages that technical progress brings, it cannot be overlooked that technical developments can weaken or even eliminate feelings of gratitude and veneration without which, say, monuments as symbols of heritages lose their significance.

Furthermore, a fundamentally problematized world poses an affront to self-respect inseparable from self-esteem. This affront occurs because self-respect consists in the refusal to allow oneself be degraded to the level of an instrument.[31] In fact, if I allow myself to be degraded to the level of a tool I betray my being, that is, my personal truth as a certain quality implied in self-respect.[32] Personal existential truth exceeds particular truths about a person that another may learn or discover after study. Personal truth also defies precise formulations. Truth considered under its existential aspects engages the living being that a person is. This means that personal significance roots itself in one's reality. In effect, the intention of wanting to destroy another person's sensitivity to or sense of truth

---

30. Marcel, "Reply to Kenneth T. Gallagher," in *The Library of Living Philosophers Vol. XVII: The Philosophy of Gabriel Marcel*, Paul Arthur Schilpp and Lewis Edwin Hahn, eds. (La Salle, Illinois: Open Court, 1991), 390.

31. Marcel, *The Existential Background of Human Dignity*, 150.

32. Ibid., 149.

The Priority of Mystery over Problem

seeks precisely to make a direct attach upon the person's self-respect.[33] Self-respect derives from personal truth. Self-respect heals and fosters sharing, friendliness, care and compassion. When people awaken to their self-respect, they become confident, resilient, open and affirming of others as well. Self-respect considered under its existential aspect touches on the interests of the people.[34] To lose self-respect implies interior breakdown or the loss of inner consistency.

So, where persons have been reduced to a little more than the functions they carry they tend to lose the capacity for self-respect. Without self-respect people also become impervious to the sense of justice and truth. Undermining or destroying human respect leads to the deterioration or attenuation of the sense of justice which comes to ally itself with mainly punishments. In such an atmosphere, courts of justice arouse as little affection as a tax or an immigration office. Furthermore, justice and truth hang together; both aim to restore the humanity of people. The violation of justice conceals the truth which brings spirit and light to human existence.[35]

Self-respect needs still to explicitly inform the sense of justice because justice requires reverence for a person's inviolability, that is, people's sanctified character which is inseparable and bound up with who they are. Further, the exercise of justice requires an interior freedom from biased feelings. True justice marks the beginning of sympathy, that is, the beginning of love.[36] Sympathy means that we are capable of subjectively assessing, interpreting and possessing the experience of another so that it also becomes our own. In apprehending and actualizing the experience of another in ourselves, we become changed by active sympathy. In light of this sympathy, we guide and bring creative, contingent and free spirit in communal and personal forms of being.

Every abuse of persons undercut genuine concern for justice necessary for enkindling nonpartisan protest. Concern for justice needs to arise from the fracture, weakening or betrayal of the self-respect of people. On the whole, it must be added, the problematic world as a predominantly technical world tends to diminish spontaneity and freshness in human relations. This explains why "usually high development of the applied sciences goes with great impoverishment of our inner lives. The lack of proportion

---

33. Marcel, *Tragic Wisdom and Beyond*, 83.
34. Marcel, *The Existential Background of Human Dignity*, 149.
35. Marcel, *Searchings*, 21.
36. Ibid., 13–14.

between the apparatus at the disposal of humanity and the ends it is called upon to realize seems more and more outrageous."[37] Consequently, within the problematic milieu, we tend to end up with greedy, predatory and parasitic elite.

Furthermore, in a problematic milieu, human consciousness also becomes that of anonymous masses. That is, it assumes an identity with the masses that thrive on gossip, hearsay and rumors. This means that as an individual, I think what others think. I become wholly what others think of me. Living life becomes a matter of doing what the anonymous "they" want me to think, do and want. In this light the human being debases his or her personhood by failing to make judgments and taking responsibility for his or her life. In fact, a denial of personhood engenders the anonymous "they" because "the person is defined primarily by his opposition to that anonymous and irresponsible element which is designated by the French pronoun, *on*, or the German word, *man*."[38] Stated differently, the perception of the human being becomes that of being a "technical power and appears as the sole citadel of orderly arrangement in a world which is unworthy of him; a world which has not deserved him, and has to all appearance produced him quite haphazard—or rather, he has wrenched himself out of it by a violent act of emancipation."[39] Seeing the human being solely as a technical power easily leads the human being to consider the physical environment as consisting merely of a set of technical possibilities. As a result, human beings come to engage in the catastrophic adventure of environmental degradation.[40]

Paradoxically, the ends to which people are called anticipate or participate in being that connects with and touches on the marvelous life and the joy of living. Presence truly mediates the experience and recognition of being as intrinsic value and plenitude. Presence refers to the immediate experience of personal significance. In other words, presence awakens people to their unconditional desirability, attractiveness, value and lovableness. Presence yields inward openness and personal outreach that draw people together. Conversely, the problematic world deprives people of the qualities of presence and significance.

---

37. Marcel, *Being and Having*, 186
38. Marcel, *Tragic Wisdom and Beyond*, 86.
39. Marcel, *Being and Having*, 184.
40. Gabriel Marcel, "Reply to Pietro Prini," in *The Library of Living Philosophers Vol. XVII: The Philosophy of Gabriel Marcel*, Paul Arthur Schilpp and Lewis Edwin Hahn, eds. (La Salle, Illinois: Open Court, 1991), 240.

At any rate, the more a human being is delivered over to the problematic world and its categories, the more he or she becomes individualistic and egotistic. As a person begins to see neighbors and others mainly in terms of their functions or roles, he or she also loses the capacity to be present to himself or herself. In fact, the measure in which a person fails at being present to others mirrors the measure in which he or she cannot be present to himself or herself. As people become less present to themselves they annihilate the necessary condition without which existential value ceases to be experienced or even recognized.[41]

Intersubjectivity or human kinship forms the intelligible background for experiencing and recognizing values. In effect, the more people center on themselves the more they reject value because there is no value without communion.[42] That is not all. The more people make themselves centers of reference and consider others only in relation to themselves, the more the idea of human transcendence loses its significance as well. In other words, we perceive the value of others as human beings when they become an integral part of our experiences. In so perceiving them we also begin to search for modes of existence that can bring us together towards some real and pleromatic unity where we can be all in all.[43]

In other words, we grow as human beings when we open ourselves to others in a spirit of kinship with a unity of purpose and destiny. When I open myself to the other, the other ceases to be something that bars my path or something against which I come into contact or can deal with entirely problematically. Hence:

> The other in so far as he is other, only exists for me in so far as I am open to him, in so far as he is a Thou. But I am only open to him in so far as I cease to form a circle with myself, inside which I somehow place the other, or rather his idea; for inside this circle the other becomes the idea of the other, and the idea of the other is no longer the other *qua* other, but the other *qua* related to me; and in this condition he is uprooted and taken to bits, and at least in process of being taken to bits.[44]

When the other becomes for me a *thou*, that is, as a presence, I encounter him or her in his or her being. In a moment when a man, for instance, feels himself weighed down by distaste for life and self-disgust,

---

41. Marcel, *Presence and Immortality*, 155.
42. Ibid.
43. Marcel, *The Existential Background of Human Dignity*, 141.
44. Marcel, *Being and Having*, 107.

the presence of another who takes him into account can act as a vehicle of renewal that re-establishes him in his condition as a subject. He then becomes re-integrated into the living and loving world of people.[45] The awakening process can further become pierced with personal involvement and warmth. When we become *present to one another*, we become interior to one another.[46] That is also to say, encounter can only be accomplished at the level of presence. There is true encounter only if there is the experience and expression of *being with*, that is, where we pour out our very selves.[47] This participation constitutes a culmination of hope. When persons awaken to the consciousness of being as intrinsic value and plenitude, they make active and liberative, faithful and fruitful presence sensible and concrete. This is also a presence in which their very selves are poured out. In a word, mindfulness that characterizes presence radically discloses and affirms the unconditional truth, desirability and lovableness of persons.

Certainly, the world of the problematic is also the world of technical progress. This is not to say that technical progress is bad. No doubt, technical advancement enhances flows of people as tourists, immigrants, machinery and plants as well as repertoires of images and information through newspapers, magazines, televisions, videos and films. What is more, when put to the service of people technical agriculture and industry make available basic goods and services and opportunities for expanding material satisfaction and wealth of human communities. At the same time, however, unless we make a consciously ascetic (disciplined) effort to master the techniques and put them in their proper subordinate place of serving ends that anticipate or participate in being, they tend to assemble themselves or organize themselves against the man or woman who rejects or refuses them.[48] In sum, it may be affirmed that in the problematic world people can dominate and exploit one another, as they turn themselves into means to their selfish ends and interests. In other words, when egoism and self-centeredness take center stage in the drama of life, who persons are and what they can be as human beings become impeded as well. When, however, technology fulfills its proper function it remains subordinated to something higher. In other words, technology submits to the mode of thinking that grasps the intrinsic significance of the human reality. The grasp of such significance belongs to disclosive truth.

45. Marcel, Marcel, "Desire and Hope," 285.
46. Gabriel Marcel, "Some Reflections on Existentialism," *Philosophy Today*, Vol.8, No.4 (1964), 254.
47. Marcel, "Reply to Gene Reeves," 273–74.
48. Marcel, *Man Against Mass Society*, 260.

The problematic world easily abandons individuals and human relationships to extrinsic and material gains. Spiritual wellbeing of people then suffers diminishment. In this framework, life becomes impoverished and existentially insecure. Where existential rootlessness marks life, the temptation to despair easily enters into existence.

The Problematic, Techniques of Degradation and Propaganda

A world given over to problematic categories easily yields to the notion of the massive and systematic employment of the techniques of degradation, which just control and dominate. Control and domination make extrajudicial killings, torture, blackmail, kidnapping and arbitrariness common methods of settling scores. Techniques of degradation signify a whole body of methods deliberately put into operation in order to attack and destroy the self-respect of people who belong to some definite class or other. Techniques of gradation steadily destroy people's self-respect. In making people conscious of themselves as of little or no significance, techniques of degradation force them to despair of themselves from the very depths of their being.[49] A prison system can constitute a series of techniques of degradation of a people. Again social and economic bigotry against a group of people may build within its mechanisms techniques of degradation.

A technique of degradation seeks to humiliate men and women, who, nonetheless, sometimes still become pierced by flashes of awareness of their intrinsic worth and, hence, know the depth to which they have fallen or sunk. Such a technique destroys people's awareness of themselves as of intrinsic desirability, worth and lovableness. In the circumstances, people come to appropriate and inhabit distorted stories, judgments and imaginations that others have of them. Such people then come to lose all sorts of living links with anything of enduring value and sense of significance. Accordingly, for such people the moral fabric of life and conduct collapses. In contrast, persons who retain the awareness of their own intrinsic desirability and value remain capable of challenging and reacting against their own mistreatment and abuse.

In the application of a technique of degradation one forces on others one's incorrect and mistaken claims to superiority. Therein lie the vicious and hideous dynamics of obfuscating the awareness of the sacred existence of others. A man or woman who degrades others, in effect, refuses to regard them as made in the image of God.

---

49. Ibid., 42.

Furthermore, close kinship exists between propaganda and the techniques of degradation. Both systems insult, mock and abuse human dignity in frightening, awful and ruinous ways. Here propaganda needs to be understood as the malicious spreading of misinformation about others' views on issues. Through misconception, misplacement, manipulation, misnaming and labeling, propaganda literally attempts to stifle the fine shades of truth. Propaganda tapers off and restricts common nouns with exclusivity and self-serving distortions. Propaganda seeks to neutralize and reduce people to conditions in which they lose their capacity to alertly and attentively react to their situations. Propaganda refuses to recognize the competence of individual judgments. Impatience, intolerance and presumptuousness mark the appreciation of the individuals who submit to its devices and caprices. Therefore, propaganda condemns those it manipulates. For, it claims the right to manipulate the consciences of other people in abusive, violent and discriminatory ways. The imposture of propaganda refuses to the transcendence of truth. This refusal impoverishes human existence.

Besides, an effective propaganda exploits as skillfully as possible the weaknesses of the other' position while pretending there is no hostility. Also, propaganda incorporates hegemonic forces of domination, exploitation and pillage which disrupt mutual respect among persons. This parody of promotive wisdom systematically tramples universal values in principle and in actuality. Universal values confer on every human being his or her proper dignity.

Together passions and propaganda foster a culture of deception. Propaganda incites passions which lends credibility to its excesses. Of course, propaganda thrives best in a world of resentment which has an arrogant propensity for the arbitrary use of force. Resentment tends to draw out negative urges over which people tend to lose control. People easily lose authentic self-awareness when resentment yields anger directed against the others perceived as imposing themselves against one's will. Within the logic of resentment lies the desire to conquer, rule and subjugate some reality where that desire results from the struggle for power or some valued actuality. As people strive for lordship in the forms of riches, honor, power and privilege, they enslave and oppose others. Oppressors make the oppressed feel disgust for themselves as they are not merely content to torture and kill their victims.[50]

---

50. Marcel, *Awakenings*, 168.

The Priority of Mystery over Problem

The victims of psychological manipulation and oppression find themselves reduced to the status of a mere thing, a psychic thing.[51] Mass enslavement breeds contempt for the intrinsic value of life. In the end, "all that is not done through Love and for Love must invariably end by being done against Love."[52] Accordingly, whims of propaganda degrade life's own greatness, nobility and privilege. The world of the problematic easily gives itself over to paralyzing fears and covetous desires that close the self on itself or lead to obsessive tendencies. Finally, propaganda psychologically assaults people's identities and relationships. It does so by turning people into stereotypes. In this contrived perception we find that selective attention which distorts or ignores the actual experiences of people and human relations. Often victims of propaganda suspect, slander and violate others and one another. Although not uncommon, the resulting antagonism breeds anxiety, depression and stress in victims of propaganda. In this way, too, propaganda undermines political trust and confidence.

The Problematic and Hope

The following consideration on the relationship between the problematic and hope throws important light on the relationship between the human subject and hope. As we shall see, hope and problem inversely relate. In fact, the capacity to hope diminishes in proportion as people become increasingly chained to conventional experience and to the categories which arise from it and as that experience is given over to the problematic world.[53] Given that the problematic world and technique coincide, together they create desire and fear. Every technique serves some desire or some fear. Characteristically, hope eschews technique.[54] Also, hope belongs to a different order from desire; unlike desire, hope involves active waiting.[55] In addition, the subject of "I hope" excludes all possessive claims of ownership or having.[56] When *having* dominate life people fail at communion. Therefore, dividedness rules human relations.

In fact, the problematic world has close links to despair. The world of technique remains opaque to the fundamental issues of human kinship or meaning of life and death.

---

51. Marcel, *Man Against Mass Society*, 19.
52. Ibid., 75.
53. Marcel, *The Philosophy of Existentialism*, 43.
54. Marcel, *Being and Having*, 76.
55. Marcel, "Desire and Hope," 278, 280.
56. Marcel, *The Existential Background of Human Dignity*, 142.

> The world of the problematical is the world of fear and desire, which are inseparable; at the same time, it is that world of the functional—or of what can be functionalised . . . finally, it is the kingdom of technics of whatever sort. Every technique serves, or can be made to serve, some desire or some fear; conversely, every desire as every fear tends to invent its appropriate technique. From this standpoint, despair consists in the recognition of the ultimate inefficacy of all technics, joined to the inability or the refusal to change over to a new ground—a ground where all technics are seen to be incompatible with the fundamental nature of being.[57]

In the problematic world, people have the fragility to lose control of their techniques resulting in negative consequences for persons and human relationships. In effect:

> [Man] can achieve as much as his technics; yet we are obliged to admit that these technics are unable to save man himself, and even that they are apt to conclude the most sinister alliance with an enemy he bears within him . . . man is *at the mercy of his technics* . . . he is increasingly incapable of controlling his technics, or rather of *controlling his own control*.[58]

Our present ecological crisis illustrates this well. Any attempt to situate hope within the realm of technique subverts hope.[59] Hence, the more one engages the problematic world and its categories, the less can one control techniques, the less one hopes or becomes a true sign of hope. Besides, "technical progress provides no guarantee for the foundation of a just social order. Technical progress could ultimately lead to a world of robots in some sense bereft of conscience."[60] Technique offers only a means-end schema of dealing with the practical and functional world of objects.

Mystery

Mystery as Meta-Problematic

To begin with, when a problem becomes personal, it crosses the threshold of the problematic. The experience touches on the meta-problematic, the mysterious. The mysterious does not coincide with the unknowable. "The unknowable is that on which thought is bound to stumble. It cannot be

---

57. Marcel, *The Philosophy of Existentialism*, 30.
58. Ibid., 31.
59. Marcel, *Being and Having*, 77.
60. Marcel, "Reply to Otto Friedrich Bollnow," 202.

considered otherwise than as a wall, an obstacle, or, if you like, a chasm."[61] An example of an unknowable is whether or not I will die tomorrow. "The unknowable is in fact only the limiting case of the problematic, which cannot be actualized without contradiction."[62] In fact, "a problem which does not allow of a solution is no doubt a problem that has been badly posed."[63] However the existence of a problem presupposes that there is something which stands above it. That is, the meta-problematic precedes a problem. Within this perspective, then, mystery coincides with the meta-problematic. The realm of mystery places a person beyond the parameters of problem in the strict sense. Connectedness with the mysterious vista of life alters self-perception, personal participation and practical attitude.

Mystery should not be confused with a lacuna in our knowledge or a void to be filled. Mystery entails the profound.[64] Mystery possesses certain plenitude and expresses the profound. A human being lives in the presence of mystery whenever he or she confronts reality that stands above and beyond the domain of the problematic properly so called.[65] An example of meta-problematic is the presence of HIV in my body. If I am HIV positive, it is not just a problem. It is something that disturbs me as a total person. Being HIV positive touches me in the proper and active sense of the word. The experience brings my vital energies into play. Even a suppression of the viral load in my body using anti-retroviral drugs does not solve the problem. It only mitigates the situation.

Properly speaking, then, in the encounter with an illness like HIV/AIDS, a person puts accent on the dramatic energy and tonality of affectivity which brings with them feelings, sentiments and confidence in the self and life. As an experience of interior awareness, affectivity touches on passion and personal meaning in the world. Affectivity involves an individual's perceptive sparks of valuation, value-differentiation and communication. It implies human subjectivity that freely leads its life within a system of beliefs and existential meanings. In this way, affectivity ignites and impacts the directedness and definition of personal life. What is more, with affectivity comes the experience and expression of human presence. So, mystery endows concrete life with spiritual values, meaning and vitality. Indeed, the meta-problematic of being HIV positive involves

---

61. Marcel, "Some Reflections on Existentialism," 255.
62. Marcel, *Being and Having*, 118.
63. Marcel, *The Existential Background of Human Dignity*, 82.
64. Marcel, *Creative Fidelity*, 152.
65. Marcel, *The Philosophy of Existentialism*, 21.

a participation in my reality as a subject. The experience touches on my being. I am not outside the experience. I cannot be outside it. And my being transcends all inventories.[66]

In effect, mystery involves realities closely bound up with a person's existence, identity and sense of significance. Mystery envelops whole realities of persons and human relations. Before a mystery, like the family or freedom, we may become worried, tired and terrified or enchanted, overwhelmed and ecstatic. Within this perspective, mystery becomes something I am immersed in. In a mystery I cannot make an abstraction from and of myself. I cannot create a dichotomy between some ever-present principle of my life and myself. In mystery, "I am involved *in concreto* in an order which, by definition, can never become an object or a system for me, but only for a thought which over-reaches and comprehends me, and with which I cannot identify myself, even ideally."[67]

What Is a Mystery?

A mystery refers to something I am involved in with the totality of my person. I cannot place myself outside or before a mystery. I am inside a mystery in a certain sense. A mystery envelops and comprehends me, even if I do not comprehend it. To say that evil, for instance, is a mystery means that "I am implicated in evil—just as one is implicated, for instance, in some crime. Evil is not only in front of my eyes, it is within me . . . in such a realm the distinction between what is within me and what lies outside of me becomes meaningless."[68] A mystery then acts on me as an inward principle.[69] In being closely bound up with a person's existence and realities mystery engages the individuated identity of persons. In this light, we can speak of the mysteries of evil, freedom, family, and of ourselves insofar as these realities cannot be separated from who we are. Also, mystery encompasses such profound realities like forgiveness, reconciliation, love, kindness and salvation.

In addition, a mystery can be doubted and rejected. "Just because it is of the essence of mystery to be recognized or capable of recognition, it may also be ignored or actively denied."[70] It is rather by analogy with light that we have to think of mystery—light, insofar as it is "*lighting*" and "en-

---

66. Marcel, *Being and Having*, 102.
67. Ibid., 128.
68. Marcel, *Man Against Mass Society*, 91.
69. Marcel, *The Philosophy of Existentialism*, 22.
70. Marcel, *Being and Having*, 117–18.

lightening": in other words, as a vitalizing cognition. It is precisely because it is light*ing* that mystery cannot be "lit" as an object may be "lit."[71] Thus, the mysterious must be looked for in the direction of light rather than in the direction of obscurity.[72] This light may be understood as an experience that cannot commute itself into evidence before us. No possibility of confining-within, of reducing to something else or "to something" exists in a mystery. In mystery, we find ourselves well within the sphere of the unquantifiable. We find ourselves caught up in the complexity and depth of a reality that confront our human existence.

In a basic sense, speaking of mystery implies our involvement with being which has a supra-physical quality. This is also to say, we engage who *we are* and our whole tasks consist in defining ourselves in relation to plenary Reality.[73] The more we actually participate in being the less we are capable of knowing or saying in what it is that we participate. At the same time, the reality of being will resist all critical dissolution. When it comes to mystery, I am, by definition, led beyond any "system for me." I am involved in an order which by definition can never become an order or a system for me. Rather I become immersed in a consciousness of being which transcends and includes me and with which I cannot even ideally identify myself.[74] It makes no sense then to speak of the problem of being or of a problematic approach to being.

In the confrontation with mystery I face who I am as a subject. In a way then mystery implies positing the omnipresence of being and the immanence of thought in being. There is the transcendence of being over thought.[75] This is also to say, in order to think or know we need, first of all, to be. In fact, being can only be conceived as that in which thought participates.[76] In other words, knowledge presupposes something beyond itself and from which it distinguishes itself. We conceive of knowledge in relation to a context that marks out intelligibility. Particular knowledge implies a blindfold sense of being. In asserting the immanence of thought in being we recognize that thought always refers to something, being, which transcends it. Thought is a way to being; it is a means of encountering the mystery of being. Logically, thought is subordinate to being. Any

---

71. Marcel, "Some Reflections on Existentialism," 255.
72. Marcel, *The Existential Background of Human Dignity*, 82.
73. Marcel, *Being and Having*, 35.
74. Marcel, *Creative Fidelity*, 69.
75. Marcel, *Being and Having*, 36.
76. Marcel, *Philosophical Fragments*, 84.

attempt by thought to make objective representation or an abstract schema of being remains inadequate. Being asserts itself as interior to thought. Being is the base of thought and from which thought starts. Although omnipresent, being is accessed in the contingency of thought. In this way, being bears a perspectival context. Besides, knowledge as interpretation always refers to something already there. And knowledge refers to being as its own ontological presupposition. Knowledge is contingent on a participation in being and no epistemology can be adequate here since it would presuppose it.[77]

Being constitutes the ground on which we evaluate our lives. This means that we evaluate our lives on the basis of the unity of our persons. We evaluate our lives in accordance and in coherence with a fundamental sense of the unity of life. In evaluating our lives we account for who we are, what we have, our social context and what we do. In the process we draw the disparate elements, loyalties and roles of our lives into the unity of our personalities. The narrative and feeling of our being shape our judgments, discernment and life's direction.

Furthermore, mystery and presence are equivalent; mystery can only be properly used in a context where presence makes itself somehow felt.[78] As a notion, presence tends to defy definition though it can be described. Presence fulfills our need to belong. At the root of presence lies someone who takes us into account. Presence satisfies our hunger and slakes our thirst to be significant. Nothing can take the place of presence; no letters or phone calls, pictures or souvenirs or keepsakes can constitute adequate substitutes for presence. In this regard, many people long for the presence of their beloved or of friends. People feel the pain of separation from people about whom they care. When people are ill, they do not need flowers and cards nearly as much as they need the presence of friends or people they cherish. Presence anchors and brings people together; it bonds them. Presence reveals itself the moment persons awaken to the experience that re-creates them with warmth and significance. Conversely, absence exists in contrasts with presence. In absence people feel lonely, alienated and miss the sense of significance in their life. In absence people feel restless. Absence illuminates the human demand and aspiration for communion with another or others.

As a structure for experience, presence "is something which reveals itself immediately and unmistakably in a look, a smile, an intonation or a

---

77. Ibid.

78. Marcel, *Being and Having*, 101; *The Mystery of Being Vol.I: Reflection and Mystery*, 216.

handshake."[79] Presence refers to the gift of the self in personal openness that arises from participation in a plenitude of kinship and warm-heartedness. Not everybody takes us into account which means that not all people can be personally present to us. Hence, "presence has its full significance only in a world where the negative and depressing aspects of otherness are also manifest."[80] In presence persons become interior to one another. Hence:

> When I say that a being is granted to me as a presence or as a being (it comes to the same thing, for he is not a being for me unless he is a presence), this means that I am unable to treat him as if he were merely placed in front of me; between him and me there arises a relationship which, in a sense, surpasses my awareness of him; he is not only before me, he is also within me—or, rather, these categories are transcended, they have no longer any meaning.[81]

Presence constitutes a sincere assurance which discloses to us an immediate sense of counting in virtue of being who we are. The permanent gift of who we are also implies self-understanding in history. Presence entrust us with who we are. The experience reveals the unconditional value of our persons. In this entrustment, presence renders us more accountable, responsible, patient and humble. With presence a human subject achieves a unity of creative impulse and personal faith.[82] In fact, a renewal of presence constitutes the lifeblood of faithfulness to those persons who are present.

We may also note that the idea of mystery implies the idea of expansive power bound up with the very idea of God.[83] But here power refers to the assurance and joy of living. "Our world is certainly not a world from which the mysterious is excluded, a world in which all that has the power of communicating itself communicates itself directly and spontaneously. Hence there is an intimate relation between the idea of mystery and the idea of value."[84] Since being is spiritual the mysterious world touches on the spiritual horizon of life. A spiritual world is also at once a milieu of dialogue: "all spiritual life is essentially a dialogue."[85] Therefore, we enter the spiritual milieu through love which, in turn, implies a life that is not centered on itself.

79. Ibid., 40.
80. Marcel, "Some Reflections on Existentialism," 256.
81. Marcel, *Being and Having*, 38.
82. Marcel, *Man Against Mass Society*, 90.
83. Marcel, *Metaphysical Journal*, 161.
84. Ibid.
85. Ibid., 137.

Mystery and Hope

A direct correlation exists between hope and mystery. Hope is a mystery and not a problem. One who lives in hope obtain from oneself the assurance that one should remain faithful in the hour of darkness to that which in its origin perhaps expresses itself as inspiration, exaltation or an enrupturement of heightened awareness. But this faithfulness cannot be put into practice except by virtue of cooperation between freedom, good will and promptings from the regions of depths, that is, where values become divine gifts.[86] In the experience and expression of hope lies the radical conviction and assertion that reality overflows all possible reckoning. In this connection:

> To hope against all hope that a person whom I love will recover from a disease which is said to be incurable is to say: It is impossible that I should be alone in willing cure; it is impossible that reality in its inward depth should be hostile or so much as indifferent to what I assert in itself as good . . . beyond all experience, all probability, all statistics, I assert that a given order shall be reestablished, that reality is on my side in willing it to be so. I do not wish: I assert; such is the prophetic tone of hope.[87]

To hope, say, even as one is HIV positive consists in asserting that there exists at the heart of being beyond all data, beyond all inventories and all calculations, a mysterious or transcendent reality in connivance with me. This reality cannot but will that which I will by the whole of my being.[88]

Therefore, to hope means to carry within me the assurance that my present situations or conditions of captivity and pain, fear or insecurity do not have the final say on my destiny. As it were, the unconditional appears to grasp me. Insofar as hope is a mystery it carries with it the affirmation of the unconditional and the eternal.

Thus far, the next sections will consider freedom and the encounter with HIV/AIDS as case examples of mysteries. When understood less as problems than mysteries, freedom and evil change and transform their meanings in people's lives and imaginations. In fact, how people harness and understand freedom and participate in the encounter with concrete evil shape how they become true signs of hope.

---

86. Marcel, *Homo Viator*, 63.
87. Marcel, *The Philosophy of Existentialism*, 28.
88. Ibid.

The Mystery of Freedom

The subject matter here is personal and existential freedom. It is in the very definite sense of the meaning of mystery that personal and existential freedom exists and expands. A person, as a living being, participates in and exercises freedom. The mystery of freedom comes with the advent of human life. The mystery of freedom envelops a person's existence. Freedom constitutes the ground of thought which tries to conceive it.[89] Freedom can only be conceived through itself: it creates or constitutes itself in the act of thinking itself.[90] When I act freely I am conscious of the act. Self-consciousness accompanies every act of free choice. Or again, every act of free decision goes together with consciousness of the self. Freedom involves the awareness of self-relatedness as an original phenomenon of negation or affirmation. In a sense, my freedom is something I decide and decide without appeal. It is beyond anybody's power to reject the decision by which I assert my freedom and this freedom is ultimately bound up with the consciousness that I have of myself.[91]

In effect, to say that I am free is to assert who I am. This is also to say, the thought of being and being coincide in the act by which the individual creates, that is, affirms himself or herself liberatively.[92] We are also conscious of our freedom when we acknowledge and recognize what we and others expect of ourselves. When we make decisions about events and situations we also make decisions about ourselves.[93] Stated differently, our choices individualize and define us. Selfhood takes shape primarily by the choices that we make. When a person fails to choose, by remaining in a constant state of indecision, his or her spirit remains vaporous and, apart from him or her, hovering.[94] The act of choosing seals and sanctions a person in some concrete way. Every decision we make creates a new habit or reinforces a previous one. Our choices actuate and express our self-understanding and at the same time make self-understanding possible.[95]

---

89. Marcel, *Creative Fidelity*, 69.
90. Marcel, *Presence and Immortality*, 21–22.
91. Marcel, *The Mystery of Being Vol.II: Faith and Reality*, 113.
92. Marcel, *Philosophical Fragments*, 91.
93. Marcel, *The Mystery of Being Vol.II: Faith and Reality*, 113.
94. John C. Haughey, *Should Anyone Say Forever? On Making, Keeping and Breaking Commitments* (Chicago: Loyola University Press, 1975), 22.
95. Ibid.

Freedom, Attention and Significance

Freedom and attention link closely with human finitude because finitude is the field in which attention and freedom are exercised.[96] Only in freedom can people sustain the focus of attention which enables them to separate essential from nonessential elements of experience and, so, discriminate aspects of it. Freedom of attention root people in themselves and also enhances their performance in the world. The human capacity for attentiveness expresses a person's lived or core freedom (i.e., how he or she spontaneously is secure in himself herself and with others). In effect, my attention reflects the measure of my freedom.[97] In freedom people willingly and spontaneously awaken to their being; in other words, to *who they are most deeply*. A person's lived freedom indicates his or her degree of self-possession. Attention implies some withdrawal from one's own ordinary life in order to reflect upon it. In this way, attention connects closely with personal experience.[98] Only by arbitrary means can freedom be dissociated from some kind of reference to embodiment.[99]

As a vital and meaningful undertaking, "the free act is essentially a significant act."[100] We must, then, underscore the fact that the very word freedom does not retain any meaning when the sense of human values disappears because values are transcendent.[101] Thus, a proper quality of motivation matters for self-communication and the expression of true freedom. Consequently, it becomes absurd to think of an act as more free the less it is motivated.[102] At the same time, it is important to grant that the senseless holds a considerable sway in human lives.[103] There is a large portion of our lives that we do not deliberate about; this is the contingent part of human lives.[104] The fully free act helps mold a person while the in-

---

96. Marcel, *Tragic Wisdom and Beyond*, xxxiii.

97. Ibid.

98. Marcel, *The Mystery of Being Vol.I: Reflection and Mystery*, 78–79.

99. Marcel, *Tragic Wisdom and Beyond*, xxxiii.

100. Marcel, *The Mystery of Being Vol.II: Faith and Reality*, 116.

101. Marcel, *Man Against Mass Society*, 35–36.

102. Marcel, *Tragic Wisdom and Beyond*, 85.

103. Marcel, *The Mystery of Being Vol.I: Faith and Reality*, 116.

104. "Contingent" here refers to the habitual and instinctive patterns of behaviors and actions. This is different from the "contingent" which is an attribute of every finite being, every existent being, except God. However, between the fully free act and the senseless lie the less significant yet free choices such as what to eat, what to wear, and in what order to do our chores.

significant and meaningless do not impact self-identity or self-direction.[105] Besides, without authenticity freedom deteriorates into an anarchical disposition or it becomes a counterfeit of itself. In this light, a dishonest or corrupt person, for example, lacks an authentic experience and exercise of personal and existential freedom. His or her acts, like a person's disposition of himself or herself, caricature true freedom.[106] When people are authentic, they tell the truth and also do the truth. A person who does not tell the truth cannot be free, and therefore such a person tends to live as a captive of fear, covetousness and manipulation. Freedom and truth cannot be arbitrarily divorced from each other without each losing their own proper character.[107] In other words, when I am open to truth, it reveals itself as a power that envelops and transcends me. When I partake of truth I essentially incarnate an act which terminates the game I can play with myself under any circumstance—a game that always springs from a certain felt sense of complacency.[108] This signifies that truth as an intrinsic value constitutes the very condition upon which anchors human freedom. This freedom makes possible human communication, dialogue and communion necessary for human existence itself.[109] Subsequently, "The man who has betrayed truth—and by that one must understand truth not as a meaningless abstraction, but as one's own truth [intrinsic value]—can no longer be a free man."[110] Authenticity frees a person.

Freedom and Captivity

It is in the midst of a situation of captivity of one kind or the other that a freedom fully ready to choose and decide can be born, first in the form of the aspiration to be free.[111] To say that the freest human being has the most hope indicates that the person has been able to give his or her existence the richest significance.[112] Additionally, the freest person lives most fraternally.[113] Fraternal people live with their neighbors in ways that free

---

105. Marcel, *The Mystery of Being Vol. II: Faith and Reality*, 117.

106. Marcel, *Creative Fidelity*, 102.

107. Marcel, *The Mystery of Being Vol. II: Faith and Reality*, 124.

108. Marcel, *Homo Viator*, 140.

109. Thomas R. Koenig, *Existentialism and Human Existence: An Account of Five Major Philosophers* (Malabar, Florida: Krieger Publishing Company, 1992), 67.

110. Marcel, *The Existential Background of Human Dignity*, 150.

111. Ibid., 146.

112. Ibid., 147.

113. Ibid. Fraternity refers to the comprehensive sense of human kinship or fellowship

them from themselves and, therefore, transcend self-enclosing passions, prejudices and interests. To love one's brothers or sisters means hoping in them. In this light, fraternity brightens life.[114]

True freedom moves in the direction of fraternity without which freedom loses its content of significance. Only in freedom can there be relationships among people that evoke delight. Love which springs from delight make wishing and willing characteristically powerful agents of positive energies. The order of love contrasts sharply with domination, exploitation and pillage that destroy relationships. Love transforms the will into a maker of relationships. The order of love endows life with significance, attraction, vulnerability and authenticity. Love creates and builds relationships.

Indeed, fraternity implies dynamism of love.[115] In this regard, too, human subjects in their freedom become conjointly responsible to themselves and to everyone else. This conjunction of responsibility engages the human person individually and socially.[116] The exercise of one's freedom can constrict or enlarge and deepen another's freedom. People influence the breath and depth of each other's freedom.

Frequently and in a myriad of ways, people preoccupy themselves in ways that skew proper interpretations of issues. This situation may be aggravated by entitlements, riches or promise of material gains which make it difficult to promote self-sacrifice, patience and faithfulness. In a self-enclosing world, people cannot reach out to others with freshness since they tend to see life through some prism of unrequited or unrelieved self-pity. When a person lives from the experience of unrelieved self-pity, he or she becomes preoccupied with satisfying immediate needs, expectations and demands. Freedom of the self, of thought, of action and of speech, *ipso facto*, diminishes. The addictive, materialistic and sensual dynamism of self-preoccupation contradict the expansive exigencies of freedom. Human egoistic exigency distorts self-definition and past-time imaginations. Freedom means that people can always control how they respond to life and existence. Of course, proximate psychological conditions do affect the experience and expression of freedom as the ground for service.

Freedom identifies itself with inward unity of the self which partakes of the experience of an intrinsic sense of the self.[117] This is also to say that free-

that reflects at once and simultaneously a lived experience of human brotherhood and sisterhood.

114. Ibid.
115. Ibid., 148.
116. Marcel, *Homo Viator*, 21.
117. Marcel, *Searchings*, 53.

dom symbolizes the self-experience and self-understanding wherein persons decide for or against themselves. Hence, lived freedom cannot separate itself from realizing self-transcendence and the unconditional value of persons and human kinship. In other words, a free person hopes; in a certain sense freedom and hope coincide. Men and women cannot be free or remain free except in the degree to which they remain linked with that which transcends them, whatever the particular form of that link may be.[118]

Freedom and Grace

True freedom lies in navigating the grey areas of life and existence. To live in the grey field of existence is not a matter of choosing evil against the good; rather it is a question of choosing a better value which realizes human transformation as the object of choice. It is always a matter of desiring a better good. The test of liberty reveals itself in the dividedness of human consciousness before acts of free choice. On account of organic dialectical synthesis between the ego and being in human individual and shared existence, this test becomes inevitable. The exigencies of self-enclosure and open-heartedness attend every significant act in the world. At the heart of liberty lies grace that predisposes people and relationships providentially to discern the greater and expansive good in life.

In relation to grace human freedom grasps itself in the experience of depth and the creativity that truly accompanies it. Of course, grace refers to the experience of being as intrinsic value and plenitude. As a dynamic, grace signifies the afflux of being that can emanate from a word or a smile, gesture or event which symbolizes transcendence or the light of plenitude.[119] Within this context, freedom touches on the imagination, creativity and openness to others. This openness expresses its particularity in *agape* (charity) or *philia* (attachment).[120] In short:

> No life is creative except to the degree that it is consecrated. On the other hand, it is from this very consecration that the gift of my life becomes possible, since this gift . . . realizes only one more step on the road to consecration. To refuse to give my life in some extreme circumstances would be, not to preserve it, but to mutilate it. It is as though sacrifice were its very fulfilment as though to lose it were the means of saving it.[121]

---

118. Marcel, *Man Against Mass Society*, 23.
119. Gabriel Marcel, *Problematic Man* (New York: Herder and Herder, Inc., 1967), 59.
120. Marcel, *Man Against Mass Society*, 24.
121. Marcel, *Presence and Immortality*, 44.

Not uncommonly, sacrifice typifies authentic expression and realization of freedom. For, the human field on which freedom realizes itself always remains precarious and tenuous in character. But sacrifice can be accomplished only to the degree that consciousness ceases to treat itself as a center of projection.[122] This also means that "sacrifice takes on its meaning only in relation to a reality that is susceptible of being threatened, that is, a reality historically given and consequently exposed to the forces of destruction which are brought to bear on whatever endures."[123] Here we stumble upon the deep meaning of the act and experience of making a sacrifice.

The person who gives up his or her life for a cause is unaware of giving his or her all, the making of a *total* sacrifice. Rather, he or she does it for something else that he or she asserts means more (i.e., something that is worth more). He or she puts his or her life at the disposal of a higher reality. He or she extends to the ultimate an aspiration towards the unconditional availability. A person who makes sacrifices places being beyond life. Of course, no sacrifice can take place without hope.

Sacrifice is essentially an attachment. Whether or not a person actually believes in eternal life, the person who makes sacrifices acts as if he or she believed. On the other hand, a person who commits suicide acts as if he or she did not believe in eternal life.[124] Thus far, it becomes interesting to note that my death only prevails against me in collusion with my freedom which betrays itself in order to confer this reality or seeming reality of death. It is this freedom and it alone which can blot out, can conceal from my eyes, the unimaginable richness of the universe. If we are to speak of an ontological counterweight to death, it can only lie in the positive use of freedom which becomes adhesion, that is, love. This adhesion simultaneously counterbalances and transcends death.[125] In the last analysis, a fully free act is essentially the acceptance or refusal which is up to me to make in relation to grace, a refusal that may always disguise itself in the form of a fallacious neutrality.[126]

The very nature of grace is freedom. Grace is not capricious. Grace resides in the natural dynamics of human psychology as human interiority. Grace is at home in the interiority of human dynamics and desires. The

---

122. Ibid., 47.
123. Ibid., 46.
124. Marcel, *Creative Fidelity*, 77.
125. Ibid., 143.
126. Marcel, *Problematic Man*, 60.

immanence of grace constitutes its transcendence: grace has a transcendent source immanent in human interiority and living ties among people which urge us towards marvelous living. While immanence speaks of the closeness of grace to us its transcendence speaks of its expansiveness. The closeness of grace connects us with the experience and marvel of vulnerability. So, as a fervor and flavor of existence grace exists within the natural dynamics of liberating love. This ambiance of grace attracts and orients life towards higher and fuller existence.

Also, grace connects with belief in a way that gives life. Grace demands that we extend ourselves beyond ourselves. It manifests itself in our humanity when we act with self-transcendence which may find expression in extraordinary or meritorious acts, good intentions and honest involvement. It works through human natural powers by bringing them to self-transcendence. Thus, grace liberates, perfects and elevates human wish, imagination and attitudes by turning them into beautiful vehicles for realizing a fuller life.

In actualizing freedom grace cajoles and convicts, prompts and illuminates, invites and beseeches. In so doing, grace also transforms life with vibrancy, fulfillment and liberative sense of significance. When grace fulfills freedom, grace lifts up persons and human relations from threats of oblivion. This is not to assert that grace and suffering are not unconnected. In fact, grace makes us face our own deepest fears. When grace greases the exercise and path of freedom it wakes up people's spiritual, affective and expansive lives. This waking up, as a matter of perspective, interpretation and one's place in particular situations, expands people's ability to sympathize with others. Through sympathy real suffering puts one in touch and contact with one's feelings.

In any case, to live humanly implies being part of narratives of little stories whose headlines, heartbeats, remain elusive. In this way, freedom exercised through grace builds up human trust, confidence and assurance that enables people to recognize, embrace and deepen human narratives. The exercise of freedom in relation to grace heals human existence and begets wondrous living. In other words, through grace people's tasks and sense of mission in life become defined, as they grow in the belief and regard to the self.

Freedom and Act

It is simply a distortion and a mistake to say or maintain that the greater the number of options a person leaves open, the greater his or her freedom will be. Indeed, "reality at any one moment is capable of becoming unreality if the person allows the chaos of 'possibilities' to envelop him, imposing its 'form of indefiniteness upon the definiteness of the moment.'"[127] Nonchoice manifests or mirrors indecision and noncommitment. Freedom is not merely the ability to do whatever I want, when I want and how I want it, that is, to choose as I will or to live as I wish in the way I want. "Human freedom is not some phantom commodity that enjoys a life apart from particulars. Freedom must be exercised in order to be."[128] Hence, "It is only in the exercise of one's freedom that one assures it; by nonexercise one runs the risk of losing it."[129] By no means does this imply that freedom is an act of utter self-determination without restrictions or limitations set by a sense of purpose, responsibility and contingency. "I act freely if the motives of my action are within the limits of what I can legitimately consider as the structural traits of my personality."[130] When we exercise our freedom, it always becomes part of history, that is, a part of ourselves in that it shapes our self-definition and the way we imagine our existence.[131] Thus, the authentic approach to freedom takes place in the reflection of a subject on himself or herself.[132] "There is no meaning in the statement that man is free, and there is of course still less in claiming, with Rousseau, that he is born free . . . every one of us has to make himself into a free man."[133] Freedom is not merely a capacity for endless revision. There is no more fatal error than that which consists in regarding freedom as an attribute.[134]

The personal exigency for freedom defines human subjectivity and kinship with others throughout life. We each tend to become a prisoner to mistaken self-perception, not only in respect to material interests, passions or prejudices, but also in the predispositions which incline us to be centered on ourselves and to view everything from this perspective.[135] Encumbered existence, whether to the self or others, lacks freedom. One does not increase one's freedom by expanding possibilities so that one may have one's own way however one wants it.

127. Haughey, 24.
128. Ibid., 31.
129. Ibid., 33.
130. Marcel, "Truth and Freedom," 232.
131. Haughey, 33.
132. Marcel, *The Existential Background of Human Dignity*, 87.
133. Ibid., 146.
134. Ibid.
135. Ibid., 147.

To be free, a person must go beyond being able to act and act in a certain way. A being is free to the extent that he or she places his or her life under the sign of love.[136] Freedom that never comes to choice or an act will eventually cease to be. Thus, we must once and for all break with the idea that freedom is essentially liberty of choice being conceived as indetermination.[137] Freedom should not be confused with the suggestibility of a dilettante who is curious about everything, but without ever being ready to give himself or herself, to devote himself or herself, to anything.[138] This is not to deny that prior liberty is one aspect of freedom, but only to recognize that "freedom is a conquest [of existential insecurity or lack of security in being]—always partial, always precarious, always challenged."[139] In fact, the distinction between the I and the self in the self-consciousness which accompanies the free act means that we are yet to become identical with ourselves. Properly speaking, freedom is not an attribute with which I am merely invested—but rather that I *must* become free by growing in the plenitude of intrinsic value and expansive consciousness.[140]

Also, the insertion of freedom into existence takes place against the backdrop of the limits of the innate disposition of persons and their circumstances of life. Human freedom does not actuate itself in a social or relational vacuum; rather it always presupposes a relational or interactive world. Contextually, freedom realizes itself in particular expressions of expansive and liberating forces in and among persons. In effect:

> I find myself in strictly determined circumstances regarding my birth, the milieu in which I live, the people I have met, and so on . . . It would be altogether inadequate to maintain that these conditions are due to pure chance and for that reason, insignificant. It is in relation to them that I have to assert my freedom, and in the course of doing so I am let to appreciate my circumstances as having been—in the strongest sense of the word—given. In this way I come to think of a will which is giving and at the same time free.[141]

---

136. Marcel, "Truth and Freedom," 235.
137. Marcel, *The Mystery of Being Vol.II: Faith and Reality*, 115.
138. Marcel, *The Existential Background of Human Dignity*, 146.
139. Ibid.
140. Ibid., 87.
141. Ibid., 30.

Or again, "each of us, however he may desire to do *what he pleases*, is integrated into a certain totality."[142] Vital link and mutual belongingness exists between people and their particular space of dwelling.

Freedom and Liberty of Being

In the human condition exists a certain vital and spiritual realm (that is, a realm of moral and spiritual integrity), the realm of being as the milieu of intrinsic values. In this realm truly consists our freedom which we cannot violate without exposing ourselves to a loss not only of our firmness but also of our organic and moral integrity.[143] This spiritual and moral realm is bound up with human life itself. And far more profoundly, this realm involves the necessity of accepting risks and refusing to believe that it would be possible—and even an advantage—to succeed in removing them.[144] This realm explains why hope necessitates accepting trial as an integral part of the human person and considering it as destined to be engaged and transformed by the inner workings of a creative process.[145] In this light, then, hope appears as a response of the creature to the infinite being to whom it cannot impose any condition whatsoever without scandal.[146] In the final analysis, the philosophy of freedom may be regarded as the philosophy of being, that is, of who we most deeply are without inhibitions and/or constraints.[147] Our freedom is implied in the awareness of our participation in the universe.[148]

Accordingly, true freedom springs from the experience of liberty in our innermost being, the harmony of depths and human kinship. Freedom in this sense cannot be separated from being ourselves and responding to the gift of our own creation: this freedom humanizes life. True freedom actualizes and humanizes who we are. This entails being all that we can and ought to be. Ideal freedom involves the obligation to be human. Unless we become truly ourselves we do not feel free and authentic. Our freedom is "the soul of our soul."[149] Ultimately, even the power of death changes its character in the light of freedom:

142. Ibid., 161.
143. Marcel, *Homo Viator*, 54.
144. Ibid.
145. Ibid., 39.
146. Ibid., 47.
147. Marcel, *Creative Fidelity*, 26.
148. Ibid., 23.
149. Ibid., 55.

> ... my death is powerless against me except by the collusion of a freedom which betrays itself to give death that reality or appearance of reality whose fascinating power has already been verified. It is this freedom and this alone which can seal off from my view the inconceivable richness of the universe.[150]

Of course, personal and existential freedom expresses itself socially, culturally and religiously. Freedom roots itself in historical and personal existence. The mystery of human life winds up closely with the reality of human freedom:

> Everything goes to show with increasing clarity that the power is given to us of in some way locking ourselves more firmly in the prison in which we elect to live. That is the terrible price we have to pay for the incomprehensible power we have been given, or which, still more, makes us to be "ourselves." On the other hand, in so far as we allow ourselves to give ear to the solicitations—which come to us from the invisible world, then the whole outlook undergoes a change . . . the transformation takes place *here below* for earthly life is at the same time transfigured, it clothes itself in a dignity which cannot be allowed to it if it is looked at as some sort of excrescence which has budded erratically on a world which is itself foreign to the spirit and to all its demands.[151]

If we fail to think of freedom as a faculty or an attitude with which we are equipped, we run the danger of converting it into a fancied power outside of us—we risk losing and destroying its true character.[152] In addition, social pressure can always subvert the exercise of human freedom. When this happens, we deny the intrinsic worth and significance of persons and living ties among people. Moreover, paralyzing fear can always inhibit us from exercising and asserting our freedom.

Freedom and Autonomy

The domain of freedom, which includes others, does not coincide with that of autonomy.[153] We can only talk legitimately about autonomy in the

---

150. Marcel, "Desire and Hope," 283–84.
151. Marcel, *The Mystery of Being Vol.II: Faith and Reality*, 187.
152. Marcel, *Creative Fidelity*, 55.
153. Here autonomy does not merely refer to attaining majority and making decision for oneself. It refers to individualism as the act of radical self-administration. This is being one's own person all for oneself. In this sense, autonomy is not simply a matter of supporting and taking care of oneself. Individualism becomes the criterion for appropriating and expressing freedom, which albeit excludes others.

order of administration and the administrable.[154] Furthermore, a human subject can only administer, or treat as something to be administered, everything that can be compared to a *possession*, that is, as something which one has.[155] The idea of autonomy, then, is bound up with a certain kind of particularization of the human subject. The more a human subject enters into an activity with the whole of himself or herself, the less right have we to say that he or she is autonomous. Autonomy is bound up with a sphere of activity which is strictly circumscribed.[156] The radical formula of autonomy is, "I want to run my own life." This formula refers essentially to *action* and implies the notion of a certain province of activity circumscribed in space and time. Everything that belongs to the order of interests, whatever they may be, can be treated with relative ease as a province or a zone marked off in this manner. And legislation is simply the formal aspect of administration. What is beyond administration is by definition also beyond legislation.[157] Such ascription pertains to the nature of true freedom, for example.

Indeed, my life, considered in the totality of its implications, does not seem to be something that can be administered, either by oneself or by another. Between the administrator and the administered there must exist a certain proportionality. This relationship does not ordinarily obtain between me and my life. It only obtains in the case of self-mutilation that is sacrilegious. Hence, at a certain depth within the self and in a zone where practical specializations melt away, autonomy becomes inapplicable.[158] What we can show belongs to us so that there is a sense in which a person does not belong to himself or herself and this is exactly the sense in which the human subject is absolutely not autonomous. While we can show what we have, we only reveal who we are though, even then, only in parts.[159] In effect, as soon as we participate in being we are beyond autonomy. In the sphere of being, autonomy becomes inconceivable. The realm of being involves the whole person. In other words, the more *I am*, that is, the more I assert my being, the less I think myself autonomous. The more I manage to conceive of my being, the less subject to its own

---

154. Marcel, *Being and Having*, 130.
155. Ibid., 132.
156. Ibid., 131.
157. Ibid., 132.
158. Ibid., 131.
159. Ibid., 135.

jurisdiction does it appear to me to be.[160] Autonomy properly belongs to the domain of having.

In order to *have* effectively, it is necessary to be in some degree, that is, to be immediately for one's-self, to feel one's-self, as it were, affected or modified. However, mutual interdependence exists between having and being.[161] The nearer people come to creation, the less they can speak of autonomy. In creation, people are drawn to a fuller future, which incorporates others. In the strict sense, people can only speak of autonomy at the level of exploitation as when an artist exploits his or her inspiration.[162] In creation abides the liberation from the order of having or possessing. In fact, consciousness as such is not a possession or a manner of having, but it may be an enjoyment of something which it treats as a possession. Also, a human act goes beyond possession but may, after the event, be considered a possession as a result of degradation.[163]

Accordingly, the idea of autonomy cannot mean the same thing as freedom. While the human subject may legislate itself, it does so within the network of assumptions, beliefs and psychological possibilities made possible through the historical and cultural contexts of the acting human subject. The choices and actions which the human subject actuates frequently involve the interests, trust and image of others.

Freedom and Its Social Embeddedness

Even well-intentioned personal choices cannot ignore their social embeddedness. Choices cannot be indifferent to the interests of the community and society. Frequently, our choices engage cultural assumptions, values and attitudes. The interrelatedness of personal choices and societal judgments calls for a consistent ethic of life. As a result, the choices we make need to recognize the sacred dignity and wellbeing of others through listening and dialogue. Choices that suppress or destroy life undermine responsibility and heartening respect. Freedom has an effect in shaping individuals, communities, institutions and regulations so that these creations do not become oppressive or repressive. In this regard, the expression of freedom entails a multiplicity of forms and functions, mobility and flexibility which build up others and humanize life and existence. Lived freedom expresses itself in courageous and honest speech. Freedom

---

160. Ibid., 132–33.
161. Ibid., 134.
162. Ibid., 130.
163. Ibid., 134.

also comes with the attitude of nonservitude to the cult of persons or to possessions, pleasure and domination.

Indeed, freedom refreshes life with a sense of purpose and confidence. Freedom actuates the experience and expressions of liberation for life, service and love. When this happens, freedom makes possible the solidarity of the rich and poor, the privileged and disadvantaged, the learned and unlearned as well as men and women in the human community. In taking the welfare of people seriously and fraternally, freedom rejects contempt for people. In freedom, people treat one another with respect. Of course, the authority that freedom nurtures promotes common welfare. Such authority cannot but be truly fraternal.

A fraternal authority exhorts and guides, inspires and persuades, directs and pleads. It is also representative, consultative and participatory. In so being, such authority assumes responsibility, respects rights, promotes the common welfare and brings people together in a committed service of love. Such an authority also grounds communication, dialogue and understanding. This interactive perspective likewise implies that such an authority will not lead to an encapsulation of the society in a sectarian fashion. Such authority strives to serve the unity which exists among people. Yet this unity will always require continual effort to bring people together in a committed service of love.

Fraternal authority prefers appeals to commands, responsibility to prohibitions, the hortative to the imperative, reconciliation to revenge, appeal to coercion, and consultation to unilateralism. Such authority honors human fragility, weakness and fallibility through patience, accommodation, compassion and humility. It also takes risks, inspires confidence, encourages initiatives and arouses enthusiasm for self-belief and belief in others. In the end, freedom shapes individuals, communities, institutions and liberates the enforcement of human regulations. This further means that the experience and function of freedom which humanizes life require honesty, plurality and courage.

Mystery of Evil: A Statement of Context

At the outset, it may be pointed out that as a negation of light, life and love, evil symbolizes the darkness of human experience. Evil has no positive ontological standing; it is a profoundly distorting *lesion* which attacks a certain vital or living order. In this sense, the experience of evil threatens people with the loss of inner equilibrium. Evil may be seen as a resistance against being, where being is understood as intrinsic value and plenitude. We interpret evil well when we see it as a resistance to the creative processes of life. In the concrete, evil refers to and symbolizes the experiences and expressions of the nastiness, wickedness and pain of living that penetrate the fiber of human existence. Fundamentally, the encounter with evil takes place in the experience and expression of all that opposes, frustrates, obstructs or hinders human flourishing or the human openness to the joy of living. Evil is a mystery in the sense that it involves the whole human person. A person who suffers evil finds himself or herself embraced by it. Its alternative does not really lie outside the self. When evil is suffered, it engages the whole existential fabric of the human being and of human relations.

In this section, I proceed into the exploration of the mystery of evil through the concrete example of HIV/AIDS. I explore the existential drama of hope and despair in an adult person who is HIV positive and suffering from an advanced form of Acquired Immune Deficiency syndrome (AIDS). The existential drama of this person engages the bodily, mental, psychological and social aspects of the victim's life. This person's emaciated and distressed body gives way to something grotesque and fearful. Besides, the ability to interact, walk and meet people comfortably also tends to be restricted by the harsh circumstances of the illness. Not only does this person suffer passionately from a certain loss of public reputation, good will and standing in the community, but an ominous or portentous fear of death also grips this person. The victim faces the decline of physical health, loneliness, emotional stress, mental distress, a tendency to spiritual anguish and alienation as well as social desertion and physical exhaustion. The totality of the victim's suffering not only tends to wear down the mind, psyche and spirit, it also appears to drive this person towards the edge of personal disintegration and self-destruction. Before focusing the considerations, however, it is important to have some overview of suffering in its many forms.

In analyzing HIV/AIDS as an evil suffered, I begin with a distinction between mystery and problem as setting the context and categories for speaking about evil that is suffered as a mystery. Concrete evil that is suffered is not well understood when envisaged merely as a problem. After exploring and discussing issues of personal engagement, meaning and meaninglessness, despair and hope, I end with a consideration of transcendence as a vivifying power for life even amidst the febrile confrontation with unspeakable evil like HIV/AIDS.

Suffering and Its Multiple Manifestations

When we confront people who grieve in the face of senseless death, the bleeding bodies of the victims of war, or starving children, we confront evil in the concrete. Think, for example of people in northern Uganda or southern Sudan where people die daily of starvation, pestilence, war and abandonment. The grief of these people surpasses the limits of any philosophical argument. Why do so many people suffering needlessly? Why do the innocent end squalid and oppressed? How can one live meaningfully in the midst of evil? Of course, if one recognizes one's suffering as a mystery, one grasps it as a presence, or as a modification of a presence that a person may have to live with or for which a person may play the role of intermediary. In the experience of suffering, the co-articulation of the vital and the spiritual become palpable and this co-articulation cannot give rise to knowledge.[164] The spectacle of detentions without trial, prison walls, dark cells, unspeakable tortures, incarcerations and executions supply all too familiar concrete cases of evil.

Think of people in relational subjugation or victims of sexual abuse, violence and crime. The inhumanity mounts with the passage of time. The experience begets anger, disappointment and a sense of despair. People experience such evils as more than privations. They experience evils as lesions. A raped woman or a person suffering from HIV/AIDS knows more than privations. We also encounter evil in systemic injustice or oppression that a person or groups of persons experience. Such experiences shatter the life-giving relationships and kinship that bind people together. Take the state prison systems which oppress so many. Here we may note briefly that the United States of America prides itself on freedom and democracy yet six-and-a-half million Americans now languish in prison or in the penal system. People of color often convicted of non-violent crimes associated with poverty or drug addiction populate the American prison system. Their poverty deprives them of an adequate legal defense and eventual exoneration. More than four million American poor minorities cannot vote, many for life, because of felony convictions. As a result, more affluent voters decide the outcome of key elections. The United States runs the largest prison system in human history. The system buds and maximizes punishment, degradation and brutalization.

---

164. Marcel, *The Mystery of Being Vol.I: Reflection and Mystery*, 210.

Concrete Evil as a Mystery

Concrete evil as a mystery involves me. I cannot place myself outside of it or before it. It envelops and comprehends me, even if I do not comprehend it. Concrete evil acts on a suffering person as an inward principle. It envelops a person's subjective and trans-subjective reality. The envelopment may not present itself at once in its entirety. Concrete evil as mystery implicates the whole human subject. In this regard, the struggle with HIV/AIDS, for example, confronts the victim with an inescapable mystery.

HIV/AIDS as Evil Suffered[165]

In dealing with HIV/AIDS as evil suffered, the question of experience in general touches on the fabric of experience in particular. Particular experience engages practical experience. Practical experience shapes our sense of history and identity. HIV/AIDS as evil arises for persons whenever their suffering and pain call into question the meaning and purpose of life. As a result, HIV/AIDS as an experience and expression of evil engages deep feelings or emotions. In short, the experience of suffering and the threat of meaningless death arise in particular human existence.

Suffering HIV/AIDS as an evil lacks any sense of higher purpose or meaning. It calls into question the physical, psychical and social relations of persons. After all, HIV/AIDS as evil is suffered by people whose motives are no worse than banal. Individual intentions correspond rarely to the immensity of pain that HIV/AIDS as an evil suffered can cause or lead to. Protest against the affliction and loneliness which the experience of HIV/AIDS brings is as personal as it is political. Ironically, too, the experience of HIV/AIDS as evil suffered may rescue a person from any complacency or uncomplicated thinking that human existence is a forgery.

One cannot reduce HIV/AIDS to a problem in need of a solution. The victim of HIV/AIDS experiences something not external. The experience rings the person round; it lays siege on the person.[166] The sufferings that HIV/AIDS brings undermine personal commitment, self-confidence and trust in life. The disease raises justice issues. The disease begets division, disintegration and confusion, not spiritual integration, growth and freedom. The encounter with it, then, easily comes to constitute an attack

---

165. HIV/AIDS as evil that is suffered means that it diminishes and thwarts human wellbeing and flourishing.

166. Marcel, *Man Against Mass Society*, 127.

upon a vital or living order without this attack being truly defined as a privation. This attack is properly speaking a *lesion*.[167]

Victims of HIV/AIDS feel suffused with enormous pain. Their struggle and grief defies philosophical analysis. They want to know why they suffer pointlessly and needlessly. They want to know how to live meaningfully and creatively in the face of evil. In this light, confrontation with the damaging and unspeakable experiences of HIV/AIDS can inspire the imagination with a sense of the profound and the tragic elements in life. In the end, however, HIV/AIDS makes the pain and darkness of human life concrete.

The Personal Character of Evil in Suffering

The encounter with HIV/AIDS as an evil suffered frequently breeds despondency, frustration and alienation. In other words:

> . . . evil which is only stated or observed is no longer evil which is suffered: in fact, it ceases to be evil. In reality, I can only grasp it as evil in the measure in which it *touches* me—that is to say, in the measure in which I am *involved*, as one is involved in a law-suit. Being "involved" is the fundamental fact; I cannot leave it out of account except by an unjustifiable fiction, for in doing so, I proceed as though I were God, and a God who is an onlooker at that.[168]

The evil of HIV/AIDS involves a person at the deepest levels of affectivity and consciousness. The evil lacks any adequate explanation. It forces people to question the depths of their existence. When we treat HIV/AIDS as a mere problem, we make the following blunders:

> I treat evil as an accident befalling a certain mechanism which is the universe itself, but before which I suppose myself placed. Thereby I treat myself, not only as immune, to the disease or weakness, but also as someone standing outside the universe claiming to put it together (at least in thought) in its entirety.[169]

In solving a problem, I am exterior to it; I also bring my mind to bear on the elements with which I must work. When we reduce evil to a problem, it ceases to touch us. We disengage ourselves from its personal and wounding aspects. Within this framework, "I make evil problematical when I treat it as a kind of breakdown that might happen in a piece of

---

167. Marcel, *Awakenings*, 127.
168. Marcel, *The Philosophy of Existentialism*, 19–20.
169. Marcel, *Being and Having*, 101.

The Priority of Mystery over Problem

machinery or as something lacking or as a functional failure."[170] In reality, I cannot treat evil that is encountered as something external to me. I cannot reduce it to something whose contours I simply map out.

HIV/AIDS invades the organic, moral and spiritual integrity of a person. Of course, to speak of suffering from HIV/AIDS already admits of some interpretation. We commonly interpret HIV/AIDS as terminal illness which leaves one powerless. So, HIV/AIDS radically threatens us with compromise. It hurts and harms our wellbeing.

The evil of HIV/AIDS generates and spreads anguish. In anguish a person struggles with fright, sadness, anxiety, doubts, bouts of depression and loneliness. People in anguish wrap themselves up in their concerns. The experience of anguish leads to a personal sense of trouble. In trouble, one's lived time shrinks. Trouble makes a person distrustful of others and oneself. Consequently, people in anguish lose sensitivity to and sight of others around them. One lives anguish more than one thinks it. The alternative to anguish does not lie outside the self.

The encounter with HIV/AIDS as an evil affects the total person as his or her equilibrium shifts. Tragic questions arise such as, Who am I? What am I living for? In these questionings people recognize the extremity of an experience which yesterday, perhaps, they did not think would or could become theirs today. Yet it may be noted that:

> evil appears as wholly unsusceptible of being characterized and classified like an object, which we cannot control to the extent that we describe it. Free of our control, evil takes us unawares, it surprises us with its treachery, and does so in such a radical way that we are quite unable to locate who or what is to blame.[171]

In addition, the experience of HIV/AIDS as an evil suffered communicates inclusively a sense of the betrayal of life or by life. The questioning of life can lead to guilt, shame or a sense of inferiority. The sense of the tragic consciously and affectively disrupts the joy of living. At the same time, one cannot really objectify the encounter with HIV/AIDS. The felt distress which results from the encounter with HIV/AIDS includes an element of domination the nature of which is in some way refused to us, without of course our being able to say by whom or by what.[172] The experience precludes appeal. Life itself feels betrayed. The disorientation which the encounter with evil brings plunges one into darkness. The wonder and

170. Marcel, *Man Against Mass Society*, 90.
171. Marcel, *Tragic Wisdom and Beyond*, 135.
172. Ibid., 137.

abundance of life appears truly broken and threatened. It is like being in the presence of a genuine treason which one does not know how to interpret.[173] Not only can one not understand what meaning the poignancy and agony of HIV/AIDS have, but one doubts if the encounter with the deadly disease has any meaning at all.[174]

Evil Suffered and the Question of Meaning and Meaninglessness

One who suffers from HIV/AIDS can see it as a nuisance, that is, without any positive significance at all. The formidable suffering can keep suffusing life with meaninglessness. Because the experience is not curable, HIV/AIDS tends to leave one impotent or powerless. As a consequence, one cannot reduce HIV/AIDS to a malfunction. HIV/AIDS devastates concrete lives, ruins love relationships and disrupts traditional communities.

The encounter with HIV/AIDS as evil suffered can betray us into reducing people to objects. But the reduction of people to instruments and means ends in nihilism, which makes people expendable. Within this perspective, life can be caught up in the urge to serve one's immediate sense of purpose. When that happens, "what I cannot stomach is somebody else just insofar as he *is* somebody else, a clog on or an impediment to my life."[175] When we objectify people, we diminish our humanity by losing our ability to be selfless, self-sacrificing and generous with others. We fail to touch life with freshness, spontaneity and light-heartedness. We do so because we lose the ability to commune with ourselves and others. That way of living leads to death. In other words, the encounter with HIV/AIDS can deprive people of a living sense of human dignity.

People infected with HIV who face the reality of AIDS, also can treat HIV. As a result, the creative future depends on human freedom and responsibility.[176] In addition, those confronting the evil of HIV/AIDS need to open themselves up to a wider community which, perhaps, includes ancestors. Community resources can introduce and construct new meanings or perspectives to a suffering person. In becoming *ours*, the sting of pain is diluted and the burden of suffering becomes tellingly light. Life with others who share in one's memory, heritage and hopes tends to broaden and regularize the horizon of positive self-definition.

---

173. Ibid.
174. Ibid., 138.
175. Marcel, *Man Against Mass Society*, 64.
176. John Heagle, *Suffering and Evil* (Chicago: The Thomas More Press, 1987), 103.

Of course, the policy and practice of confidentiality can spurn a virtual shroud of secrecy, shame and fear around the pandemic as something that should not be openly shared and discussed. It seemingly sends a message that HIV/AIDS is a burden of the individual and not the community. The effect is that many who are HIV positive carry their crosses alone. This loneliness can fuel isolation, anger and resentment which could lead to deliberate infection of others. Besides, people who have tested HIV positive also come to fear that their status will be found out. Such a secret itself constitutes an incredible burden of ill-health. In the circumstances, many people also avoid to find out their HIV status. This also means that HIV/AIDS prevention strategies and programs work better when people can test and comfortably share their HIV status.[177]

Communal conversations can forge culturally broad and effective responses to the HIV/AIDS pandemic. In this light, the African wisdom of "I am because we are, and we are because I am" can offer an effective approach to HIV/AIDS prevention and care. Our troubles affect our neighbors. For better or for worse, we are together in sharing each other's troubles, burdens and cares. Vital relationships form part and parcel of a person's health. Moreover, given the socially driven face of HIV/AIDS, the spread of the pandemic cannot be adequately addressed by an exclusive focus on an individual's physical systems and treatments as a private secret of the infected and the affected. An individual always exists within communal and social relationships.[178]

Communion with others in life's tragedy can prevent the victims of HIV/AIDS from failing into despair. Facing HIV/AIDS in a community invites public discourse, conversations and shared decisions and actions. Frequently, in the course of human communication new perspectives emerge that lead to shifts in dealing with a concrete case of HIV/AIDS. Moments of grace include those times when shifts in consciousness yield liberating and life-giving responses to the sick person.

In the face of evil, radical protest heightens the human sense of value and of interiority as well as of kinship. Also, every such protest presupposes a remedy or listener to which it beckons or which it seeks.[179] Of course, the experience of HIV/AIDS frequently appears to reduce persons

---

177. Musa W. Dube, "*Adinkra!* Four Hearts Joined Together: On Becoming Healing-Teachers of African Indigenous Religions in HIV/AIDS Prevention," in *African Women, Religion, and Health: Essays in Honor of Mercy Amba Ewudziwa Oduyoye*, Isabel Apawo Phiri and Sarojini Nadar, eds. (Maryknoll, New York: Orbis Books, 2006), 138.

178. Ibid., 139.

179. Marcel, *Creative Fidelity*, 76.

to their biological functioning. HIV/AIDS does involve explainable malfunction.[180] But HIV/AIDS must not be understood as a malfunction, pure and simple. In this regard, it may be noted:

> Evil can perhaps find no place in the world considered as ground, that is to say as the field of action or play common to all, or again as the place of an objective thought . . . It could appear only within the perspective of the subject as subject, within my universe in as much as it is mine; or more precisely, the evil would be a blow felt from any point of view as subject, something like an inquiry.[181]

HIV/AIDS may disclose the limits of physical human life. Nevertheless, HIV/AIDS may also bring a new wakefulness, responsibility and agency that never would occur without its experience. In fact, a sense of the precariousness of human life frequently fosters a sense of unity, coherence and purpose to daily living. In other words, human misery can serve as a springboard for human recovery and good spiritual advancement. In realizing the shortness and precariousness of life one may also awaken to its unmistakable significance.

A sense of life's shortness and precariousness can awaken a person to a sense of depth which re-establishes one's relationship with meaning and with passionate creativity. When that happens, hope overcomes nihilism. Even amidst pain, hurt and injury human beings can wake up to the wonder of life and recognize the madness of nihilism.

Wonder at life re-connects a person to the integrity and wholeness of hope. Hope stimulates the creative imagination which can open a person to the transcendent meaning and the fullness of life. Wakefulness to the wonder of life points a person both outward and inward with expansive freedom and a sense of life's richness. That is to say, hope enables a person to believe against all evidence to the contrary that life has a purpose. In spite of all else, we can always reshape life in liberating ways. A positive and creative imagination can yield a new sense of self. The experience of HIV/AIDS can re-enforce one's giftedness, one's capacity for relationships and a sustainable sense of identity. The tragedy of HIV/AIDS can also sharpen one's ability to support and encourage those in pain. Pain can teach people to honor others in appropriate and authentic ways.

Without a doubt, a person afflicted with the disease may fear vulnerability and what others will think of one in a degraded or weakened form. The victim of HIV/AIDS may only foresee death as the end of the disease.

---

180. Marcel, *Presence and Immortality*, 223.
181. Ibid., 221.

It is in such a situation that the use of language can alter the meaning of the experience. Language can lead to positive self-realization even in the midst of much pain. It can help the sufferer realize the possibility of a wondrous life in the present. In order to instill in the sufferer the courage to live, one must sympathize with the other person in pain. Imaginative sympathy overcomes exteriority through identification *with* the sufferer. This identification requires depth and openness to the other.

People can, of course, simply identify with their suffering and proclaim them completely meaningless. Then, as suffering becomes the center of their world, the world itself appears absolutely meaningless. They can then begin to view their sickness as the beginning of the end or as punishment of their guilt. In other words, suffering people can contribute to the shared sense of meaninglessness.

Or again, people who suffer can focus attention only on themselves. When that happens, they set themselves up as victims of a cruel and meaningless world. When suffering people see their situations as meaningless, no remedy can be conceived. They simply give up. This situation resembles a protest made by the man who thought that he was addressing somebody else but who immediately becomes stifled, when he perceives that he, in fact, is alone.[182]

On the other hand, people can discover meaning in their suffering but not if they regard their suffering as meaningless. One cannot merely affirm meaning. Furthermore, the absence of meaning cannot be merely affirmed either. A meaning can only be re-created or discovered by an act of mind. One way by which the mind comes to discover and establish meaning is by creative interpretation. Similarly, people may see their suffering as a struggle in which they need to take initiative and change the meaning of the inevitable. Coping with HIV/AIDS as an evil suffered can disclose to people, not depth of their decline but an extraordinary capacity for transforming the sting of pain. HIV/AIDS can inspire marvelous magnanimity in coping with suffering meaningfully. In short, HIV/AIDS can lead people to acquiesce to meaningless despair or to interpret their existence in spiritual terms which transcends the problematic.

The encounter with HIV/AIDS frequently causes an existential crisis which calls for its creative interpretation in community. Creative interpretation widens the horizons of life and existence. An expansive understanding embraces the world and its tragedy. The encounter with HIV/AIDS strikes at the foundations of human existence. It can engender profound disillusionment and loss of identity with life and of purposeful

---

182. Marcel, *Creative Fidelity*, 76.

directedness. It can destroy confidence in existence. The ambivalence of human existence requires prudence in those who strive to help the victims of HIV/AIDS.

Suffering and the Sense of the Self

How people respond effectively to the experience HIV/AIDS as evil suffered is very much connected with their own self-understanding or sense of the self. The sense of self that confronts HIV/AIDS as evil suffered defines the meaning of the experience. A conditional sense of self that premises the worth of persons on extrinsic validation suffers forever from gnawing anxiety, a felt sense of inner emptiness, covetous desires, paralyzing fears and tenuous fascination with the spotlight. Such a fragile self is frequently preoccupied and self-absorbed with the drama of self-evaluation for one's own sake. Such a self also tends to affirm itself over and against others. When such a self experiences HIV/AIDS as evil suffered, the response can be one of rage or capitulation because such a self also easily runs short of inner resources. Such a self already battles with a catastrophe of inner powerlessness that may already occupy a large field of a person's consciousness. The experience of evil then exposes the fragility of such a self and depletes it of inner resourcefulness.

On the other hand, a person who is awake to being as a milieu of intrinsic value and plenitude can understand, in the first place, human limitations. Such a person also grows in a certain respectful reverence and humility. The test of pain initiates and shapes one's existence. Then, a person does not confront HIV as evil suffered with desperation. A person confronts HIV/AIDS with resourcefulness and conviction about life's ultimate meaning. Such a grounding attitude tends to value and cherish connectedness with others so that the experience with HIV/AIDS as evil suffered becomes bearable. The key issue then becomes how one appropriates the experience of HIV/AIDS with groundedness in meaning and hope.

Therefore, any realistic and sound inquiry into or reflection on HIV/AIDS as evil that is suffered includes the question of the self. A certain realism about oneself changes the way one responds to the experience of HIV/AIDS as evil suffered. Of course, people who attempt to address the question of HIV/AIDS as evil encountered need not focus exclusively on the explicit questioning about it. They only need to understand the dynamism and flow that underlie behavior patterns in the face of their pain and suffering. The more deeply people understand the meaning of behavior patterns, the more freely and truly would the authentic self respond to concrete evil suffered. In the face of concrete evil suffered, people need not sacrifice depth for the sake of breadth. Doing so would problematize evil suffered. And evil would no longer be dealt with properly. Only a liberating interpretation and disposition empowers persons to respond effectively to the question of concrete engagement with evil suffered. Such a response normally inspires a dynamic of love, openness and transcendence.

The question of HIV/AIDS as evil suffered leads to the search for what one has never really known, that is, oneself. The journey can be dark, painful and threatening. It can generate many feelings of fear, sorrow, or anger. The experience of HIV/AIDS as evil suffered can create the sense of burden. This sense leaves survival and living at risk. One then loses the struggle for patience, responsibility and probity. Any concrete evil suffered cuts deeply into the defensive mechanisms of the self so that it generates much pain and affliction. This in-breaking of concrete evil into people's lives tends to undermine their restraint, responsibility and touchability. The darkness and suffering that attend the experience of concrete evil suffered challenge defense mechanisms in a global way. One tends to lose self-respect and to question one's most basic values. One tends to imagine oneself in a way which one perceives others doing so. After all, the human sense of self marks itself by ingrained emotional habits and responses. There exists in human beings a reservoir and body of memories and interactive or interpretative experiences that form their worlds.

A Matter of Despair or Hope

When painful suffering forces one to face one's limitation, the past enters the present shrouded in fear and uncertainty. The puzzle, alienation and disruption of suffering can seem utterly inexplicable and senseless. In the personal encounter with horrendous suffering, previous trust seems vain. Lived faith appears childish and cherished confidence, illusory. Illusion can breed a dangerous indifference. In this endangerment, dreams turn to ashes, the future becomes closed and expectations, impossible. The desire to live or to hope withers. In one suffocated by suffering and suffused with self-doubt, fear, anguish and bitterness can spring up from within. Distress, weariness and delusion people imagination with threatening chimeras. Instincts of self-preservation, self-defense and pride may yield to oblivion of life. Behind self-preservation usually lies a lack or need. No straightforward answer exists for the anguish of suffering. After all, there is also innocent suffering.

Despair or hope: before the experience of HIV/AIDS as evil suffered people can either hope or despair. On the one hand, despair means that in the confusion and bewilderment of suffering people become suspicious, resentment, cynical and give up. Despair saps energies, confidence and good will. Despair can express itself through forms or layers of silence. On the other hand, hope focuses on life, freedom and dignity. When hope penetrates suffering, it engenders a new sense of self. To hope within suffering takes humility, a paradoxical assurance and the perception that still contains value and the capacity for fulfillment. In gazing into the very mystery of plenitude, hope suffuses a difficult experience with an expectation of a new future. Nothing purely external can effect the transformation of suffering in hope. Frequently, people who pass from condemnation and ridicule know how to hope amidst affliction or struggle.

When hope confronts the evil of HIV/AIDS, it tends to fluctuates. It grasps first at this then at that. A rigid interpretation of hope almost certainly distorts it because the itinerary of birthing forth a particular vision of full life within a given context of HIV/AIDS never works itself out all at once. As the sting and pain of HIV/AIDS frustrate people's dreams, it can leave them weakened. The deep suffering caused by HIV/AIDS can lead to the rupture of relationships, both organic and social. But a suffering person can always hope and strive for a better life. How a person deals with an experience of evil depends on how he or she interprets and participates in the world. Strong hope can overcome engulfing fear, separation and pain. Hope means *not giving in* to the suffocating choice of defeatism. Along the path of life persons can, with support, muster strength to keep their faith in life alive and hope for liberation. Hope can hold up the promise of a wondrous life even when one stands on the threshold of death or when one feels fear or fatigue before existence itself.

In fact, when suffering persons give in to defeatism or despair, they long for death in order to end excruciating pain, crushing fear, exhausting fatigue or the bewilderment of illusion. When people have no reason for living, they lose their desire to fight for life. When life becomes a burden and its significance dwindles, existence itself loses all allure. Nonetheless, the human organism can always choose the noble aspiration for life in spite of everything. In short, the exercise of freedom in the midst of horrendous suffering can always make the difference between life and death. In effect, when freedom is exercised its actuation can constitute an expansive moment of grace.

Suffering and Transcendence

The victims of HIV/AIDS who question life itself face a major crisis. The crisis threatens confidence in life with the face of disappointment and disillusionment. In such circumstances, the transcendent act explores possibilities for reaffirming life. In such a case, transcendence must engage a new order of availability and charity. Also, every act remains transcendent which proclaims that one does *not* belong entirely to the world of objects in which illness threatens to imprison one. In such a circumstance, the need for transcendence presents itself as a kind of dissatisfaction that is not a part of depression. That dissatisfaction implies an aspiration towards renewing contact with an invisible and limitless reality of wondrous meaning and life that surpasses mundane existence.[183] In other words, theologically, human transcendence always seeks God.

The act of transcendence responds to an exigency and an appeal; it involves more than a claim because claims remain autocentric. And the transcendent One to whom one appeals transcends all possible extrinsic experience as well as of all rational conception, which is but experience anticipated and schematized (i.e., reduced to details).[184] Such transcendence implies an experience of plenitude that exceeds all experience of conditional values. We experience and grasp plenitude in the inner awareness of the creative sense of life.[185] Inner awareness awakens people to personal significance. On his or her own a person cannot confront resourcefully the question "What am I?" out of pain, difficulties and struggle because the question arises from the very conditions which raise it. But, such a questioning keeps the vital energies of the self-quest from drying up.

Indeed, suffering can awaken us to the consciousness that we can love each other, give ourselves to each other and feel thankful for ourselves and for each other. In this way, suffering can lead us to realize that we do not control the meaning or definition of reality. Suffering can force us to come to terms with our humanness, vulnerability and need. As persons emerge organically, emotionally and intellectually from difficult or painful experiences of darkness and weakness to light and joy, they gain greater strength of confidence, hope and appreciation of life. In other words, we can experience evil as wrenchingly tragic or maeutically[186] uplifting.

---

183. Marcel, *The Existential Background of Human Dignity*, 94.
184. Ibid., 145.
185. Marcel, *The Mystery of Being Vol.I: Reflection and Mystery*, 45.
186. When maieutic is ascribed to something it means that the thing brings out, reveals, clarifies and furthers awareness, definitions and understanding latent and implicit in

Thus far, it has become notable that HIV/AIDS as evil confront men and women with names, histories, locations, desires, beliefs and attitudes in this world. The complex reality of suffering begins with some felt experience of inward conflict, dilemma and darkness. The character of the suffering itself remains profoundly personal, but it also has a collective and social dimension. We do not suffer alone, and too often our sufferings spread to others. We are all responsible for and victims of suffering: this implies an entanglement of good and bad in our human existence. In fact, our suffering resembles a drama more than a linear history: life has a dramatic form in process of playing itself out fully. Every suffering conveys the sense that the big story is unfolding and that our little stories remain incomplete. Some sense of significance frequently undergirds and points beyond our experience of suffering.

Paradoxically, we know suffering in its contrast with bliss or fullness. One cannot suffer without presupposing the good, that is, without anticipating and participating in a greater abundance of life. In other words, knowing bliss gives human life its tragic character. In the midst of suffering, thus, human goodness demands an explanation. The question of humanity is at stake in every suffering so that a purposive take on it involves a certain dimension of catharsis which calls for transcendence. A promise of openness to transcendence inheres in human experience without which the human subject despairs of the self, others and the world. And despair easily metamorphoses into the real sense of living for the moment which has its own ruinous consequences in life. A human being stops to care when he or she ceases to experience the sense of the tragic.

Emancipatory Wisdom and Suffering

In the best sense of the term, wisdom, before the experience and expression of suffering, implies a certain perception and love of the joy of living. A guiding question becomes: what sort of attitude do we develop when things do not work out right? A positive and purposive attitude in the face of suffering often involves living for others or someone else: an openness to others that leads to encounters. In other words, our suffering acquires purpose when we live lovingly for others. Freedom from nihilistic despair in the face of suffering requires love of the joy of living through a sense of human connectedness. In this perspective, undeserved suffering can transform itself into a gift of love for another. Suffering acquires

---

one's assumptions, beliefs and knowledge about value, life and existence.

The Priority of Mystery over Problem

a purpose to one who puts trust in a third person who matters or on whom one counts.

Delight in the joy of living sets up the conditions for suffering. In this context, transcending suffering requires one to perceive it as an anticipation of a fuller purposeful life. The diminishment of life turns suffering into a tragedy. Suffering can make it difficult even to imagine what the full and abundant life which religious faith calls seeing God. Heroic suffering involves some joy in living even amidst much struggle. Ironically, what makes people human and likable is their vulnerability.[187] People suffer vulnerability when they bear the burden of concrete reality. This particularly takes place when they suffer innocently and with love. When people love even amidst suffering, something transformative and good happens to them.

The answer to suffering lies less in finding a way out of it than in transforming the evil encountered by becoming free of its sting. When suffering transforms, it changes the humanity of people. We transcend our suffering by engaging it and not giving up. One engages suffering by trying to get rid of it: this involves patience and determined courage. The fact that initially we do not comprehend the meaning of our suffering makes the struggle dramatic. We struggle less for some good action than for our own identity as humans. This way of perceiving suffering focuses on human brokenness as closely woven into the question of suffering. We are frequently caught up in the bondage of the disintegrating forces of inhumanity. The sense of human brokenness points to a tragic flaw in the goodness of our humanity. We all participate in the brokenness of the world and of our humanity. We routinely experience this brokenness when we fail to live up to the best which we as humans can achieve. When it enslaves our will and capacity for expansive vitality, this brokenness clouds our existence and hampers our liberty with selfishness and greed. More than an act, this brokenness involves the imagination which shapes both individual as well as human relationships.

Human suffering frequently begins with brokenness in our human relationships. When we connect with others, we unite with them by sharing in their interests and pain. The beauty of this union liberates us from

---

187. Of course, it may be noted that suffering may be approached in a number of ways: it can be dealt with through a second person-approach, which is a moral approach to suffering. In this approach suffering comes to be seen as caused by what people do. In the first person-approach, suffering becomes a profoundly personal and felt reality in *my suffering* so that it is understood strictly in terms of how it affects me. In a third person approach, suffering is approach rationally, scientifically, abstractly and objectively. This approach is capable of getting rid of suffering in specific form but not suffering *per se*.

resignation and enables us to bear suffering with dignity. When borne with dignity, suffering resets our priorities, frees us from the idols of life and awakens us to the joy of living. With support, suffering furnishes us with new perspectives, luminous strength and the courage to live.

The making of life lies at the heart of most human suffering despite the fact that its particularity tends to make the sufferer feel very alone. Long suffering can especially call into question our very identity as we begin to feel like aliens in a world largely indifferent to our own survival. When life becomes a solitary struggle, inevitable questions about its own intrinsic sense of purpose arise in acute ways. In the restlessness of loneliness, however, also lies an invitation to openness, to presence and to imaginative living. In this way, difficult experiences have, in many people's lives, yielded an unparalleled and bounteous outcome that exceeded all expectations.

Participation in Problem and Mystery

Having probed the meanings of problem and mystery, let us consider how human beings participate in both of these realms. The human subject participates in problem and mystery through primary and secondary reflections which correspond to calculative and meditative thinking respectively. Let us see what this means.

Primary Reflection

Primary reflection characterizes thinking in a problematic world. Primary reflection assumes that the universe contains some verifiable order or pattern which the human consciousness can discover. The universe does not exhibit a random logic; it has a quantifiable or mathematical pattern. The intelligent pattern of the universe grounds understanding. Primary reflection is a scientific thought that is abstract, probable and verifiable. Science recognizes probability. Further, scientific thinking can be detached, analytical and reductive.[188] In this way, primary reflection solves problems.[189] Through primary reflection we solve problems. Anyone can engage in primary reflection. This is also to say, a solution to a problem can be reproduced and handed on through an empirical or probable proceeding.[190]

---

188. Marcel, *Tragic Wisdom and Beyond*, 15.

189. Marcel, *The Mystery of Being Vol.I: Reflection and Mystery*, 78.

190. In *Tragic Wisdom and Beyond*, page 140, Marcel cites the case of a mechanic to the effect that a problem is solved through the reflective method of primary reflection.

To solve a problem, the human mind tends to fling itself on the elements with which it sets itself to work.[191] However, this need not happen with self-critical scientific thinking. Because it is highly analytical, primary reflection tends to dissolve the unity of experience. It dissolves the concrete into its constitutive elements.[192] Because of its problematic milieu, primary reflection requires existential detachment; however this detachment involves some interest in the validity and soundness of analysis and interpretation.[193] In fact, the ambiguity of human existence calls for primary reflection. *"It is impossible to discard primary reflection. It would be sheer nonsense to try to discard primary reflection."*[194] Insofar as problems exist, the relevance and development of primary reflection remain necessary or needful in life.

Primary reflection employs techniques in dealing with problems. A technique offers a group of procedures, methodically elaborated and, consequently, capable of reproduction. When people use these procedures, they aim at some definite results. A technique exemplifies something good because it merely applies human reason to reality. Because we can acquire a technique, it exemplifies a habit or complex of habits. Just as one can always become a slave to habits, one can also become a prisoner to techniques. When that happens a technique becomes, not a means, but an end in itself.[195]

Rational thinking which produces techniques frequently enhances progress in communication that produces excellent results. The advancement of communication improves and expands contacts, businesses, discussions and policies. At the same time, a world obsessed with technical progress tends to suffer a certain loss of feeling for living reality and for the handing on of life. When that happens, progress in communication can sacrifice local beliefs, local customs, native traditions, local costumes and local craftsmanship.[196]

Uncritical primary reflection can have a devastating influence on human communal or relational living because it offers openness to only

---

191. Marcel, *Man Against Mass Society*, 91.

192. Marcel, *The Mystery of Being, Vol. II: Reflection and Mystery*, 83; *Tragic Wisdom and Beyond*, 235.

193. Ibid., 92.

194. Gabriel Marcel, "Reply to Erwin W. Straus and Michael A. Machado," in *The Library of Living Philosophers Vol. XVII: The Philosophy of Gabriel Marcel*, Paul Arthur Schilpp and Lewis Edwin Hahn, eds. (La Salle, Illinois: Open Court, 1991), 157.

195. Marcel, *Man Against Mass Society*, 82–83.

196. Ibid., 86.

certain perspectives. This happens since one who has mastered one or more techniques tends to distrust anything alien to these techniques.[197] In primary reflection, technique can function as a milieu of the covetous desire and fear which accompanies greed. Then, covetous desire and fear conflict. Greed aims at an anticipated satisfaction of an action in question.[198] Also, greed tolerates no delay. It shows itself impervious to delay and becomes increasingly entrapped in the conflict between desire and fear. Haste to acquire the object of one's greed betrays one into treating human persons contemptuously as objects. In fact, primary reflection can produce a dehumanizing bureaucracy, charades of power politics and predatory market forces.

Thinking predominantly in problematic terms, that is, in terms of primary reflection, can desensitize one to life and a human sense of kinship. The bomber pilot exemplifies primary reflection. In obeying orders with precision and effectiveness gone mad, a bomber pilot kills people invisible to him. He cannot hear the screams or see homes and bodies he shatters.

Without a doubt, primary reflection goes hand in hand with technical development; but "the development of techniques does inevitably tend to give a primacy, at the practical level, to the idea of output."[199] With an emphasis on output, technical progress easily leads to thoughtless consumerism and materialism. Often, multitudes of people, considered unproductive, also find themselves deprived of dignity and human recognition.[200] When we turn people into objects they begin to resemble units of productions.[201] In other words, "when man seeks to understand his condition by using as his model the products of his own technical skill, he infinitely degrades himself and condemns himself to deny, that is, in the end, to destroy, those deep and basic sentiments which for thousands of years have guided his conduct."[202] It is of far-reaching significance that "man is tending more and more to consider himself in relation to the products of his own techniques, and by a singular paradox he even undervalues himself in comparison with the far more precise and effective apparatus which his technical skill has perfected."[203] Or again, "a machine

---

197. Marcel, *The Decline of Wisdom*, 11.
198. Marcel, "Desire and Hope," 279.
199. Marcel, *Man Against Mass Society*, 95.
200. Ibid., 96.
201. Marcel, *The Decline of Wisdom*, 17.
202. Marcel, *Man Against Mass Society*, 98.
203. Marcel, *The Existential Background of Human Dignity*, 160.

must be in the service of man, although tragic experiences have taught us that this relationship can be perverted so that man is put to the service of his own machines."[204] Oddly enough, all pragmatic, economic and political decisions need to start with and flow from the dignity of the human persons and kinship ties among people.

In fact, technical development does tend to fragment human society and in the process create a world unfavorable to the cultivation of enlivening wisdom.[205] The tragedy of primary reflection entails that:

> If man is thought of on the model of a machine, it is quite according to the rules and it conforms to the principles of a healthy economy that when his output falls below the cost of his maintenance and when he is "not worth repairing" (that is, not worth sending to hospital) because the cost of patching him up would be too much of a burden in proportion to any result to be expected from it, it is quite logical that he should be sent to the scrap heap like a worn-out car, thus allowing any still useful parts of him to be salvaged . . .[206]

Technical representation of the world may fascinate but it does not enliven individuals and kinship ties among people. In fact, to rely mainly or exclusively on technology brings boredom, superficiality and social confusion. These experiences are becoming increasingly evident in many industrialized nations whose economic and political standings in the league table of the world are based precisely on their technological superiority. Or again:

> The astonishingly high incidence of psychosis in these countries is enough to show that the system which they seem to have adopted involves a tragic oversight of certain deep exigencies, and this is perhaps the more convincing because these are the countries which are prosperous and where all the basic needs seem generally speaking satisfied.[207]

Primary reflection tends to divide reality into the microworlds[208] or into the scientific worlds. With its particular object of study, science tends to specialize and explain specified features of the world. In other words,

---

204. Marcel, *Tragic Wisdom and Beyond*, 36.
205. Marcel, *The Decline of Wisdom*, 12.
206. Marcel, *Man Against Mass Society*, 182.
207. Marcel, *The Decline of Wisdom*, 16.
208. Microworld refers to a world system with restricted number of objects, relations and rules. The microworld is a scientific world, say the world of physics or chemistry. It is not to be confused with the microcosm.

microworlds rest on a limited number of assumptions and presuppositions. A microworld differs from an environment as a life-world. We live in environments. The microworld of technology only controls a limited world of the external reality.[209]

A microworld of technology, for example, cannot tell us how to handle complications in human relations which belong to the realm of presence. As problems arise in human relations, attempts to deal with them problematically will only be partially successful. "It is indeed far simpler for an action to be pure if it bears on things, while to act on people, or to be more accurate, to bring to bear on them the techniques which are rightly applicable to things is, as we shall see, an abuse pregnant with the gravest consequences."[210] Science only says something about the world, but it does not say everything about the world. A technical microworld falls far short of the environment or the lifeworld. A lifeworld provides a cultural climate of presence and sympathy, a life rich in relational understanding and imagination, feelings, friendships, fraternity and tradition. A particular way of life or civilization typifies particular environments.[211] We must always interpret a microworld within the context of a given cultural-historical world before we introduce its creation in the social and relational world. We should never absolutize technologies.[212] Here we need to note that:

> . . . technical progress in the strict sense is a good thing, both good in itself, and good because it is the incarnation of a genuine power that lies in human reason: good even because it introduces into the apparent disorder of the outer world a principle of intelligibility . . . The fact is that to the average man today, whose inner life tends too often to be a rather dim affair in any case, technical progress seems the infallible method by which he can achieve a sort of comfort, apart from which he finds it impossible to imagine happiness.[213]

The relationship between scientific constructions and the environment or lifeworld needs to be in terms of interactive collaboration, proactive

---

209. Gabriel Marcel, "Reply to Richard M. Zaner," in *The Library of Living Philosophers Vol. XVII: The Philosophy of Gabriel Marcel*, Paul Arthur Schilpp and Lewis Edwin Hahn, eds. (La Salle, Illinois: Open Court, 1991), 334.

210. Marcel, *The Decline of Wisdom*, 9–10.

211. Ibid., 3.

212. Professor Fritz G. Wallner in a public lecture at Arrupe College, Harare, Zimbabwe, on "Goals and Methods of Philosophy of Science," February 8, 2001.

213. Marcel, *Man Against Mass Society*, 56–57.

exchanges and complementarities. At the heart of these processes needs to lie the conviction that "every kind of outward technical progress ought to be balanced in man by an effort at inner conquest, directed towards an ever greater self-mastery."[214] Scientific discovery and innovations that do not encourage and promote basic human values and aspirations can often lead to the opposite: street crime, oppressive relationships that violate rights of people, terrorism, bullying, deception and manipulation, the destruction of human life and property, and environmental blight. When technological advances the manipulation of life, they violate human dignity. Then they fail to promote truth, or honor human relationships and the common good of humanity.

In conclusion, the world of primary reflection offers empirical procedures, methodically explained, teachable and reproducible with a view to the achievement of some concrete end.[215] Such a world can easily lead to a materialistic philosophy which denies the possibility of authentic human existence. In a problematical, technical world speed and complexity also exert greater and greater influence. As an increasing sense of speed takes over human existence, the sense of the sacred in human life tends to flag.[216] Indeed, the limitations of primary reflection point to the importance of secondary reflection, the subject of the next section.

Secondary Reflection

Secondary reflection fosters recollection, inner stillness. As imbued with presence, it involves mindfulness and attentiveness to the deep significance of people and human kinships. It celebrates the intrinsic desirability, attractiveness and lovableness of their persons and lives. It fosters existential freedom and a sense of significance. It encourages openness and generosity. It reconstructs and expands personal and interpersonal identity.

In secondary reflection, human consciousness reaches towards a fullness of communication and communion which arises out of a dynamic solitude sensitive to value and plenitude. Through secondary reflection, the human subject awakens to the resonances of human plenitude which enliven people. The human subject encounters the self as source of interior liberty. The experience increases tenderness, warmth and affection. Secondary reflection fosters existential assurance. It discloses that a person may always remain caught up in the mysterious and delightful depths of

---

214. Ibid., 55.
215. Ibid., 82.
216. Ibid., 84.

the wholeness or integrity of human experience and existence. It probes the unconditional attractiveness, desirability and lovableness of persons and of human relations. The vitality of secondary reflection frequently impels persons to reach out to life and to others with a liberating and fresh availability and spontaneity. It connects and becomes coextensive with luminous experiences and fosters hope. It opens human consciousness to the sense of the sacred.

Secondary reflection contradicts any hard, sterile and dichotomizing use of abstraction. Vicious abstractionism depreciates the integrity of the concrete reality. Vicious abstractionism absolutizes particular abstract categories by isolating them from all other categories and from the concrete conditions of lived experience.[217]

As an act of recollection, secondary reflection involves solitude and watchful vigilance over the self so that people may return to themselves. It implies a cultivation of an inner state of stillness so that nondiscursive symbolic thinking and awareness may emerge. Then persons interconnect with the gift and goodness of their being. In this context, the human subject encounters the unifying, true and expansive self which generates a liberating understanding and interior liberty. One encounters the worth and lovableness of persons. The felt experience of wholeness and inner harmony renews and suffuses thought, passions and imaginations.

Secondary reflection bursts forth and stirs the human consciousness with illuminating light, imagination and the sense of purpose. Rooted and called forth from the past, secondary reflection actuates new and/or surprising experience, the energies of liberty and enthusiasm, of joy and generosity. Secondary reflection enkindles active awareness, impelling attentiveness and an expansive being, which keep persons and human relations warm-hearted.

The transformation that secondary reflection brings consists in applying to the realm of presence categories which relate to the world of perceptions and of objectivity.[218] The solitude which characterizes secondary reflection, say, in meditation or examination of consciousness, invites persons to listen attentively to what is happening in their worlds. Secondary reflection is experiential thinking. It is itinerant and narrative. The sensibility of secondary reflection relates with tact, courtesy, and pleasant taste to the self. As a participation in mystery, secondary reflection exhibits the distinctive quality of presence. Secondary reflection explores the significance of lived experience but in a reconstructive or synthetic way—it seeks

217. Ibid., 156.
218. Marcel, *Presence and Immortality*, 236.

The Priority of Mystery over Problem

to reconstruct or re-conquer the unity of experience.[219] Secondary reflection retrieves the unity of experience and also rediscovers the unity of our being with others. The truth and unity of lived experience grows in and expands the depth of human understanding and the intersubjective sense of community. As it emerges and expands, secondary reflection concerns itself with a personal realm of mystery because it engages the whole being of the questioning subject.

The understanding of secondary reflection shows that it "is a reflection whereby I ask myself how and from what starting point I was able to proceed in my initial reflection, which itself postulated the ontological, but without knowing it."[220] Hence, as a movement of retrieval, secondary reflection facilitates our becoming aware of the partial and even suspect character of the purely analytical procedure. It tries to reconstruct, but now at the level of thought which qualifies and understands concrete state of affairs, that analytic thought merely glimpses or fragments.[221] Secondary reflection restores and explores vital experiences which spring from the unity of living, thinking and responding. The reflective process of secondary reflection attempts to recover and relive the lost immediacy of experience by means of reflective examination. In the end, secondary reflection clarifies and confirms personal existence through reflection.

Self-intimacy makes secondary reflection possible. We can close in on ourselves or open ourselves up to life. This means:

> There is in me something intersubjective, that is to say, some possibilities of intimacy with myself, but also a possible deficiency with regard to this intimacy which can drop almost to zero. I can become wrapped up in myself to the point of no longer communicating with myself at all, much less with others.[222]

Intimacy with oneself grounds secondary reflection. Self-intimacy negates the contraction or the falling back on the self in self-enclosure. Intimacy renews personal contact with the ontological basis of being through generosity and self-giving.[223] While in self-enclosure one refuses to set values outside oneself, in self-intimacy one opens up and partakes of intrinsic value and plenitude. In self-intimacy, a person opens out to

219. Marcel, *Tragic Wisdom and Beyond*, 15; *The Mystery of Being, Vol.I: Reflection and Mystery*, 83.
220. Marcel, *The Philosophy of Existentialism*, 25.
221. Marcel, *Tragic Wisdom and Beyond*, 235.
222. Marcel, *Presence and Immortality*, 153–54.
223. Marcel, *The Philosophy of Existentialism*, 34.

life's grandeur. One welcomes surprise and allows oneself to be uplifted by goodness that discloses itself in experience. People capable of communing with themselves and so of renewing contact with being can reveal themselves as capable of transcending the spontaneous course of life.[224] In this way, secondary reflection makes the joy of living real and concrete.

Ascendancy of Mystery over Problem

First, all problematizing requires the meta-problematic. The metaproblematic refers to being. So, the ascendancy of mystery over problem refers to the priority of being over the problematic. Being connects people with the inexhaustible in human existence. This means that a human being:

> . . . participates in the inexhaustible plenitude of the being from which it emanates. This is the reason why it is impossible to think of both the person and personal order without at the same time thinking what lies beyond them, that is, a suprapersonal reality that presides over all their initiative and, at the same time, their origin and their end.[225]

Furthermore, the ascendancy of mystery over problem refers to the ascendancy of existential truth in life. "The essence of truth is such as to be a form of awareness related to what is already in essence beyond the limits of abstract objective facts or subjective desire."[226] Truth provides life with hope and resourcefulness that enable us to let go not so much of the things we love as the way we cling to them. Or again, truth enables us to let go not of delight in gifts but the habit of turning gifts into possessions. Truth shapes the way we participate and engage experiences.

Also, the priority of mystery over problem provides a framework for respecting people. Truth of persons refers to their human dignity or significance as persons.[227] Respect for human dignity implies a certain restoration of the spiritual integrity of individuals in societal living. A society by itself cannot conceive or master its own destiny without the insights and inputs from individuals.

Indeed, as subjects of secondary reflection, we rejoice in the inexhaustible gift of being. Being makes us joyful people in hope. In being, we define ourselves less by extrinsic validation than by an affirmation rooted

---

224. Marcel, *The Existential Background of Human Dignity*, 94.
225. Marcel, *Homo Viator*, 26.
226. Koenig, 67.
227. Marcel, *Searchings*, 15–16.

in the intrinsic desirability, attractiveness and lovableness of our persons. In the world of being, people live by quality presence and live for the fullness of promise. When we rejoice in who we are, we care for one another, grow in trust and open up to others. We walk and live in hope. We promote human wellbeing by encouraging hospitality, life in the family and the local sense of community. In other words, as we expand the joy of living, true wisdom blossoms in everyday experience:

> . . . true wisdom lies in setting out, with prudence to be sure, but also with a kind of joyful anticipation, on the paths leading not necessarily beyond time but beyond *our* time, to where the technocrats and the statistic worshippers . . . and the tyrants and torturers . . . not only lose their footing but vanish like mists at the dawn of a beautiful day.[228]

True wisdom discriminates and illuminates concrete experience. True wisdom constitutes itself in respecting, serving and valuing others. This also means, however, that we can reduce people to items of economics. We can develop the habits and tendencies of human expendability and frightful coercion.

Conclusion

Human beings are technical and vital beings. Because they are more than units of production or technical progress, people have a spiritual dimension to themselves. They can expand life and engage it from the perspective of plenitude. The priority of mystery over problem prompts a stance that rejects the absolute character of calculative mind that subordinates everything to utility. This stance gives priority to dignity, community and human kinship. This stance also promotes flexibility, tolerance, understanding and care.

On the other hand, when primary reflection controls our relations, they become tenuous. We come to define ourselves in terms of what we have or do and less in terms of who we are. The desirability, attractiveness and lovableness of people stop at the door of utility. We know only conditional love. We hold little space for the weak, sick, old and marginalized. We even empty justice of its authentic meaning. We prize and cherish justice that we understand as offering utilitarian guarantees. We even problematize language. We say one thing when we mean another. Our language becomes a phony device. We use it to veil truth. Yet we build our

---

228. Marcel, *Tragic Wisdom and Beyond*, 213.

lives together well through a culture of honesty and warm-heartedness that opens us out to others.

Our lives participate in mysteries and problems. In our lives, the constructs of mysteries and problems need each other. We enkindle the flame of hope and love in existence when we harness and integrate the constructs of mysteries and problems. When we understand these constructs well, we give them right perspectives, proportion and priorities in concrete existence. In light of this backdrop, the following chapter explores the constructs and complementarity of the scientific and sapiential in human existence.

4

Precincts of the Scientific and the Sapiential in Existence

Scientific Knowledge

As the previous chapter discussed, tensions exist between mystery and problem, primary and secondary reflections. These tensions could be posited as one between the scientific[1] and sapiential ways of interpreting and dealing with the world. In this connection, it becomes imperative to inquire as to what makes the scientific, scientific, and what makes the sapiential, sapiential. Already one thing to grant is that the realm of the scientific coincides with the problematic while the domain proper to the sapiential relate to the mysterious in that it is deeply relational and qualified by the property of presence. In this way, any scientific theory whatsoever remains in the last analysis a tributary to the *percipio* as the quantifiable can be always seized.[2] On the other hand, kinship ties belong to the sapiential order.

Because the realm of science coincide with the problematic, science consists of infinitely various and ever-expanding techniques.[3] The scientist as scientist strives to keep up with the level of thinking thought while the scientific popularizer moves only on the level of thought thought, that is, on the level of thought already digested. The domain of the scientific popularizer is that of empirical findings that he or she tends too often to raise to an *absolute* status by taking them out of the context to which they properly belong.[4] This implies that scientific findings are not absolute; tentativeness about them perdures. And the common nonscientific think-

---

[1]. Scientific refers to being methodic and systematic, exact and verifiable and specialized. In this light, we can speak of positive and human sciences.

[2]. Marcel, *Being and Having*, 128.

[3]. Gabriel Marcel, "Science and Wisdom," in *Bulletin de la Société Américaine de Philosophie de Langue Francaise*, Vol.VII, No.1–2, 1995, trans., Maurice Cranston, 31.

[4]. Ibid., 38.

ing rarely suspects the part that approximation plays in science, even in the discovery of unquestionable natural laws of physics which describe phenomena that change. It is also commonly assumed that scientific experiment can be reproduced as often as you like.[5] Even where unquestionable scientific laws are concerned, approximation plays a very crucial role in science. Each repetition of a scientific experiment is no more than an approximation. Scientific data cannot be absolute.[6] The truth of every scientific statement remains preliminary and subject to changes both in understanding and grasping reality as well as in expressing it more adequately. Scientific discoveries remain provisional answers. They perdure insofar as they can serve as reliable basis for confidence in dealing with reality. The best scientific theory gives the best explanation of events at a given time, circumstance and place.

The real scientist always guards himself or herself against the scientific popularizer and against the temptation to define human conduct, say, in terms of the theory of evolution passing off as a definitive discovery of truth.[7] The good scientist, as a person of research, gives good proof of wisdom in regard to those hasty, absolute and unreflective conclusions that men and women outside the field may draw from his or her work. In fact, a scientist who claims that a certain scientific theory exists forever beyond any methodological doubt ceases simultaneously to be scientific. Practical purposes or pragmatic certainty sufficient for action verify the validity and soundness of a scientific theory. In fact, scholars and researchers tend to speak of the results of their labors in terms of wisdom. So, science has something in it that really belongs to the realm of wisdom.[8] Science needs wisdom so that scientific prudence essentially implies a cautiousness which would never express itself in the name of objective certitude. It expresses itself rather in the name of those exigencies to which scientific research itself must submit if it is to remain an authentic research.[9] In other words, as a whole and with all its technical developments, scientific progress can offer a permanent inducement to the most excessive pride and restless expectation.[10] This is because the moment that we are endowed with a power of some sort, we are exposed to the temptation of abusing it. Thus,

5. Ibid.
6. Marcel, *Searchings*, 31.
7. Marcel, "Science and Wisdom," 38.
8. Ibid., 39; See also *Searchings*, 31–32.
9. Marcel, "Science and Wisdom," 39.
10. Ibid., 42.

the exercise of any sort of power should, by right, be accompanied by the exercise of control over the power itself.[11] In effect, humans developing mastery over nature needs to go hand in hand with the triumph of what is right.[12]

Today, to conduct a scientific research undoubtedly involves work in the company of others and this requires a minimum of good will. Scientific research thus implies a disposition that moves in the realm or spirit of peace and lies on the threshold of love.[13] Scientific techniques become dangerous from the moment they do not serve ends higher than the technical or when science, without denying those ends, ignores them. More precisely, techniques always remain in danger of being used for ends which occupy a decidedly inferior place in the hierarchy of values.[14] No progress will be made in our understanding of scientific inquiry if we grant in principle that it is not the personality of the scientist with its good and evil capacities that is involved, but an impersonal mind instead, which for some unknown reason a contingent individual embodies. As a matter of fact, we may thereby be prevented from grasping a feature of that inquiry which is at once personal and dramatic. Scientific inquiry belongs not merely to history in general, but is, more importantly, the fulfillment of the individual destiny.[15]

Precincts of the Sciences

Science consists of a methodic means-end process that brings reproducible results by which we come to belief with regard to certain phenomena or events. Particular sciences, besides working within set subject-matters and requiring verifiability, are also controlled by a number of key values or judgments. In the concrete, a science needs to be or must permit puzzle-formulation and solution. This means that the terrain of the sciences addresses problems. Science also requires the value of prediction for it to be consistently satisfying within its given field or specialty. The scientific value of prediction implies a number of other values as well: accuracy, simplicity, self-consistency, plausibility and compatibility with other theories already in use. Additionally, quantitative predictions are usually preferred in science. Moreover, scientific theory needs to be socially useful. Of course, dif-

---

11. Marcel, *The Decline of Wisdom*, 10.
12. Ibid., 2.
13. Marcel, "Science and Wisdom," 44.
14. Ibid., 45–46.
15. Marcel, *Creative Fidelity*, 30.

ferent usefulness and values require or dictate different scientific choices. Besides, different personalities and contexts affect the application of scientific values. Furthermore, the points at which values must be applied are invariably also the ones at which risks must be taken. And scientists resolve most scientific anomalies by normal means and that most proposals for new theories do prove to be wrong.[16]

Moreover, there is an entire constellation of beliefs, values, languages, symbolisms, criteria and techniques which define behaviors and sharing within particular scientific communities as they strive to address a particular set of problems.[17] Of course, a scientific community consists of the practitioners of a particular specialty or discipline. Marked by the limits of their subject-matter, members of a scientific community usually undergo similar educational and professional initiations and use similar kinds of procedures. Typically, scientists solve a scientific problem by interrelating symbols and attaching them to physical nature in ways that are proven or seen to be effective. Scientific symbolism enables a scientist to see the similarity or the likeness in a variety of situations. In a word, a scientific methodology proceeds through the assumptions of similar relationships.

So, the practitioners of a particular science see themselves as responsible for producing and validating a species of scientific knowledge and pursuing a certain set of goals.[18] There are often problems which provide the prelude for self-correcting or self-improving mechanisms and dynamics within particular sciences. This is not to deny that particular sciences and scientific communities reconstitute and reconstruct themselves constantly, perhaps in very small ways. The power of sciences normally also increases with the force of symbolic generalizations, definitions, particular models or their heuristic varieties that its practitioners have at their disposal in addressing relevant problems of life or existence.[19] Scientific knowledge, insight and understanding remain intrinsically the common property of the communities that create and use them.[20] In this way, the sense of shared purpose becomes a basic principle of the scientific process.

It is also important to understand that scientific hypotheses and postulates ground themselves in personal and subjective intuitions. An intuition refers to an act of awareness and recognition that could arise

---

16. Thomas S. Kuhn, *The Structure of Scientific Revolutions* (Chicago: The University of Chicago Press, 1996), 185–86.
17. Ibid., 175.
18. Ibid., 177–78.
19. Ibid., 183.
20. Ibid., 210.

involuntarily. This is also to say, intuitions, *of themselves*, do not come through set criteria, rule or experimentation. Intuitions follow perceptions which have to be contemplated, analyzed, interpreted, put to test or use. Of course, not all intuitions are formulated into hypotheses subject to experimental investigation.[21]

Furthermore, scientific theories need careful processes of verification. Permissive scientific approaches undermine the credibility of scientific processes and standards. When the scientist proceeds to carry out an experiment, he or she is forbidden to speculate in advance on what it will yield.[22] Frequently, the ordinary findings of a scientific theory demand and come under the scrutiny of peer review processes where scientists do not accept findings at face value. The process critiques, clarifies and authenticates the soundness of a scientific methodology and discovery. Characteristically, the scientific statement can be doubted and validated. As a result, mechanisms exist in the scientific community that offer some proof against misrepresentation and misinterpretation of data through some form of independent analysis, authentication and justification. Unacceptable practices and fabrication of data, for example, undermine the validity of scientific findings and conclusions. This is not to deny that much of what is accepted in science may also be taken on trust. Dialogue, research and intellectual honesty and discovery do play pivotal roles in propelling the credibility and the advances of the sciences. Scientific theories do not merely justify themselves through analysis of anecdotal data.

Scientific statements and theories can bring fundamental changes in people's conceptions of thought, knowledge, learning and how people come to understand, distort or impede the experience of human fulfillment or how people speak and think about the world. But scientific understanding needs to go hand in hand with the sense of social and common interpretative experience. This dimension in understanding scientific theories and postulates is important as sciences impact the material conditions of life. For example, it is notable that in technologically advanced countries people live longer and eat better while in technologically inferior countries life seems brutish and short in many ways. What is more, applied sciences tend to go, for example, hand in hand with medical science and medical care, health, food and education. Applied sciences can find remedies to unnecessary suffering. To situate scientific findings and consequences within the realm of the cultural and historical milieu that affect the sense

---

21. Ibid., 194.
22. Marcel, *Presence and Immortality*, 171.

of human kinship is to also speak of wisdom, which is the subject-matter of the next section.

Wisdom

The preceding considerations bring us to the threshold of wisdom, the region of the sapiential. Wisdom implies the understanding and sense which make it possible for people to conduct their lives well, preserve their individual and social health and to master some creativity. The simplicity and coherence of wisdom frees an understanding person from the snares of imagination and the yoke of passion.[23] And, insofar as it does not reduce itself to mere sagacious counsel, wisdom tends to appear as something wholly irreducible to knowledge—if not knowledge in general, at any rate to the knowledge which is expressed in empirical science.[24] What is more, in all of its flawed forms that we know, wisdom seems almost invariably to imply a sort of acquiescence in the existing order or the social system. In this regard, wisdom would tend to imply, at any rate, a resignation and, within this perspective, wisdom runs the risk of being the accomplice of the worst conservatism.[25]

Wisdom re-creates life. Wisdom sees life as an expansive and creative venture. From the moment that life is conceived as a creation, it becomes a question for man and woman to participate actively in that very creation. The milieu in which people live ceases to be a fixed datum; it becomes something that can be renewed and transformed. But this does not happen without bringing a radical renewal and change in the idea of wisdom.[26] Not surprisingly, then, wisdom exists wherever men and women seek to *order their lives around a luminous center* which makes the mere concern to sustain one's existence and interests appear peripheral and subordinate. At this point, even science itself becomes a scattered heap of knowledge if it is not *constituted around this center* around which consists the pleroma of wondrous life. Wisdom thus, perhaps, consists of a joyous effort to clarify, conquer and master ignorance and fear, just as science, on its side, is a victory over fantasies and illusions.[27] Accordingly, wisdom cannot be separated from re-discovering the common root of propriety and justice. *For justice is above all a steady reference to a certain*

---

23. Marcel, *Searchings*, 27.
24. Marcel, "Science and Wisdom," 35.
25. Ibid., 37.
26. Ibid., 36.
27. Ibid., 47.

keynote. This keynote is a liberative crystallization of the Light that is at the same time joy in being light.[28]

In the framework of wisdom, the scientific endeavor becomes truly liberative in that it tries to make the world as much as possible inward and expansive. In this sense, the pure joy of the scientist, whose work develops well, expresses the *gaudium cognoscendi* (the joy of knowing). This joy participates in that *laetitia contemplandi* (the joy of contemplating—knowing and loving) as the supreme end of our life's journey on earth. More crucially, assimilating the universe inwardly has nothing to do with possessing it or doing with it as one pleases. Rather, it is a matter of achieving a consonance with the world by a method that has its own rigor. This method calls persons back to the sacred region of their existence where they celebrate their creatureliness as desirable, attractive, inviolable and able to open itself up to others.[29]

Of course, when egalitarianism prevails, rooted as it were in envy and resentment, the sense of quality also tends to vanish.[30] Egalitarianism further implies that even if social progress were to be achieved or realized the tragedy of death would always exist.[31] In the end, it needs to be affirmed that wisdom is concerned inescapably with peace and right relations among people because inceptively people have to celebrate life and live in peace with one another. Within this perspective, it must be added that the cultivation of wisdom fosters, encourages and promotes the development of technical capacity, institutional memory and stability. Wisdom enlivens the vibrancy of living ties which bind men and women to the sense and promise of wondrous life. Put differently, the service and celebration of fraternity and living ties among people, which wisdom implies, will repeatedly involve differentiation of professional skills and deployment of resources that affirm people as friends, brothers and sisters of the same quality and each as gifted with dignity and responsibility in an inclusive existence. Further, this affirmation promotes networks of support organizations, associations and complementary leadership and forming strategic alliances.

---

28. Ibid., 46.
29. Ibid., 46–47.
30. Marcel, *The Decline of Wisdom*, 48.
31. Marcel, "Science and Wisdom," 41.

Wisdom, Heritage, and Gratitude

Wisdom signifies that there exists a hierarchy of ways of living that makes possible and gives truer harmony and meaning to life. There can be no wisdom without recognition of a certain hierarchy of living, that is, without the prevalence of an idea of a better or marvelous life. In this sense, wisdom involves the consciousness of belonging to a deeply humanized environment as the soil of existence.[32] Wisdom develops to maturity through patience, humility and continuity. In fact, patience relates closely with the visage of continuity. At the root of wisdom, then, lies a certain self-awareness and patience towards oneself and others. The cultivation and maturity of wisdom require time. Yet, at a certain level, wisdom cannot be separated or be distinguished from the pursuit of it.[33] Wisdom also implies a certain distance from events in order to link its various elements and aspects together and to bring simplicity and world harmony.[34]

Wisdom is an appanage of authentic freedom or the will to be free. In this light, the reasonable man or woman is perhaps one who perceives the limitations of reason: reason in a reasonable man or woman acts as its own brake and where this brake lacks there can be no room for reason.[35] In effect, order, stability and truth become mortally compromised as soon as the will to dominate prevails in the world and turns it into a factory. From then on, practical and metaphysical problems tend to merge into one for the sense of a concrete neighbor begins to disappear altogether.[36] Further, there can be no wisdom without at least the veiled presence of the universal. To the extent that the universal is debased or driven out, wisdom becomes eclipsed and its place taken up by a system of technical processes fitted tightly into one another.[37] People define themselves precisely in terms of the *tension* between their own situations, which are always singular, and the universal values which they do not have to create but to assert by embodying them in their conduct and work.[38] An authentic value can only be incarnated if it is not to be distorted. This further implies that in a value there is always and necessarily a *tension* between the individuality of circumstances and the universality of an absolute. This tension refers to the

---

32. Marcel, *The Decline of Wisdom*, 39, 44.
33. Ibid., 40.
34. Ibid., 41.
35. Ibid., 43.
36. Ibid., 55.
37. Ibid., 51.
38. Ibid., 48.

concrete human subject that is rooted in history with the power of freedom and initiative.[39] Wisdom thus entails a certain considered appropriation of a means to an end regarded as an undisputed and beautiful good.[40]

Also, common sense bears close kinship and connection with wisdom. But there can be no common sense where no common life or common notions exist, that is, where there no longer exist any organic groups like the family or village or stable neighborhood. The moment common sense goes out of institutions and civic or ordinary relationships it is also driven out from the ordinary human mind. As compassionate qualities fall off the radar of educational and professional concerns and attitudes, sensitivity to life and living realities increasingly become alienated from mundane existence.[41] And, if wisdom further implies maturity, it presupposes an attitude of respect with the past. To respect continuity with the past does not, in any way, prevent us from recognizing its mistakes of whose guilt we may perhaps have some share.[42]

Wisdom proclaims, begets and witnesses to possibilities and opportunities of new life by enabling positive energies, promoting the spirit of sharing, caring and gathering together. Wisdom seeks to reconcile, transform and celebrate the gift of each human life as well as kinship ties among people. Also, thanksgiving and uniting epitomize the exigency of wisdom. In name and reality, wisdom seeks to realize the experience and expression of peace, love, compassion and reverential respect for people. The sense and conviction of common humanity pervades the tenor and lifeblood of wisdom. Within this framework, people become brothers and sisters of the same quality, sons and daughters of one origin or source as well as endowed with the same spirit and dignity. Continual self-giving and care expand and enhance life. Wisdom nurtures and promotes positive relationships.

Furthermore, wisdom connects closely with heritage materially and, above all, spiritually. In speaking about heritage we speak about a manifested survival of the past which ensures the participation of the living in supra-personal life.[43] A heritage exists as an intermediary between us and the spirit, that is, value and dignity, which make possible the progress of piety as the feeling towards what is holy or inviolable. Force has no hold over the inviolable. A heritage reiterates a call rather than a possession that

39. Ibid., 33.
40. Ibid., 52.
41. Ibid., 46–47.
42. Ibid., 48.
43. Ibid., 26–27.

is handed on. Heritage belongs to the way of living a reality which itself refers to the visible and invisible worlds. This dynamic constitutes the very life of the spirit.[44] A heritage brings with it discordant calls and temptations which freedom distinguishes by becoming that which we truly are.[45] Only where there exists a concrete and organic unity between life and spirit shall we find ourselves in the presence of the supra-personal and only there does it become possible to speak of a spiritual heritage.[46] To be an heir to a spiritual heritage implies living in a human way, that is to say, not being crushed by the weight of care.[47] We speak of spiritual heritage where there persists an awareness of such heritage that survives in a certain climate of diffuse gratitude.[48]

In fact, the notion of heritage or, properly speaking, spiritual heritage cannot be well-understood without understanding the notion of gratitude. Gratitude implies for its subject an intense awareness of his or her receptivity. Gratitude wholly refers to the *other* as the source of some benefit received. The assertion inherent in gratitude bears on the gift that the subject has received. Gratitude directs itself to the giver of the gift. A bond, thus, unites the benefactor of a gift and the receiver of the gift in the act of gratitude.[49] Also, gratitude is purposive: it is a sort of restitution in the spirit. Gratitude expresses a response and an aspiration to respond more and more intimately to an act of generosity, kindness or mercy. The response that characterizes gratitude essentially recognizes the generosity, kindness or mercy which inspires and grounds a whole experience.[50] In this light, people offer gratitude joyfully, publicly and in community. What is more, gratitude *does not limit itself to the moment*; it seeks to last. Gratitude bases itself on memory; it is memory that brings out the reality of life in a certain way. As an evaluative response, gratitude remembers or memorializes the past in the present with a presentational immediacy. Remembering embodies, in a certain sense, the very reality and relationship recalled. This experience, in turn, makes persons not only present to themselves but also to others and to the world around them. In other words, present responses color the way persons relate to themselves and to their world.

44. Ibid., 28–29.
45. Ibid., 33–34.
46. Ibid., 27.
47. Ibid., 34.
48. Ibid., 24.
49. Ibid., 25.
50. Ibid.

Precincts of the Scientific and the Sapiential in Existence

But the memory characteristic of gratitude does not preserve; it also awakens. In this sense, recalling constitutes an act of self-recognition. Gratitude, then, refers to a vigilance of the person not to lose what he or she regards as of lasting value. The wakefulness of gratitude manifests an active struggle against the inward forces of dispersal or distraction. In this way, gratitude is also an inward disposition or an act of faithfulness. Conversely, forgetfulness is a lapse of faithfulness.[51] And when gratitude is diffused, the giver is not identified easily. Here we have the immediate case of a person receiving a gift without knowing from whom it came. So, gratitude cannot in fact be abolished by ignorance of the giver.[52] In the end, the gift cannot be separated from its recognition and recognition itself can in a sense be described as the gift. Recognition establishes all responses. As a result, to lack the power of recognition then is to be disinherited.[53] Openness to gratitude heals and enlivens human awareness. It also connects people with a sense of appreciation and life's abundance and vibrancy.

The man or woman of an agglomeration is in the deepest sense of the word a man or woman without a heritage or from whom no one will inherit anything. The element in which he or she subsists is that of non-gratitude because ingratitude would presuppose a gift or kindness which remains unrecognized. In non-gratitude, kindness disappears. The man or woman of an agglomeration replaces the notion of a gift with the always partial, inadequate satisfaction of a claim which the claimant feels to be profoundly just and also unlimited. This world of claim excludes grace of which it cannot think. It is a mechanized problematic world devoid of presence. Only implacable rules describe such world.[54] Furthermore, gratitude and admiration tend to lessen in the measure that the creative power weakens. In its place, the claim to innovate takes over life. The self-styled innovator tends to be centered upon himself or herself so that he or she finds it difficult to admire or be grateful. The independent signature of admiration and gratitude would appear to threaten such a person with diminishment or humiliation.[55]

When the scientific and sapiential exist together, they lead us to interpret the past relevantly, judge the present appropriately and foster a future of hope as people seize upon possibilities of being more fully human

---

51. Ibid., 25–26.
52. Ibid., 26.
53. Ibid., 27–28.
54. Ibid., 27.
55. Ibid., 24.

with one another. To be more fully human entails responsibility, affection, sympathy and celebrating shared existence. Herein lies the deep feeling for humanity by means of which people use their talents, aptitudes, skills, enthusiasm, fortitude and compassion to promote and serve common life. From within the sensibility of the sapiential, human life, from its humblest and defenseless, weakest and voiceless forms to its most resplendent and resurgent, healthy and convenient, remains a beautiful and precious gift. It must be added that the technician rarely exists as a pure technician. His or her techniques cannot be exercised where minimal conditions of psycho-physiological balance are not realized.[56] The scientist always lives in a given cultural and historical context within which he or she does his or her work. A scientific understanding cannot fail to attend to details, contingencies and vagaries of cultural experiences that inform configurations, nuances and subtexts of interpretations of particular scientific concerns. Cultural circumstances do change the meaning, quality, possibilities for and seriousness of scientific realities.

The Micro-world of Science and the Lifeworld

The dialectics between the scientific and the sapiential plays out concretely in the dynamics that goes on between the microworld of particular sciences and the lifeworld, the domain of the sapiential.

The lifeworld refers the world of engaged human experience and activity, that is, of human concern with socialization and attitudes, meaning and value, motivation and communication and with personal and social identity and integration. The lifeworld coincides with the plausibility structure or lived experience of the human community that forms the background of common pre-understanding, understanding and ongoing conversations among different people. The lifeworld exists in contradistinction to the microworld of the particular sciences. The dialectics between the microworld and the lifeworld, as the engaged socio-cultural world, plays out in the privileging of primary and secondary reflections in dealing with this-worldly affairs.

Primary reflection is ordained or oriented towards management and control of things and people through a certain rigid framework of thought. Secondary reflection, on the other hand, has as its basic sensibility and concern with cultural and existential meaning and meaning-change, and their consequences in terms of progress or decline as reflected in people's growth towards greater Truth, Justice and Love. Secondary reflection deals

---

56. Marcel, *Being and Having*, 127.

with the lived field of experience and understanding in terms of practical language, culture and community. The set of cares, which characterize secondary reflection, gives meaning, structure and the sense of purpose to the experiential world of commonly lived experiences. The realities that secondary reflection deals with permeate the human subject's life's experiences, be they at the conscious, subconscious or unconscious levels. Secondary reflection underscores the fact that the ontological dimension of human experience precedes the epistemological.

Nature as the human ecological niche in the cosmos and culture locates the lifeworld and the inquiry of particular sciences. In Nature we confront the realities of historicity, contingency, contextuality, emergence, and the role of religion and human culture. Most particularly, we confront the embodiment of human consciousness in the everyday lifeworld. Through new technologies in the cultural lifeworld, researches direct, shape, produce and, in this way, give meaning to new scientific phenomena and change the meaning of old phenomena. By these means particular sciences shape the cultural lifeworld with significant consequences for progress or decline for individuals and for communities.[57]

Postulates or theoretical constructs bridge the gap between the microworld and the lifeworld which holds the ups and downs of individual lives as well as core historical development. Within this framework, hermeneutics and narrative become important media which close the gap between life and understanding, theory and practice, existence and language, history and change, or between medical science and clinical practice. All the discourse of using abstract thoughts and scientific theories depends in a metaphorical way on the structures of the bodily senses and on converting action verbs denoting processes into nouns denoting things. There are no disembodied ways of thinking about disembodied ideas. Concreteness is what sustains life and provides the meaningful physical space in which people performatively live.[58]

The lifeworld is concerned with life and verisimilitude. While the scientific world needs testability, the lifeworld requires believability. Common attitudes, common ways of life, common standards and patterns of behavior, common approaches and social assumptions establish the lifeworld. In other words, the lifeworld coincides with the cultural

---

57. Patrick A. Heelan, "The Lifeworld and Scientific Interpretation," in *Handbook of Phenomenology and Medicine*, Philosophy and Medicine Series, Vol. 68, Baylor University, Waco, Texas, Kay Tombs, ed. (Dordrecht and Boston: Kluwer Academic Publishers, 2002), 47–48.

58. Ibid., 50.

world. At the same time, people retain their individuality and freedom in the lifeworld.

In the intersection between the microworld and the lifeworld, human understanding functions by interpretation, meaning and language. Meaning is a public domain accessible by common habits of actions and the use of shared languages. Through meaning, people understand one another, converse with one another, justify their points of view or actions, establish aims, set up norms and offer definitions to different kinds of experiences. Meaning arises from history which includes local interests, demands and the exigencies of social communities or groups. Or again, the historicity of language, local interests, human temporality and human forgetfulness affect meaning. As a result the lifeworld has gains and losses over time. Indeed, meaning is the locus where truth manifests itself historically, practically and contextually.[59] Of course, the pre-conditions for truth manifesting itself are human openness and freedom.

Furthermore, human interpretative process begins in the lifeworld and ends in the production of a phenomenon in the lifeworld. Interpretation uses thought but it does not end in thought. Moreover, it does not primarily seek control. In order to be a successful praxis, interpretation must lead to the production of some cultural phenomenon.[60] In effect, interpretation constructs meaning through common action, theory, language and with common action involving the body or body-situatedness, which connects science with technology. In other words, to be meaningful and generative of imagination, language needs a self-supporting context of uses and the user's community and there are infinite varieties of contexts of use and of users' communities.[61] Scientific theories make available possibilities and opportunities that cultures embody.

The plasticity of the human genome, for example, is such that there is no one way in which it realizes itself. In other words, we can instruct and bring up people in more than one way. Nurture and nature affect the phenotype through human understanding and control. Our experience of nature constructs and shapes our conceptions of it. Human beings are not free of *either* their genomes *or* their cultures. Human culture simply provides *ways and terms* of human development. These *ways and terms* offer the prescriptions about human growth relative to cultural contexts.[62]

---

59. Ibid., 51.

60. Ibid., 53.

61. Ibid., 54.

62. Jerome Bruner, *Actual Minds, Possible Worlds* (Cambridge: Harvard University Press, 1986), 135.

Any scientific theory of human development thus needs to recognize the primacy of the lifeworld in relation to the microworld of science. Culture offers the grounds for scientific thinking. A scientific theory relates to culture through language. In constituting an unarticulated backdrop, cultural values, beliefs and forces enshrine commonplace attitudes, habits, perceptions, judgments and practices which inform scientific discipline and procedures. Particularities of cultures imbue scientists with some forms of maxims, anticipatory judgments, biases, or partiality. Overlap of interpretations, visions, judgments, critiques and self-criticisms in the lifeworld provide for common feelings and affectivity in the scientific world.

Accordingly, we are fundamentally creatures of biology and human culture. We are constituted by the dialectical interplay between nature and history in which thought and speech become vehicles for planning and carrying out actions. Thought helps organize perception and action. The unity of perception, speech and actions, within a cultural context makes it possible to internalize and produce the field of human behaviors and intentions.[63] Cultural concepts, ideas and theories create meaning, renew thought and transform concepts. Hence, language and the way we use language reflect particular histories.

In the lifeworld truth expresses itself as a property of meanings with individual, local, variable, sensory-based, material, technological and historical origins and uses. We transmit meanings about things through local praxes which relay them through texts, speech, actions, empirical procedures, images, symbols and other public expressions.[64] While the language of scientific theory and the language of praxis belong to different genres and domains of thinking, culture defines and provides the basic ways of interpreting their relationships.[65] The praxis-laden cultural world coincides with the lifeworld while the theory-laden world coincides with the scientific world. Being truly belongs to the lifeworld that can grow or decline historically.[66] Through the senses, language and cultural environments the theoretical entity like a positive Wasserman Test can become a lifeworld phenomenon.[67] Through lifeworld involvement perceptual space, color, sound and syphilis, for example, exist as true products of interpretation through which they become intelligible phenomena of hu-

---

63. Ibid., 72.
64. Heelan, 53, 54.
65. Ibid., 57.
66. Ibid.
67. Ibid., 58.

man experience.[68] In effect, the scientific world can renew, transfigure and revolutionalize the lifeworld.

Importantly, however, the metaphorical constructions of the scientific world should not replace the pre-scientific lifeworld meanings. Failure to do so would lead to much confusion and poor discourses. For example, often enough scientific terms like cells, organs and bacteria are treated as things, that is, like replaceable parts of a machine violating their natures as integral parts of a living organism. Yet these organic terms are constituted by the continuous flow of chemical exchanges across their interfaces with the surrounding tissues. What follows from the non-recognition of metaphorical transitions has led, for instance, to confusion in the public debate about abortion, cloning, disease prevention and artificial intelligence where scientific model terms such as *fetus, genotype, bacteria* and *neural workings* become filled with meanings taken from related practical everyday contexts, making them falsely synonymous with the everyday uses of the related everyday terms. In the above cases, the everyday terms would be child, adult, cause of disease and intelligence, respectively. This usage may be good in politics but it is itself a form of cultural disease.[69]

Let us take the example of abortion within the context of the lifeworld in order to illustrate further the preceding considerations. Barbara Duden, the historian of the woman's body in clinical medicine does question the scientific term "fetus" that belongs to the context of scientific imaging and biology and asks whether it is being abused in public fora of discussions when substituted for the term "child" that is used in the lifeworld context of pregnancy and maternity. Has the separateness of contexts between model-scientific, pre-scientific lifeworld processes and post-scientific lifeworld processes been illegitimately suppressed in our modern medical culture, in the media and in public policy discourse? The terms "fetus" and "child" are, of course, correlative; each in its own context reveals something about what the other term refers to but they are not isomorphic and interchangeable. A "fetus" is a term whose primary owner is the medical profession. A living fetus is recognized by sonographical and other imaging techniques apart from the mother's context in the everyday lifeworld. Even while it is inseparable from the living tissue of the mother, the fetus is described as a "thing" as if it had an existence separate from the mother. Accordingly, it may be noted with concern that in many countries, ethical rules and legislation concerning pregnancies are being written in terms of the "fetus" where the term blurs the difference between the fetus as a part of the sci-

68. Ibid., 60.
69. Ibid., 61.

Precincts of the Scientific and the Sapiential in Existence

entific model, the fetus as an organic part of the post-scientific lifeworld and the child as an element in the mother's pre-scientific pregnant life. In effect, should the difference between the two cultural perspectives be recognized and an accommodation found that defers the special cultural role of the mother in decision-making about the child?[70]

Without a doubt, scientific theories have been a very positive force in shaping the contemporary lifeworld. But scientific practices, of course, have to be carefully designed and implemented. Besides, as scientific theories grow and change, new issues emerge. What is more, new cultural practices found to be effective also lead to new scientific theories, which in turn can lead, for example, to better medical practices which may lead further to better scientific theories. Scientific theory is in fact no more than a tool for, or a way of coping with, some living function of the human body constituted as meaningful by a lifestyle. Because of the zone of uncertainty between theory formulation and cultural practices and between pre-scientific and post-scientific lifeworld terms, an inescapable tension exists in the public consciousness that can—and often does—result in changes, possibly also in confusion, concerning conditions of meaning, contentment and policy norms. Noting such changes, one recognizes and captures something about the historicity and cultural hermeneutics: its manifestation is not independent of available possibilities and opportunities to a particular culture.[71]

Since the theoretical and the practical do not coincide, it makes no sense to predicate the theoretical models literally on the lifeworld. The two must come together consciously in some unambiguous but metaphorical way guided by the prudent action and, if possible, some consensus about soluble lifeworld issues.[72] Herein also lies the question of definitions and perspectives congruent with values that prevail in particular cultures. Without alertness to the cultural exigencies and contingencies of the lifeworld, scientific formulations, implementation or even underperformance easily come to serve selfish interests that can only thrive at the expense of the common life and wellbeing. Human progress requires the affirmation of subjectivity and intersubjectivity in order to truly establish the individual in his or her own right. This affirmation recognizes and cherishes the unconditional desirability and worth or lovableness of persons and the

---

70. Ibid., 62.
71. Ibid., 61.
72. Ibid., 63.

intrinsic significance of human relations. It further implies a complementary understanding of experiences that makes community possible.

Every scientific world, then, generates and establishes an ontology. Simultaneously, then there is not and there cannot be any science in whose name the refusal of being can be either absolved or condemned.[73] The scientific criterion only helps to bring out into the open the elements and qualities that enable people to deal with problematic elements in particular experiences in the world. A scientific realm offers a genuine version of what there is but not all that there is. But the interpretation of the scientific world goes on by means of communication, open-mindedness, tolerance and experimental spirit. A specific scientific world opts for a conceptual system in the light of which advantages play the more important role in the human effort to deal with the problems that confront people in the lifeworld. The specific sciences justify themselves continually by means of pragmatic validation.

Thus, scientific statements are not true by virtue of their meanings alone, independently of how life is experienced and lived in the lifeworld. The ontology of particular cultures, which is also to say, a network of beliefs and convictions, grounds the particular sciences. As a result, the microworld of particular sciences consists of an entire network of interrelated statements or propositions. This network consists of logical principles and observational conclusions that can be accepted, validated, rejected or modified. This is also the way of changing scientific positions.

In determining the truth and knowledge of the scientific truth in lived experience, we should not consider merely an individual scientific proposition. A scientific proposition does not exist apart from its interrelations with other propositions and assumptions in a total network of beliefs within the scientific microworld. Always, then, in the face of a challenge by observational experience and conclusions, it is not a single scientific proposition that is being tested but a whole network of beliefs and assumptions. Thus, the network of scientific statements faces the interpretative tribunal of experiences and values of the lifeworld. Even scientific synonymy depends on empirical, sociological, historical experience and expression of linguistic usage and meaning. The scientific world presupposes usage. No scientific statements exist which cannot be revised or rejected. Cultural scrutiny and interpretation can modify or replace scientific beliefs.

Use and appropriation in the lifeworld determine the meaning of a scientific expression. A scientific meaning refers to what we understand when we know what an expression means in the lifeworld in that it offers a correct explanation of some experiences. In the end, we need to know what is for

73. Marcel, *Creative Fidelity*, 143.

one kind of proposition to be true as opposed to another or what counts as knowing one sort of proposition rather than another. Within the scientific world, what is held rigid is a way of understanding, interpretation and description of concrete experiences in the lifeworld. However, wholesomeness of science entails the sapiential dimension of life.

The forthcoming section illustrates how harnessing elements or dimensions of the sapiential can help forge a humane, civic and mature human relationality in ways that fulfill and expand human capacities for greater peace and harmony. The context for the forthcoming considerations are the issues of mass violence as set against the inevitable need for reconciliation and forgiveness since people cannot live well or normal lives without others.

Violence, Reconciliation, and the Sapiential Exigency

Existentially, the whole question of atrocity and mass violence roots itself in a contextual or interpretative paradigm of the problematic world, that is, in a world imbued by the will to dominate that engenders a masterslave, defensive and/or offensive self-affirmation and attitudes of over-and-againstness towards life. Such worlds control people by the survival exigency, namely, the urge to dominate or triumph over others through corresponding relations of enslavement or slavehood mentality. In such a world, the patterns of initiation into the world necessarily imply orientation of how to acquire the power to accumulate, conquer, order, rule, subjugate, punish and reward. Personal glory and honor assume preponderance over all values. In such contexts, human relations primarily define themselves by the readiness to obey, to surrender, to please and appease, or to praise and be rewarded or, if not, accordingly face the risks of humiliation or punishment. As some people are consumed by the frantic quest for prestige and lordship over others, many others are, out of necessity, subordinated, oppressed and enslaved or referred back to being servants of or below others.

Understandably, direct and scandalous violent reactions tend to occur because of the fierce struggles for survival and domination. Within such contexts in which networks and dynamics of survival and the quest for lordship predominate, people readily violate and abuse others and the physical environment. Essentially, people perfect the art of destroying one another. In such a problematic milieu, basic stances towards life as a whole become distrustful and existence assumes a threatening and dangerous visage.

As a matter of fact, where the pursuance of dominance or lordship in problematic settings goes apace, people lose all sensitivity to the wellbeing of others. In this regard, the quest for success systematically empties humanity of its true content and enduring meaning. Fear, hypocrisy, rivalry and tyranny fill up the order of life as people use, control and dump each other like objects. Even language becomes a tool for expedience and acquisition. Consequently, relationships and life itself become bereft of the sense of intrinsic significance or dignity. The blinding urge for all honor, glory and the power leaves little room for love of self and others. The absence of positive presence and the weak sense of care among people fuel hatred and resentment, jealousy and envy as death-dealing and misery-inducing arsenals in human relations. At the existential level, we properly understand atrocity and mass violence when set against such existential logic and momentum.

In light of the preceding considerations, however, the current inquiry seeks to deal with social reconciliation and forgiveness against the background of mass violence and atrocity or mass injustice. More significantly, the following perspective intends to reflect on the sapiential exigency in the context of a disorienting and divisive social experience. For in its thrust the sapiential exigency seeks reconstruction and transformation. When the sapiential exigency of life is lifted up and harnessed, it cherishes and forges an expansive culture of understanding, care, dignity and interior unity amidst diversity. The sapiential exigency strives for healthy kinships and relations. The sapiential urge reveals the primacy of human familyhood as a value without which plenitude of this life will always remain illusory. The organic spirit of familyhood awakens in people the experience and sense of who they truly are so that they can let others be likewise. What is more, people are destined to meet and live together in this world; we are in this life together with one another, for better or for worse. The kinship of human origin and destiny urge, liberate and bind all people as friends, neighbors, brothers and sisters of the same quality and in common consciousness and fellow-feeling. When the internal momentum of sapiential awareness expands it yields common peace, freedom and joy.

Mass violence and atrocity constitute ugly scenes of despair and human bestiality as entire families perish; people wantonly kill and hatefully torture and neglect one another. Such experiences shatter hopes, dreams and trust in life itself. They bring with them not only deaths but also staggering levels of squalor, sexual abuses, disease, humiliation, despair, congestion, malnutrition and increasing maternal and infant mortality. When these ugly realities stalk people they make it difficult for them to reclaim and expand positive imagination, privacy and dignity. In any case, living conditions which haunt people with pain fracture and shatter their capacities to preserve, regenerate and develop themselves as normal human beings. Subsequently, mass violence and atrocities make reconciliation and forgiveness difficult.

On the other hand, in its dynamics, the sapiential exigency of life endeavors to situate the questions of social reconciliation and forgiveness within the broader attempts to deal with the question of evil. Forgiveness as a dimension of reconciliation is a moral option that a victim may exercise. Victimhood entitles the victim to forgive, if he or she chooses. No religious obligation to forgive overrides this moral right. In the end, not to forgive when wronged is to make the wrongdoer beholden to one who is wronged and that beholding undermines human aliveness or the capacity to be with others. An embittering and tormenting past diminishes the quality of life. Such a past can always make people angry, hateful, resentful and vengeful. In contrast, reconciliation actuates the nobility of the human spirit imbued with hope and a great capacity for goodness and wholeness. Persons can always restore and re-create the existential richness for which they are created thus. In its inner logic and momentum reconciliation encourages warm support, affirmation and restoration of positive individual and shared living.

Also, reconciliation symbolizes a certain unification of justice with mercy on what could otherwise become a shrine of pain, ruin and death. Mercy is an act and process of remembering a difficult or painful life yet with a sense of patience, restraint and sublimation. In this sense, mercy refers to the infinite capacity of compassionate love and continuing sense of care and abundance of being. In mercy guilt is established but punishment is remitted. Mercy finds continuity with, restores and encourages people to return to relational care and understanding, trust and harmony that build the humanity of people. Therein lies the conviction that people must not give up in their struggles and demands for a marvelous or wondrous life. Mercy articulates a certain appreciation and vision of fullness and oneness of destiny. It also humanizes the giving of self or self-spending generosity as a way of life.

Mercy implies the unmerited largesse of gratuitous charity and hope seeking an interpretation and enforcement of justice and communion. The largesse of mercy serves truth and promotes the common good. Charity and hope characteristic of mercy touch on the wholesome and organic reality of practical human interdependence, inner fragility and vulnerability. Charity and hope also lift up the organic and participatory character of kinship ties among people. Reconciliation which derives from mercy exposes the tragedy of abuse, pain and degradation. But beyond that, reconciliation declares faith in the future of human relationships and the capacity of people to change and make new beginnings in ways that bind and re-connect them together in a delicate network of interdependence and joyful living. After all, all life is sacred and worthy of preservation and promotion. Ideally, outcomes of reconciliation engender attitudes and perspectives of patience, friendship, humility, harmony and tolerance. The sense of responsibility which follows reconciliation seeks to foster splendid and courageous ways of living a quality life with others. Communal or social harmony enhances humanity and the personhood of the community or societal members.

Reconciliation and the Question of Evil

Reconciliation is about struggling with evil and its horrendous consequences which may numb and deafen people with a sense of wariness and cynicism. Mass violence and atrocity rob people of their relational freedom and trust, yet human relations and connections are what keep and make people human. No sense or experience of human life is possible without relational trust and peace. The issue with social reconciliation and forgiveness is that of discontinuity and continuity with a painful past, that is, how to set experiences of suffering in the context of a higher purpose, of communication and of kinship among people. Social reconciliation and forgiveness imply changing perspectives and reconfiguring the self and the community in ways and terms that look forward to a promising future, that is, a future of hope and a fuller life. While reconciliation may have different implications, it always begins with the moral imagination of evil. And, the imagination of evil which tends to precede acts of mass violence and atrocity implies that moral repugnance is not as obvious as it might be assumed. The next section discusses the moral responses that people have given to the aftermath of mass violence and atrocity. Discussions on the nature of vengeance, reconciliation and forgiveness follow thereafter.

Some Moral Responses to Mass Atrocity

A variety of circumstances and contexts will inform purposes and means in dealing with a painful past. The issues and intricacies involved in the pursuit of social reconciliation and forgiveness after the experience of abuse and collective slaughter of people always, however, remain complex. Nonetheless, atrocity always remains atrocity; the more useful question to ask in the face of atrocity is whether the particular execution of an atrocity is the whole question. The assumption tends to be that the dead are innocent, the killers monstrous and the surrounding politics insane.[74] But the language of insanity absolves people from moral responsibility. At the same time, however, it is important that no one be put on the pedestal or in the gutter. And the crime of mass violence consists precisely in wanting to make a people extinct.[75] Extermination is the crime. The central issue becomes a matter of life and death. The experience of social violence or atrocities also touches on the question of whether every onlooker or bystander is a coward, a traitor or a collaborator. Undoubtedly, the price for standing up for truth, justice and freedom may be high or stiff in particular concrete circumstances. Yet, the courage to uphold truth, freedom and the struggle for what is right must not simply be given up. The biggest tragedy in the face of social ills occurs when fear paralyzes people.

Victims and survivors of violence frequently ache for retribution against identifiable perpetrators and for a public acknowledgement of what happened. Retribution motivates punishment out of fairness to those who have been wronged and out of the belief that wrongdoers deserve punishment in direct proportion to the harm that they inflicted. In this sense, retribution becomes a way of denouncing previous wrongs and giving people their just deserts. While some might want financial compensation and redress, others may want payback through revenge. Certainly money, services and public art can constitute steps that seek to express restorative justice which emphasizes the humanity of both the offender and victim. However, money is unable to remedy nonmonetary harms like the death of a person or the humiliation or shame of being interned wrongly. In the spirit of the sapiential exigency, restorative justice seeks the repair of social connections and peace using means that enhance communications between the perpetrators and victims and fostering appropriate ties across the community.[76]

Restorative justice also seeks the re-integration of the offender into the community.[77] But, in all circumstances, the ethic of social reconciliation affirms that priority needs to be placed on moving ahead towards a fuller sense of life. Of course, the truth always remains pivotal and indispensable in this process. Truth tends to expose rumors, false pictures and

---

74. Philip Gourevitch, *We Wish to Inform You that Tomorrow We Will Be Killed with Our Families: Stories from Rwanda* (New York: Picador, St. Martin's Press, 1998), 186–87.

75. Ibid., 202.

76. Martha Minow, *Between Vengeance and Forgiveness* (Boston: Beacon Press, 1998), 12.

77. Ibid., 91–93.

myth about the past. In this regard, it may be noted that truth commissions proceed on the assumption that they are able to help individuals tell their stories and to have them acknowledged publicly and officially. The case of South African Truth and Reconciliation Commission represents an apt example of how efforts were directed at finding out what happened, creating a forum for victims to give their testimonies, developing a mechanism for reparation and granting amnesty for perpetrators who honestly reveal their roles in politically motivated violence.[78] Telling the truth and hearing the truth bring catharsis and healing. The restorative power of truth heals memories and brings forth new realization. If not handled well, however, holding accounts of people's painful experiences exacerbates people's numbness, sense of hopelessness and preoccupation with loss and injury.[79] When the process of moral reconstruction underlies the promotion of justice and truth, the process re-creates life with wholesomeness.[80] When people talk about their stories, they experience personal catharsis, they produce a social judgment and moral account of the historical record in ways and terms which lead to actions that restrain violent tendencies.[81]

Some people have held that retribution represents an ideal response to massive violations or attempts at collective extermination. Retribution can indeed correct the wrongdoer's impression that the worth of the victims was less than that of the wrongdoers. But retribution itself needs restraint as it may expand easily into forms of harm that violate respect for a person and threaten the bounds of proportionality and decency.[82] Of course, the express understanding always needs to be that expressing or communicating an outrage, making clear what is unacceptable and refusing relationships with those who carry out acts of mass violence, remain morally justifiable responses.

The social contexts that commonly call forth or beckon social reconciliation and forgiveness are those that involve wars and conflicts, massacres, systematic rapes and tortures. In all these horrendous acts exist the reality and actual attempt to exterminate a people. These horrific experiences assault human respect and dignity as well as living ties among

---

78. Ibid., 3.
79. Ibid., 61.
80. Ibid., 14–15.
81. Ibid., 79.
82. Ibid., 12–13.

people. Reconciliation attempts to forge a response of hope and justice.[83] To fear justice is to believe, first of all, that one has done wrong.[84]

The justice question arises with regard to mass violence and atrocities because these hideous acts do not happen randomly. Mass violence requires organization and careful planning. A great and sustained destruction of people and property requires some great criminal and ill-willed ambition to create a human order through blood lust by means of which perpetrators of mass violence kill their victims.[85] Mass violence is commonly carried out with assiduousness and brisk determination. In this regard, people need to be held accountable for their heinous behaviors and conduct. So, ignoring the justice question only camouflages an uncomfortable and sad existence and people's place in it. Nothing truly emerges in the experience of mass violence and atrocity which does not elicit revulsion and outrage, fear and distress, alarm and sorrow, grief and shame, incomprehension and morbid fascination.[86] Acts of mass violence and atrocity reduce life to a mere accident of fate; inherent in them is the political tactic of lying which frequently serves the intramural interests of some vampire elite. Yet ironically, justice remains the priority of all politics.

Silence is not an acceptable response to mass atrocity or violence as it will imply that the perpetrators succeeded with their destruction and that the bystanders were complicit in the wanton acts of the perpetrators. Experiences disclose that some incidences of mass violence have also brought forth, though in painful ways and complex terms, wondrous transformations of human societies and communities. Nonetheless, how to treat the continuing presence of perpetrators of violence, their victims and bystanders, after acts of mass violence or atrocities have ended, is a central issue in the ethics of reconciliation. There are also risks in dealing with social reconciliation—there could be too much wallowing in the past or forgetting, that is, either too much memory or not enough of it. There can be too much enshrinement of victimhood or an insufficient memorializing of the victims and survivors.[87] Attempts at social reconciliation and forgiveness imply that, in the face of mass violence or atrocities, merely

---

83. Ibid., 1.
84. Gourevitch, 161.
85. Ibid., 17–18.
86. Ibid., 19, 186.
87. Minow, 2.

dwelling in the frozen space of inability and incapacity remain unacceptable and unresponsive to victims and unavailing to the future.[88]

Amnesty has been another way that people have striven politically to effect some reconciliation in a society fractured by mass violence and atrocity. As such, amnesty refers to a general pardon granted by a legitimate civil authority or government to wrongdoers, especially for political offenses. In law, the perpetrators who are granted amnesty are exempted from prosecution for criminal actions. Amnesty is not meant for pleasant people. It is intended for perpetrators of political wrongs and crimes; it deals with matters of impunity. Often, amnesty involves some trade off for the sake of ending conflict or civil strife. Amnesty normally takes place when outright victory can only be accomplished at a cost too high to pay. An amnesty comes about usually as part of a negotiated strategy to end a conflict by allowing one side or other to escape the consequences of their actions. Frequently, the granting of amnesty takes place under specified set of conditions.

Subsequently, amnesty extends to a group of persons during a period of prolonged disorder or insurrection. These persons are offered a promise of immunity from prosecution on condition that they abandon their unlawful activities. The hope is that granting amnesty will provide for greater peace and re-establishes caring and harmonious relations in a broken society. This is what happened in Northern Ireland. Certain people, who were members of a paramilitary group, the IRA (The Irish Republican Army) and had committed offences such as bombings and killings, were set free as part of a negotiated settlement. This, however, does not mean that they were forgiven. They still have to live with their own conscience and many relatives of the perpetrators and the victims of their heinous acts find it very hard to forgive them. All the same, these relatives accept the perpetrators as legally set free for the sake of peace.

A program of public education, which involves people outside the law, has been another moral response to the experience of mass violence and atrocities. However, such an approach alone does not seem to be sufficient. Public education can only teach versions of what happened.

On the whole, no single response seems adequate to the question of any collective violence or atrocity. Nonetheless, the ethics of social reconciliation and forgiveness always attempts to guess how best to respond to the experiences of mass violence and atrocities. The attempt seeks to let words replace violence and to let fairness replace terror. Indeed, legal responses seem frail and insufficient in addressing situations of mass violence

88. Ibid., 4.

and violations. Yet, legal responses are necessary so that the instruments of justice may be exercised.[89] However, legal responses cannot reconstruct relationships, seek healing of the accused or heal a community divided by mass murder.[90] The law cannot make one person love another. Tribunals alone do not resolve social divisions and harm. So, trials should not be pursued unless there exists the chance for fairness or perception of fairness. Also, in such a case, every trial needs to be seen as a step which seeks to ensure peace, make those in power responsible for just laws and condemn aggression.[91] When trials signal that no individual is outside the reach of legal accountability, prosecuting human rights violations can enhance the establishment and promotion of the rule of law.[92]

When processes of reconciliation are well done or carried out, there can be a true re-creation of individuals and communities. In some places, people and communities have succeeded, as a result, to create memorials in the forms of public monuments and sculptures, museums and days of memory.[93] In all the efforts, however, justice and truth need to be essential components and values of processes and decisions. As justice demands accountability, truth requires acknowledgment.

On the Narrative Origins of Mass Violence

At the origins of mass violence or atrocities lies a successive struggle for a narrowly-based power which, to a very large extent, consists of the ability to make others inhabit one's stories in their reality. This ability may also imply killing the other to make that happen. The power that leads to mass violence and atrocities tends to be narrowly based. A broadly based power requires a truer story at its core and protects its subjects from abuses.[94] How a people inhabit their stories is important for their sense of identity. In this respect, people are frequently functions of how they imagine themselves and how others imagine them. The ideas that others have of us tend to define us sharply. As others make our lives their business, they make us vividly aware and alive. The only times when people are truly free to imagine themselves are their private times when they become in-

---

89. Ibid.
90. Ibid., 26.
91. Ibid., 50.
92. Ibid., 57.
93. Ibid., 3.
94. Gourevitch, 48, 181.

violably on their own.⁹⁵ In consequence, the stories people tell themselves tend to raise questions of the humanity of others. The motives for mass violence lie in the elimination of others perceived as rivals or menaces. This perception of others creates a unifying specter of a common enemy. And, when people see others as absolute menaces, rivals and enemies, they devise absolute means of eradication of them through suggestive messages and direct commands to kill or be killed.⁹⁶

Furthermore, the stories people tell about themselves and others shape relational expectations, attitudes and habits. And the kinds of stories that lie behind mass violence and atrocities tend to place the victims at the periphery of humanity or even deprive them of humanity. A typical tactic consists of labeling them as enemies, rivals or sources of nuisance. Such labeling neutralizes and removes the respect due to the humanity of others as human beings. Herein, too, lies the myth of superiority of one group of people over another through exclusionary educational, military, religious and economic discourses. The discussion of us-against-them scenarios of popular violence and atrocities generates mass hatred which appeals to or makes use of weakness. In order to move a huge number of people to do wrong, it is necessary to appeal to their passion for strength. And, as people surrender to hatred, they also aspire to controlling power.⁹⁷

At the origins of mass violence, then, lie the questions of the violation of the rights of people. Violation of people's rights creates physical and psychological damage which undermines people's capacities for decent existences. A wounded psyche is a source of its own affliction or torture as well as injury and harm to others. In the end, mass violence and atrocities arise from a certain denial of the common humanity of people. At times, however, human responses to mass violence and atrocities have been of vengeance, the topic of the next section.

Vengeance

Vengeance refers to the impulse to retaliate when wrong is done. But it is frequently the case also that vengeance unleashes more penalty than punishment guided by the rule of law.⁹⁸ Vengeance can make people dangerously aggressive, hateful or maliciously spiteful in ways and terms that heighten

---

95. Ibid., 71.
96. Ibid., 95.
97. Ibid., 128–29.
98. Minow, 10.

recrimination.[99] The logic of vengeance and hate develop together as they easily tend towards horrible excesses, painful and futile vendetta. Avenging can also be costly emotionally to the perpetrators.[100] Here it may be noted that reconciliation is about truth and not revenge. Truth is important in the process of reconciliation because the violence perpetrated against victims lies in a falsification about their existence and intrinsic significance. Additionally, truth and justice hang together. So, justice without the pursuit of truth easily turns into revenge. It is truth that prepares the grounds for liberative justice. Truth and justice that effect reconciliation focus on right relations among the parties in a conflict and establish positive ways of defining the self and others.[101] In this light, reconciliation and forgiveness stand in contradistinction to vengeance or hatred.

Reconciliation and Narrative

Reconciliation begins with the victim whose humanity the wrongdoer tried to call into question, wrest away or destroy. In reconciliation, the victim calls the wrongdoer to repentance and forgiveness that create space for healing and new possibilities. The process of reconciliation strives to build safe places for exploring and untangling the complexity of a painful past and for cultivating a culture of truth-telling in order to overcome the lies of injustice and wrongdoing.[102] When people see the truth they develop the praxis of truth.[103] The enterprise of reconciliation seeks to restore the humanity of both the victim and the wrongdoer. Yet the restoration of the humanity of the victim must include the painful experiences of violence which now mark the victim's memories and identity.[104] Reconciliation transforms as it addresses the past as adequately as possible.

Through reconciliation, people learn to tell their stories in new ways. Stories are a powerful means by which people shape their identities. People give forms to their identities by the kinds of stories that they tell themselves, their families, friends and communities or other people important to them. In fact, as people retell their stories, they gain new perspectives and realizations into their current situations in life. They also

99. Ibid.

100. Ibid., 13.

101. Ibid., 99–100.

102. Robert J. Schreiter, *The Ministry of Reconciliation: Spirituality and Strategies* (Maryknoll, New York: Orbis Books, 1998), 15.

103. Ibid., 51.

104. Ibid., 17–18.

reintegrate anew the important experiences of their lives so that the stories also become new stories. It is the shift in perspectives that frequently offers people a sense of healing. This healing tends to come with realization and awareness that guide in new directions and imbue life with a noble or resplendent sense of purpose.[105] Re-description of painful experiences can reveal perspectives that evoke a sense of common morality through the complex and deep-rooted nexus of degrees of responsibility.

The healing of memories, with which much of one's identity is tied, tends to take place in telling and retelling of stories. In other words, reconciliation realizes itself in a context where memory can be gently unfolded and its wounds healed.[106] Reconciliation and healing occurs when perspectives shift so that a new meaning and realization is found. A pathway which leads out of the deep tangle of memories, emotions and stories of death emerges and clarifies itself. Reconciliation truly comes to exist when it transfigures people's living continuity through history.

In recounting their experiences of pain and suffering, it is important to recognize that the victims' memories of death focus attention and awareness on experiences of loss, absence and pain that the victims of violence or atrocity felt or faced. The resulting sense of abyss can reveal the enormity and complexity of a painful past. Through absence, victims of mass violence and atrocities acknowledge who they have become because of the past and the need to transcend the past so that it no longer controls their current direction of existence. Mass violence and atrocities leave human wreckage in their wake. The yawning abyss of absence which confronts the victims of violence provides them with the loci for feeling and recognizing the sense of loss and the skein of emotions that surround their painful experiences. Out of the loci of absences tend to flow memories through which new relationships may be imagined and worked out. Yet, the strength to deal with absences positively and creatively requires steadfastness in faith, trust and hope.[107] Establishing a focus for grief then becomes important. When people grieve they proclaim that they cannot allow acts of violence or atrocity to engulf their world. It is in this regard that burial locations and memorial monuments offer places where people can engage in the rituals that re-establish a foothold in an otherwise shaky and unstable world. One cannot hold onto the dead; a new relationship

---

105. Ibid., 19–20.
106. Ibid., 44.
107. Ibid., 37–39.

has to be worked out and established.[108] Memorials bring presence to broken or changed relationships. Memorials offer creative intuition that renews and taps on the transcendence of life. A memorial allows presence and communion with another.

The telling and retelling of stories can also take place through the language of human rights which can make known the circumstances, antecedents, factors and contexts of violations and the needed process of reconciliation and reconstruction. The rhetoric of human rights, as a response to unjustified suffering, provides people with the grammar to speak about their stories of suffering. The human rights language, it may be noted, springs out of concrete sufferings of individuals in particular histories and cultures. Of course, in all of this also lies the affirmation of fundamental human dignity as an individual and collective reality which endows abuses and violations with moral significance. Human rights language enables people to see mutual and relational obligations that they owe to one another for harmonious coexistence. The language of human rights grounds itself in the conviction of the sovereign and relational self so that the language of such or said rights touches on one's legitimate interests. As a moral vocabulary, the language of human rights offers ways of talking about the experiences of people and ways of perceiving, imagining and interpreting suffering. In effect, as providing tools for telling stories about suffering, the language of human rights allows people to name the prejudices and violations of their persons and relationships. It also makes possible the imagination of new ways of describing behaviors and conduct appropriate to social reconstruction.

The grammar of human rights helps further in disclosing the historical progression of the violations of persons and human relations. Conditions that precede mass violence and atrocities are often nurtured over a long time. They often follow a long-standing toleration of violence and systemic distortions that threaten people's rights to subsistence, security and liberty of participation in social and political life and processes. Through abuses of rights, a gradual distortion of the basic humanity of some people tends to take place. Erosion of human agency through the creation of conditions that make it difficult for some people to realize a fuller sense of their dignity is a common and critical marker in the degradation of life that culminates in mass violence and atrocity.

In the light of the common good, the grammar of human rights makes possible certain narratives of people with respect to shared liv-

---

108. Ibid., 35. A later section in chapter five that deals with the question of our beloved dead pursues further this question in important respects.

ing, heritages, aspirations and common humanity. The dignity of people touches on their sacredness as people; and dignity is honored by forbearance and liberative acts and obligations in and for the moral community. In implicating people in the moral community, dignity implies that people are responsible not only for themselves as individuals but also for others and shared heritages. The language of human rights enhances the experience and expression of human historical agency in justice.

For its efficacy, reconciliation requires a spiritual orientation. Spirituality here refers to the question of a new self-perception and self-definition. The restoration of the humanity of both victim and wrongdoer, through liberating self-perceptions and self-definitions, lies at the heart of reconciliation. Socially, reconciliation involves the provision of structures and processes by means of which a fractured society can be reconstructed truthfully and justly. This further implies coming to terms with a painful past which includes some measure of reparation for the victims. In this regard, creating a social atmosphere of trust is important for reconciliation.[109] It is not enough to denounce abuses and violations; these need to be redeemed through structural compensation and protection.

Social reconciliation is about the reconstruction of a more just and safe society in which the violence and abuses of past wrongs will be prevented from occurring again in the future. But a successful process of social reconciliation will require the leadership of reconciled individuals.[110] At the spiritual level, reconciliation signifies bringing people's stories of suffering into contact with faith or the stories of their sacred traditions especially the stories which deal with betrayal, humiliation, torture, abandonment and death.[111] The meaning that people derive from connecting their stories with those of their sacred traditions needs to convey the conviction and/or assurance that there can now be no deliberate turning back to the old and destructive ways of living and doing things.[112] What is more, forgiveness is yet another dimension in the process of reconciliation.

Forgiveness and Reconciliation

Forgiveness is a particularly difficult dimension in the process of reconciliation. To be forgiven is to receive love and be reunited with another from whom one had separated or been separated. Forgiveness activates again

---

109. Ibid., 4.
110. Ibid., 65.
111. Ibid., 5.
112. Ibid., 8.

the sense and reality of bonding and oneness among persons. To forgive is not to wipe out the memory of what happened. Rather, in forgiveness, there takes place the proffering of life and a transfiguring of a wounded, problematized or broken relationship with the perspective of letting go. As an act of freedom, forgiveness involves both process and decision. In releasing a person from the bondage of the past and as an act of learning to speak truthfully, forgiveness implies the possibility of having a different and liberative future. In forgiveness one ceases to be bound by the power of a painful past. It is about not holding the wrongdoer in one's own thrall. In this sense, it is the wrongdoer's experience of being forgiven that frequently leads to the wrongdoer's repentance. Ideally, forgiveness requires reciprocity but this frequently remains only an ideal.

There is a common belief that if a person who has been wronged forgives and continues to love, that person is stupid. The existential logic and conviction of forgiveness is, however, that if a person who has been wronged does not forgive and love, he or she fails to liberate himself or herself. The person deprives himself or herself of life, light, peace and expansive possibilities of fullness. In other words, people can always bridge every chasm of inner divisions and outward separatedness from others. Painful experiences need not have the last say on their lives and choices and deny them liberating responses. By means of forgiveness, people take a first step into the future unburdened by a certain experience of newness and light-heartedness. The magnanimity and nobility of the spirit which comes with forgiveness is extraordinarily liberative—the experience recreates possibilities and opportunities for responsible trust, expansive goodness and a radiant sense of new life.

The freedom or the ability to forgive is an ennobling capacity and part of the dignity to be reclaimed by those who survive wrongdoing. The exercise of forgiveness cannot be commanded. Forgiveness is a power held by the victimized and not a right to be claimed; this power must be exercised with good reason without which the offended accepts the violation and devaluation of the self.[113] A right can always be recognized and safeguarded from without; this does not apply to forgiveness which involves a personal living relation with another. Forgiveness seeks reconnection and recognition of the humanity of the other. As an act, forgiveness underscores the strength of the common humanity of all people. The healing of forgiveness can reconnect the offender to the victim and establishes or renews a relationship for constructive alliances in life.[114] In marking a change in how

113. Minow, 17.
114. Ibid., 14.

the offended feel about the offender, forgiveness enables victims to reassert their own liberative power and reestablish their own dignity.[115] But forgiveness can too easily produce exemption from moral reproach, retribution and holding the wrongdoer to account. When injury is ignored it is left to fester. In effect, if forgiveness is announced by someone who was not wronged, then it becomes a call to forget or put aside painful memories. Such an act cannot truly be an act of forgiveness itself.[116]

Of course, it will always remain that political concerns that relate to the question of social reconciliation and forgiveness pertain to creating a climate conducive to human rights, promoting harmony across divisions created by collective violence or atrocity and restoring dignity to victims and perpetrators of collective violence.[117]

Reconciliation is a creative power of life and love and a prelude to some fullness of communion within and among persons. In the process of reconciliation, forgiveness gives others peace, acceptance, joy, wellbeing, a sense of security, strength and new life. Reconciling truly tends to mercy itself. In this light, mercy implies that one is able to conquer one's bad feelings, or rise above them and keep loving, forgiving and uniting with another who has wronged one. Indeed, one can always remain open to a fuller life even when one is hurt. Mercy respects, gives without taking, believes beyond disillusionment and hopes beyond present time. Reconciling manifests a human itinerary of love and sense of oneness.

Reconciliation, Politics, and Truth

The strategy of effecting reconciliation will always depend on circumstance, time and place. This further implies that different contexts and cultures and availability of resources or political feasibility will influence the process of reconciliation in different ways. Identifying players in the process of reconciliation is a matter of knowing who needs to be considered in the process of reconciliation and their relation to that process.[118] The nature of the players in a conflict situation shape the way reconciliation is carried out at personal and social or cultural levels.

A sense of social trust and commonwealth are very critical in the process of working out and negotiating peace in situations of conflicts. The process of the administration of justice needs to proceed within a broader

---

115. Ibid., 15.
116. Ibid., 20.
117. Ibid., 23.
118. Ibid., 108.

framework that includes justice mechanisms of the local people for the promotion of peace and harmony. An inclusive reconciliation strives to initiate meaningful dialogue and interaction which include victims, perpetrators and bystanders in local communities. Such reconciliation efforts are helpful in furthering the resolution of personal grievances that make possible a realization of some community peace and a deepening of continuing harmony. As a matter of practical politics and according to facts and circumstances, it is important that exit options be offered for perpetrators of harm if that would help strengthen the prospects of enduring peace.

A robust, expansive approach to justice and reconciliation involving much more than punishment of specific individuals or reconciliation of perpetrators and victims is necessary for a society affected by mass violence. A just and lasting peace requires that a mechanism be created that extends peace-building beyond the elite to the local level and covers a wide range of actors including women and children. In circumstances where people have limited capacities to account for their crimes, a Truth and Reconciliation Commission would be appropriate and needful. Such a commission would make possible and facilitate storytelling before an audience. When people remember and retell their stories before a listening audience they become capable of moving forward in the light of goodness. In this way, storytelling builds a common and inclusive memory, a sense of community, shared hopes and shared lives. At the same time, transitional reconciliation and justice strategies need to serve several goals: offer physical guarantees, make possible truth telling about what took place in order to rebuild communities, recognize victims and their sufferings, work out reparations as tokens of acknowledgment of harm suffered and negotiate meaningful and just forms of punishment.

Reconciliation is a moral and spiritual, political and structural work given concrete expression by particular contexts. It is a process of personal and social reconfiguration for the service of common life and a promising future. True reconciliation discloses truth and abuses, pain and degradation that people have faced and suffered. In other words, reconciliation takes place within a prior context or history in which is acknowledged some rejection, hurt, indifference, repudiation or alienation. True reconciliation deals with the problematic past in order to make for and create a noble and viable future on some painful history. In this light, justice becomes a matter of addressing violations of human rights yet with a sight on a purposive and fulfilling future so that similar violations do no reoccur. But at all times, reconciliation affirms that there is a great deal of goodness in people and in the world, despite all tensions and hurt, ruptures and struggles.

Social reconciliation will always require individual reconciliation that opens individuals to the welfare and experiences of others. The truth that engenders an enduring sense of reconciliation is one that illuminates human experiences. "Truth in reconciliation has to be understood in terms of the lies that wrongdoers perpetrate in a situation of violence, and the environment of untruthfulness that is created."[119] This is not to deny that truth that is sought in the process of reconciliation is in the first instance a retrieval of what happened. Seeking the truth establishes a pattern of truthfulness upon which a new and a more liberative self-definition, relationships and society can rebuild themselves. The truth also makes possible the forging of a new and shared civic discourse. Further, it is important to be clear about what kind of justice is being sought in a given context of reconciliation. In the end, to imagine, to remember and to redress evil constitutes elements of personal responses that make liberative reconciliation meaningful and engaging.

As an ingredient of human existence, reconciliation recognizes and asserts that people can always transcend the divisions and strife of the past. Seeking reconciliation is a way and an instrument of ending a struggle and strife, restoring people's own humanity, and promoting understanding and a future founded on the recognition of human rights and peaceful co-existence. Reconciliation demands steadfastness, skill and illuminating insight. It bequeaths a legacy of settlement and respect, reassurance and creative responsibility for continuing conversations and communication between people. At the same time, the pursuit of reconciliation also demands the pursuit of justice or some form of reparation on the basis of truth, for unless the alienating and polarizing experiences of the past are dealt with properly and prudently, they will always haunt the present and future. Dealing with the past efficaciously implies knowing what happened so that people pledge or renew their commitment and responsibility for a future of hope. A close relationship exists between truth and freedom. No healing of the past takes place without truths that spotlight and illuminate it. When people can account for the past well they also come to account for the future.

Conclusion

In life we see and meet desperate people battered by their upbringings and the pains of life experiences. We also meet people with, for example, serious medical difficulties or people affected by homelessness. All these

---

119. Ibid., 118.

issues demand different forms of responses yet which do not abandon the sense and experience of common engagement, solidarity and love. In order to achieve much and promote responsibility for one another, the scientific, ethical-political and sapiential exigencies need to work together. In other words, it is, for instance, of little effectiveness to promote family values while at the same time supporting scientific, political and economic thinking and structures that enhance a merely instrumental understanding of human life and human relationships. Scientific, moral and sapiential issues hang together and enlighten one another in shaping and integrating the various facets of life and existence.

The scientific and sapiential exigencies of life all serve the course of life by validating the strength and meaning of existence. They make possible some concrete realization of ideals, qualities and convictions by which people live and judge life. This is also to say that it is the diversity and complexity of contexts that allow people to see and refract these exigencies in an ever new light. When differentiated and harnessed well, the scientific and sapiential exigencies help illumine, address and resolve some emerging problems and needs that arise in life. They also help promote a sense of togetherness in community and establish bases for discerning and determining responses to issues that attend the constantly dialogical human life. They further supply tools for pressing forward and responding fittingly to challenges posed by the contexts that affect and shape cultural ideas, beliefs and practices.

Of course, it must be recognized that serenity, patient dialogue, depth of knowledge and good will are important ingredients of existence without which the scientific and sapiential exigencies will yield illusory results that do not expand the sense of meaning and justification for living. Perhaps to these preceding attributes must be added persistence, tenderness and unyielding adaptability. Life's goal consists in bringing forth, affirming and upholding common humanity, freedom, openness and goodness of people in spite of all else. The scientific and sapiential exigencies not only enrich and expand imaginative thinking and understanding, initiatives and conscious efforts, they also establish possibilities and opportunities for service, friendships and collaboration which allow for and promote trust, confidence in life and inclusive fellowship.

The question of the scientific and sapiential exigencies considered in this chapter cannot be a matter of plebiscites. The questions of science and wisdom come from prevailing perceptions, categories of thought and practices that pertain to living life. In the midst of all the complexities of life, people can always make a positive difference in the demanding world in which they live and work. It is the case that people repeatedly seek meaning and truth in the beauty, ambivalence and depth of life. Technological and scientific advancements need to be at the service and promotion of people's liberative freedom and wellbeing. In the last analysis, the deepest meaning of being human lies in a certain inward and practical integration of science and wisdom through communion and transcendence which the next chapter explores.

5

Communion and Transcendence

Preamble

To begin with, I would like to state briefly what will become clear in its full import in the course of this chapter that communion and transcendence express authentic experience of hope. Communion and transcendence taken together underpin the patience, chastity and humility that typify hope. In the light of communion and transcendence, hope "coincides with the spiritual principle itself."[1] The spiritual principle mentioned here is the principle of being as intrinsic value and plenitude.

Specifically for the subject matter of this chapter, it may be asserted that communion and transcendence inform the inception, evolution and concrete experiences, expressions and process of hoping. Both communion and transcendence participate and authenticate themselves within the realm of availability and mystery that constitute hope. Communion and transcendence make possible the possibilities and availability that transfigure and surmount perverted, polarized and often conflict-ridden human relations.

In communion and transcendence a person grows in humility because:

> . . . the only genuine hope is . . . hope springing from humility and not from pride . . . [which] consists in drawing one's strength solely from oneself. The proud man is cut off from a certain form of communion with his fellow men, which pride, acting as a principle of destruction, tends to break down. Indeed, this destructiveness can be equally well directed against the self; pride is in no way incompatible with self-hate . . .[2]

Besides, communion and transcendence suggest a counsel of common sense by which I cannot affirm the compassion, generosity or truthfulness when in my life I do not genuinely strive to incarnate these values.

1. Marcel, *Homo Viator*, 36.
2. Marcel, *The Philosophy of Existentialism*, 32.

Compassion laced with disdain, generosity permeated with self-importance, or truthfulness pierced with self-righteousness, leave a person vulnerable to justified contempt. In the last analysis, communion and transcendence imply that the dimension of Hope coincides with that of Love.[3]

A blossoming of the experience of communion and transcendence means that we do not lead our lives as focused solely on ourselves, that is, only on our memories, our hopes, our worries, our concerns, our ideas and whatever belongs to us. As vehicles for fullness of life, communion and transcendence entail noticing others, reaching out to and becoming a neighbor to them. Further, these activities imply lifting them up and, where necessary, helping them to overcome their fears, worries, sufferings, complexes and disabilities. The experiences of communion and transcendence can also help people come out of themselves and reach out to others as brothers, sisters and companions. In a context of responsibility, communion and transcendence mean fulfilling responsibilities as a service of love in order to initiate, create and safeguard the conditions that allow and build peace, wondrous life and the joy and fervor of living.

With this prelude, we now consider communion and transcendence as vistas of empowering availability and freshness.

Communion

At the heart of the experience of communion lie human cohesive interactions, being together, common ground rules of civility, comparable opportunity and equal respect.

Communion as Openness and Bonding

There exists an intimate connection between communion and hope. Communion is closely tied with the fabric of personal openness. There will never be any real communion between individuals centered on themselves, namely, between morbidly hardened people who thrive in the heart of the masses. The very notion of intersubjectivity or the genuine experience and expression of human kinship presuppose a reciprocal openness between individuals without which we cannot conceive of any kind of spirituality.[4] Communion expresses a subject-subject union or bonding among persons. It involves a network of relationships among people which reinforces, enlivens and indwells one another. When people are bonded

---

3. Marcel, "Desire and Hope," 283.
4. Marcel, *Man Against Mass Society*, 267.

together they become permeable to one another and come to share in a milieu where one person becomes accessible to another. In a bonding experience a relaxation of tension takes place. This bonding enables persons to grow in their responsiveness towards all of life from the point of view of expansive self-definition.

The human propensity towards communion arises from the intersubjective nexus or pleroma of human kinship. In fact, human kinship and connections characterize the whole of human life. In other words, intersubjectivity plays its part within the life of the subject. This is also to say, in its own intrinsic structure subjectivity is already and, in the most profound sense, genuinely intersubjective.[5] In addition, communion as intersubjectivity signifies that if trust and companionship are not the points from which we begin in human relationships we fail at realizing and harnessing the wellspring of joy. For, "joy is fundamentally bound up with a consciousness of being *all together*, which *all together*, moreover can affect even the consciousness which the organism has of its own functioning."[6] In this sense, the freshness of joy lies in its characteristic symbol of warm-heartedness. Human life is structured in such a way that it becomes itself when it opens up to being with others; it gives of itself and realizes itself in the reaching of one person to another. Human existence has inbuilt in it a self-identification of being-for-others: it is deeply a relationship. This trajectory of self-giving availability and freshness constitute the vibrancy of spontaneity, sacrifice, warm-heartedness, steadfastness and delight in the joy of living.

An experience of communion, say, between you and me, is enacted by "the discovery of a certain bond between us which transforms a relationship so that it becomes one of subject to subject."[7] Literally, we communicate; we become who we *are* in and by the very act of communication. In such a circumstance, the word *with* comes to reflect truly a relationship and an experience not merely of togetherness but of increasing intimacy. The word *with* only has meaning where some unity is felt, that is, where some harmony, however feeble, become manifested between people.[8] Between two people, in fact, who have an intimate relationship, a kind of unity tends to be created which makes a third person, who has not been initiated

---

5. Marcel, *The Mystery of Being: Vol.I: Reflection and Mystery*, 182–83.
6. Marcel, *The Mystery of Being Vol.11: Faith and Reality*, 119.
7. Marcel, *The Existential Background of Human Dignity*, 40.
8. Marcel, *Metaphysical Journal*, 170.

into the relationship, who does not participate in it, feel an intruder.⁹ The sense of common fate or the indistinct awareness of which workmates, allies, partners or persons sharing some experience together can be relevant examples signifying that people cannot be merely reduced to units of utility. The feeling of community in effort and struggle or in common supportive experience that people have when they are with others is in itself enough to deprive persons of the right to treat people as simple units of force that can be added to each other. Supportive common experience enriches itself further in the extent to which people working together learn to know themselves, communicate with and understand one another in the uniqueness of their diverse beings and in the single color of common purpose, fate or destiny.¹⁰

In person-to-person bonding, a relationship imperceptibly becomes a way of seeing oneself in the other and the other in oneself. In such a context it also becomes possible to see one's personal illusions, fears, insecurities and compulsions as one reckons inevitably with personal vulnerabilities in the process of interacting and bonding with another. This dynamics also points to the experience that a touch of intersubjective experience lifts me out of the stifling here-and-nowness in which my ego sticks to me as an adhesive plaster sticks to a small cut.¹¹ In fact, the way I relate with others can become an "expression of that intersubjectivity which opens philosophic reflection to the discovery of the concrete *thou* and *us*."¹²

Communion and Betrayal

Through the notion of *us* that comes to be forged, created or established through the experience of internal bonding, people in communion touch on, share or participate in the groundswell of personal trust and shared confidence. Trust and shared confidence signify that relationships between people are internal, that is, my relationship *with* you makes a difference to both of us and so will any interruption of the relationship make a difference.¹³ The notion of internal bonding is what, for example, underlies or authenticates the experience of pain people live in every act of betrayal.

9. Marcel, *The Mystery of Being Vol.I: Reflection and Mystery*, 181.

10. Ibid., 180.

11. Ibid., 177.

12. Marcel, *The Existential Background of Human Dignity*, 50. The language of thou touches on presence and invocation of another in a context of felt unity and togetherness. This is particularly efficacious in a context where living relations exist between people.

13. Marcel, *The Mystery of Being Vol.I: Reflection and Mystery*, 181.

People suffer much pain when they are betrayed or when their trust is breached. Accordingly, with every act of betrayal or breach of trust, we come up against the notion of shared secret. But this is secret in a deeper sense, that is, as really incommunicable experience—generally a painful one—about which others, who did not share it in the flesh, have no right to speak.[14] The notion of shared secret constitutes a mainspring of intersubjectivity because relationships between people are more internal than external.[15]

In fact, betrayal always begins with the experience and expression of letting down another in a context of trust and love. It also engenders the experience of guilt. Guilt is something we feel when love is betrayed. In this light, guilt tends to be experienced by both the perpetrator and victim of an act of betrayal. In fact, guilt impedes a kind of innocence that enables us to realize a fuller humanity. At the same time, it also provides fertile ground from which a wondrous humanity can rise up through a new way of life. This rising up is a process of human justification wherein people can realize a certain unity of the problematic and uplifting beauty in their persons and in their relationships.

Communion and Presence

An experience of communion has also to do with presence:

> When I say that a being is granted to me as a presence or as a being . . . this means that I am unable to treat him as if he were merely placed before me; between him and me there arises a relationship [union] which, in a sense, surpasses my awareness of him; he is not only before me, he is also within me [that is, part of my very being]—or, rather these categories are transcended, they have no longer any meaning.[16]

Presence makes the other a *thou* and creates an experience and expression of a privileged *us*. At the root of presence there is a being who takes me into consideration, that is, a person whom I regard as taking me into account. Within this perspective, presence may be regarded as truly involving the gift of oneself. Presence belongs only to the being who is capable of giving himself or herself.[17] Presence is the lifeline of the experience of communion. As a participation in the experience and expression

14. Ibid.
15. Ibid., 178.
16. Marcel, *The Philosophy of Existentialism*, 38.
17. Marcel, *Presence and Immortality*, 153.

of significance within the structure of shared life presence "exists in an immediacy beyond all conceivable mediation."[18] When I am in a context of living presence, that which becomes relevant is the act by which I expose myself to the other person instead of protecting myself from him or her, which makes him or her penetrable for me at the same time as I become penetrable for him or her. So, in the presence of a *thou*, that is, before another person offered as being present to me, I attain inner unification which makes possible a dyadic relation or a sense of an immediate living relation with him or her.[19] Thus, the more we rise to generous love, the more closely we approach a dyadic relationship where we supersede all control and render it superfluous.[20]

Presence as an experience of personal relationship and significance through another awakens persons to an existential security as they come to participate in a certain plenitude of life. In the experience and expression of bonding that characterizes presence:

> The indistinctness of the I and the thou, of the thou and him, does not imply the existence of a neutral environment in which one can lose oneself and abdicate, so to speak; on the contrary, it is a kind of vital milieu for the soul from which the soul draws its strength and where it is renewed by testing itself . . . a will to participate must operate . . .[21]

The intersubjective quality characteristic of presence is important because "it is where I am open to myself that it is given to me, not as something additional but by that very fact itself, to be open, to be available to the other."[22] In fact, "I communicate effectively with myself only insofar as I communicate with the other person, i.e., when he becomes thou for me."[23] When the other is a thou, he or she comes to be available to me and can be with me with the whole of himself or herself. The person who is at my disposal is the one who is capable of being with me the whole of himself or herself when I am in need. The characteristic of the soul, which is present and at the disposal of others is that it cannot think in terms of *cases*, that is, it ignores merely individual characteristics. In its

---

18. Marcel, *The Philosophy of Existentialism*, 15.
19. Marcel, *Creative Fidelity*, 36.
20. Marcel, *Searchings*, 70.
21. Marcel, *Creative Fidelity*, 35.
22. Marcel, *Presence and Immortality*, 151.
23. Marcel, *Creative Fidelity*, 34.

eyes there are no cases at all.[24] *To be at the disposal of* signifies a relation of one unique individual to another and not one function to another. The sharing involved in this felt and lived experience of human kinship and bonding or intersubjectivity is charity itself.[25] We may note further that fidelity is the active perpetuation of presence that precedes, makes and renews intersubjectivity. Fidelity renews the benefits and virtue of presence in human kinship which consists in a mysterious incitement to create.[26] Fidelity arises with the question of keeping and nourishing commitments to the being of another; fidelity is always posited in terms of another.

Communion as Lived Intersubjectivity

It also needs to be emphasized that intersubjectivity is frequently lived within relational forms of friendships, loyalties and communities formed by joint tasks and responsibilities, lived memories and hopes. Observably, we enrich ourselves with an intersubjective experience by knowing ourselves and knowing one another in the uniqueness of our diverse being and in the single color of shared destiny or fate.[27] In this world, human beings can be linked to each other by a real bond only because, in another dimension, they are linked to something which transcends them and comprehends them in itself.[28] In other words, the intersubjective situation in its minimal terms comprises an I, a thou and a common purpose, endeavor or trial, or peril, as living tissues which bond persons, communities and nations.[29] The experience and expression of intersubjective kinship embraces the sense of commonwealth, shared lot and a feeling of community in effort and struggle.[30] Without a doubt:

> What brings me closer to another being and really binds me to him . . . is not the knowledge that he can check and confirm an addition or subtraction I had to do for my business account; it is rather the thought that he has passed through the same difficulties as I have, that he has undergone the same dangers, that he has had a childhood, been loved, that others have been attracted to him

---

24. Marcel, *The Philosophy of Existentialism*, 40–41.
25. Marcel, *The Mystery of Being Vol. II: Faith and Reality*, 170.
26. Marcel, *The Philosophy of Existentialism*, 36.
27. Marcel, *The Mystery of Being Vol. I: Reflection and Mystery*, 180.
28. Marcel, *Man Against Mass Society*, 259.
29. William Ernest Hocking, "Marcel and the Ground Issues of Metaphysics," *Philosophy and Phenomenological Research*, Vol. XIV, No.4, 452.
30. Marcel, *The Mystery of Being: Vol. I: Reflection and Mystery*, 180.

and have had hope in him; and it also means that he is called upon to suffer, to decline and to die . . . it is only in these terms that a meaningful content can be ascribed to *fraternity*.[31]

The experience and expression of intersubjectivity as a quality of bonding between people involve living communication, a binding together.[32] As such, "it is the relationship expressed by the preposition *with* that is eminently intersubjective."[33] However, the bond or harmony of living communication in the felt experience and expression of concrete intersubjectivity always remains imperfect. When a musical metaphor is employed as an analogue for understanding the experience of intersubjectivity, it becomes recognizable that the perfect chord, at any rate, is inconceivable for wayfarers. Man and woman are fundamentally *en route*—which means being on the road to somewhere. Even if there can be no question of the perfect form, there must certainly be room here for a certain harmony.[34] "Belonging to the common lot involves human weakness, sufferings incident to the finitude of human knowledge and of power, the long journey from semi-darkness to semi-light, common handicaps that drive us to partnership even if we are not drawn to it.[35]

In the experience of intersubjectivity, I, as a participant, recognize the other as a being who has been granted to me as a presence, that is, as a source into the joy of living. That is also to say, the experience and expression of intersubjectivity involve acknowledging and loving another person as a bearer of unique value to which eternal bliss has been promised.[36] What is implied further is the light of personal participation in *this life* that enlightens every man and woman. Any attempt that seeks to define the human being in a way which excludes the possibility of conceiving light or radiance merely sets up a false picture. In its spontaneous upsurge and freshness, the truth of human life cannot be thought of without reference to the illuminating light. This is the intelligible light of being which invades and accompanies people the more they become forgetful of themselves.[37] The metaphor of light in relation to people signifies the sacred element that cannot be separated from any and every human existence.

---

31. Marcel, *Creative Fidelity*, 8.
32. Marcel, *The Mystery of Being Vol.II: Faith and Reality*, 15.
33. Ibid., 177.
34. Ibid., 127.
35. Hocking, 457.
36. Marcel, *The Mystery of Being Vol.I: Reflection and Mystery*, 179.
37. Marcel, *Tragic Wisdom and Beyond*, 209–11.

In this perspective, "man's essential characteristic seems to be his ability to let himself be penetrated by this supra-personal light, an ability which is evidently linked . . . to . . . human dignity."[38]

The ambivalent and significant character of the human social reality implies that a "community is only possible when beings acknowledge that they are mutually different while existing together in their differences."[39] Other persons are fellow-travelers that lead us towards a certain plenitude of our existence. Thus, *I concern myself with being only insofar as I have a more or less distinct consciousness of the underlying unity which ties me to other beings of whose reality I already have a preliminary notion.* Other people regarded as other beings are above all my fellow-travelers—my fellow creatures.[40] I communicate effectively with myself only insofar as I communicate with another person, that is, when, at least, some other person becomes a *thou* for me. The transformation that the experience of another as a *thou* brings accomplishes an inward relaxation and enlivenment which abolish self-enclosure or self-centeredness that shrinks and deforms the self.[41] Human growth requires that I open myself to others and welcome them without being effaced by them.[42] Or again:

> The being whom I love can hardly be a third-person for me at all; yet he allows me to discover myself; my outer defenses fall at the same time as the walls separating me from the other person fall. He comes more and more into the circle with reference to which and outside of which there exist third persons who are the "others."[43]

Communion and Compassion

Still, participation in the experience of intersubjectivity is an important vehicle and architect of human community and relationships of compassion that ground empathy and sympathy. The experience of compassion is more than affective sentimentality—it deeply embraces volition and establishes an implicit choice and commitment to another. Compassion unifies by rejecting the abstraction of the other. Compassion makes us grow in awareness of the vulnerability, nobility and lovableness of indi-

---

38. Marcel, *The Existential Background of Human Dignity*, 95–96.
39. Marcel, *Creative Fidelity*, 8.
40. Marcel, *The Mystery of Being Vol.II: Faith and Reality*, 17.
41. Marcel, *Creative Fidelity*, 34.
42. Marcel, *Tragic Wisdom and Beyond*, 39.
43. Marcel, *Creative Fidelity*, 33–34.

vidual people and the intrinsic significance of living ties among people. This sensibility is important because:

> [Whenever] circumstances prevailing here and now lead to men being not only regarded as masses but actually treated as such—treated, that is, as aggregates, whose elements are transferable according to the demands of temporal vicissitudes—it becomes more and more difficult to keep the inalienable characteristics of uniqueness and dignity . . . attributes of the human soul created in the image of God.[44]

Also, compassion expands and strengthens the vibrancy of fidelity. And we may observe immediately that fidelity as a participation in the bonding of persons or the intersubjective experience coincides with a compassionate connectedness that runs deep into the fibers of life. Its form is, "'Even if I cannot see you, if I cannot touch you, I feel that you are with me; it would be a denial of you not to be assured of this.' *With me* . . . is of the essence of genuine *coesse* . . ."[45] The power of compassion reveals the presence and security of waking up to the consciousness of the unconditional desirability, attractiveness and lovableness of people and human kinships. Accordingly, a compassionate soul is an available soul that is at the same time protected against temptations to suicide and despair. Indeed:

> . . . the soul which is at the disposal of others is consecrated and inwardly dedicated; it is protected against suicide and despair . . . because it knows that it is not its own, and that the most legitimate use it can make of its freedom is precisely to recognise that it does not belong to itself; this recognition is the starting point of its activity and creativeness.[46]

The effervescence of intersubjectivity offers an orientation of existential security and self-definition that represent a certain nonacceptance of temptations towards ultimate despair. Subsequently, at the intersubjective level the despairing person ceases to be an object about which one asks questions. He or she is re-established in his or her condition as a subject and become reintegrated into a living relation with the world of men and women, from which he or she had cut himself or herself off.[47] The

---

44. Marcel, *The Mystery of Being Vol.II: Faith and Reality*, 147–48.
45. Marcel, *The Philosophy of Existentialism*, 39.
46. Ibid., 43.
47. Marcel, "Desire and Hope," 285.

experience and expression of intersubjectivity enhance positive imagination, expansive self-perception and purposeful existence. To be sure, we may affirm that the recognition and promotion of human dignity take place within a context of a strong consciousness which unites all men and women than in the consciousness of the solitary self.[48]

Communion and Possession

The experience of communion further implies that human relations cannot be reduced to the level of possessions. That is to say, a human community does not belong to you or me; it is not a property that someone owns or the possession of which someone can contest or dispute.[49] In every belonging there is a cleavage between the one who owns and the owned. Therefore, as an intersubjective reality, the experience of the bond of communion cannot be possessive because it cannot be fully objectified. The fundamental surrender in community and communion is, "I belong to you." In this regard:

> I belong to you . . . means: I am opening an unlimited account in your name [I am at your disposal] . . . I give myself to you . . . I freely put myself in your hands; the best use I can make of my freedom is to place it in your hands; it is as though I freely substituted your freedom for my own; or paradoxically, it is by that very substitution that I realize my freedom.[50]

"I belong to you" is a situation that cannot be objectified without its nature being radically changed.[51] In contrast, "you belong to me" is an attitude that destroys communion and, by extension, community: "you belong to me means you are my thing; I will dispose of you as I want."[52] In "you belong to me," there is no experience and expression of communion or community, for "insofar as I accept being treated as a thing, I make a thing of myself, and it is then significant to ask if I am not betraying myself."[53] Of course, a relationship of enslavement develops when a person surrenders himself or herself to the habits, activities and tasks of commanding, dominating, coveting, rewarding and punishing others in ways

---

48. Marcel, *The Existential Background of Human Dignity*, 135.
49. Marcel, *Creative Fidelity*, 39.
50. Ibid., 40.
51. Ibid.
52. Ibid.
53. Ibid., 41.

that systematically diminish and, ultimately, eliminate humanity from the order of basic living. All this implies that "our structure is capable of being totally perverted, for a human being is capable of devotion to what seems to be a positive principle but what is in reality a negation of such principle."[54] Subsequently, true self-love means that I regard myself, as a seed which must be cultivated, as a ground which must be readied for the spiritual or even for the divine in this world. To love oneself is rather an attitude towards the self which permits its maximum development towards warm-heartedness and the joy of living.[55] When love becomes fake, conditional and enslaving, it also breeds paranoia, paralyzing fear and neurosis as common staples of life and existence.

The efficacious means to realizing the experience or bonding of communion is appeal and not coercion. The individual who tries to coerce us forgets or pretends to forget that when we are coerced we cease to be present to ourselves; we become alienated from ourselves. On the other hand, appeal mysteriously restores us to ourselves. Not inevitably, of course, since it is always within our power to refuse to give of ourselves.[56] *Response* should be reserved for the wholly inner reaction evoked by an appeal.[57] When I am coerced I become less disposed to others as I close in on myself in self-defense and this becomes more so "just so far as I construe my life or being as a having which is somehow quantifiable, hence as something capable of being wasted, exhausted or dissipated."[58]

As a form of nonobjective participation, the experience of communion involves the unfathomable mystery of love or wondrous life inseparable from a certain connectedness with the plenitude of our being. The mysterious quality that characterizes love may be articulated thus:

> The being I love is exposed to all the vicissitudes to which things are liable, and there is no doubt that it is in so far as he participates in the nature of things that he himself is subject to destruction. But . . . the whole question . . . turns upon knowing whether this destruction can overtake that by which this being is truly being. Now it is this mysterious quality which is aimed at in love . . . "quality" is inadequate . . . [because] ontology transcends all

---

54. Ibid., 45.
55. Ibid., 46.
56. Ibid., 51–52.
57. Ibid., 51.
58. Ibid., 54.

logical predication; it is here more than anywhere else that speech reaches a deadlock.[59]

As pointed out in chapter two, the experience of communion is essentially an openness and bonding, the fact of being together with others in light, the radiance of warm-heartedness and the joy of living. As a result:

> If, in the presence of another person I am burdened with mental reservations about him, or if, which amounts exactly to the same thing, I attribute to him some ulterior motives concerning me, it is obvious that we are not together in the light. I put myself in the shade. At once he ceases to be present to me, and reciprocally, I cannot be present for him.[60]

The light that is referred to here is the light of being which enables people to see themselves in one another and in their ties with one another. The notion of being is significant because "The more I actually participate in being, the less I am capable of knowing or of saying in what it is that I participate, or more precisely, the less such a question has any meaning for me."[61] The experience of being that persons partake of in bonding or in the mystery of communion gives off a certain light which is not that of the understanding but which, in a metaphysical sense, encourages the bourgeoning of the understanding as the sun encourages the growth of a tree or the blooming of a flower. The metaproblematic or the experience of being applies to a participation on which my reality as a subject grounds or anchors itself vicariously.[62]

The sense of closeness that typifies communion signifies that we belong to each other. The experience of communion consists essentially in the experience and recognition of human kinship as vibrant, liberative and expansive. As an accompaniment, communion opposes *otherizing* others—it stands in contradistinction with seeing some people as simply *the others*, as those who are demonized and can or may be dispensed with or even obliterated. *Otherizing* as a distancing of oneself from the humanity of others or as putting others at the periphery or outside a circumscription of a local *us* also often implies an insensitivity which negates the notion of pluralism intrinsic to human communities. In communion experience, there exists no dichotomous *us* and *them*. A reverent and an ever-expanding *us* come to mark the itinerary of living. Communion embraces a reverence

59. Marcel, *The Mystery of Being Vol.II: Faith and Reality*, 153–54.
60. Marcel, *Presence and Immortality*, 239.
61. Marcel, *Creative Fidelity*, 56.
62. Ibid.

for the contours and complexity of human predicament that constitutes *our* world. In *our* world, there is not a moral chasm between *us* and *them*. Not surprisingly, a sense of closeness, compassionate love, kindness and tenderness marks the experience of such liberating togetherness. Without going out of oneself or self-giving disposition or acts, it would be very difficult or impossible to realize inclusive communion experience that enhance and lift up respect, unity and authenticity. So, it may also be set forth that communion is a way of transcendence which is the topic of the next section.

Transcendence

Meaning of Transcendence

The notion of transcendence implies that "there are categories of lived experience that cannot be transformed by any scientific discoveries."[63] This understanding touches on the appreciation that the philosophy of being coincides with the philosophy of transcendence. The exigency of being, as the desire for the totality of our lives which we do not yet fully possess, coincides truly with the exigency of transcendence.[64] While transcendence is an exigency and an appeal, it is not a claim because every claim is autocentric. The transcendent is definable in terms of the negation of all autocentrism which is a completely negative property only conceivable in terms of participation in a reality that overflows and envelops the human subject, without his or her being able to view it as external to what he or she is. The act of transcendence, in the fullest sense of the term, is characterized by the fact that it is oriented; it entails intentionality.[65]

At the same time, "Not only does the word 'transcendent' *not* mean 'transcending experience,' but on the contrary there must exist a possibility of having an experience *of* the transcendent as such, and unless that possibility exists the word can have no meaning."[66] The metaphysical in transcendence consists in a deepening of experience. The stuff of transcendence relates to the elements of ordinary experience: the world and people around it, encounters and human history. But experience is not so much an absorbing into oneself of something as a straining of oneself towards something, as when we attempt to get a distinct perception of some far-off

---

63. Marcel, *The Mystery of Being Vol.I: Reflection and Mystery*, 41.
64. Marcel, *The Mystery of Being Vol.II: Faith and Reality*, 128.
65. Marcel, *Creative Fidelity*, 144.
66. Marcel, *The Mystery of Being Vol.I: Reflection and Mystery*, 46.

noise. Experience goes far beyond the domain of the external senses.[67] Experience may also be understood as massive presence that is the basis of all affirmations. At the same time we need to recognize that an experience can be saturated with prejudices: this also means that the prejudice which obstructs it at the same time prevents it from being fully experienced.[68]

The reality of prejudices need only lead us to recognize that human experience is always one of finitude: in every experience I encounter limits in things, people and myself. Besides, human thoughts and perceptions are constantly subject to error. Life is always open to the dialectics of suffering and death. There is radical insufficiency in life: "our condition is that of creatures, who can never cease to be such and who are compelled to think of themselves only in this perspective."[69] Even if I experience God, the transcendent being, the experience remains finite and that of a creaturely being. Within this perspective, the transcendent is not identifiable merely with a conceptual point of view. All this means that the urgent inner need for transcendence should never be interpreted as a need to pass beyond experience whatsoever; for beyond all experience, there is nothing that can be felt.[70] In effect, then, the inner need for transcendence, in its most fundamental nature, coincides with an aspiration towards a purer and purer mode of experience.[71] The subject of transcendence is a human being in his or her consciousness, behavior and conduct as he or she searches, expresses and realizes him or herself in life, striving for purer and more open modes of experience. Transcendence aims at the experience of plenitude as a fullness that enlivens and fulfills the human being and human experiences of kinship.

As such, hope reflects and signifies the exigency of transcendence; hope is this exigency itself insofar as it is the driving force behind the wayfarer.[72] Within this perspective, it must also be qualified expressly the particularities of our lives express themselves through attitudes.[73] Transcendence implies going out of oneself towards the richer experience of warm-heartedness and the joy of living together with others. This experience, in turn, implies an ascendancy of being over having and the prob-

---

67. Ibid., 47.
68. Ibid., 55–56.
69. Marcel, *The Mystery of Being Vol. II: Faith and Reality*, 172.
70. Marcel, *Creative Fidelity*, 47–48.
71. Ibid., 55.
72. Marcel, *The Mystery of Being Vol. II: Faith and Reality*, 162.
73. Marcel, *Tragic Wisdom and Beyond*, 107.

lematic. Concretely, then, transcendence may find expression in a love that respects and gives without taking. In the rise towards an ever greater realization of generosity and open-heartedness, controlling power is not merely superseded, it also becomes superfluous. In a transcendent act, a human being aspires towards a richer, fuller and wondrous life rooted in the security and consciousness of being as intrinsic value and plenitude.

In a transcendent act like reconciling with another person who, for instance, has hurt me, I am able to recognize that discord and hatred undermine the sense of marvelous peace, acceptance and security with the self and another. The transcendence of reconciliation implies a certain soaring above pride and felt hurt. It, for example, requires that I place and value my being, my *I am*, beyond my life. When I reconcile with a person who has hurt me I endow myself with vitality, light and an assuring strength of magnanimity that also comes to constitute joy (the upsurge of being or warm-heartedness in life). I proclaim *ipso facto* that I am greater than my pains of hurt. By means of such proclamation I also signify that who I am is simply more than "my life." I am able to love even when I am hurt or crucified. Besides, I become a subject of a transcendent act when I am consistent in the practice of honesty at the office, at home and in my private relations—not exercising honesty solely on the basis of self-serving utility.

Moreover, a transcendent act may also be enacted in being with and caring for the deprived and suffering, in single-minded commitment to duties and relationships, or in an unbudgeted yet discerned or spontaneous generosity. Furthermore, the transcendence of the liberating power of love epitomized in the unselfishness of people like Nelson Mandela, Mother Theresa, Julius Nyerere and Martin Luther King Jr. who labored for a better world, remains a challenge and an invitation to everybody concerned for the joy of living in the world that involves all people. Still, a transcendent act may, for instance, involve a realization and a gradual change of attitude where I discover that another person has a reality, an intrinsic value of his or her own and that I come to value him or her as existing in his or her own right and I make sacrifices for his or her sake.[74]

The preceding cases serve to exemplify that a philosophy of transcendence must never divorce itself *even in principle* from a type of reflection which is directed on the hierarchy of the various modes of adoration, culminating in an understanding of saintliness apprehended as something given in the purest form in its *intention*.[75] To transcend is to partake of human excellence, which involves a rising above the precincts of the

---

74. Marcel, *The Mystery of Being Vol.I: Reflection and Mystery*, 48.
75. Marcel, *Creative Fidelity*, 146.

conditional self and its categories of mortal existence and self-enclosure, of fear, of death and of the inability to go beyond the exigencies of the spontaneous course of life. In an act of transcendence the visible becomes the actual symbol of a particular spiritual reality and, hence, appears to be suspended from it.[76]

Transcendence and Crisis

It is particularly within a context of crisis that the creative principle of transcendence and the demands it makes on us, to which each must answer in his or her own way through decisions and choices, come into active play.[77] A crisis situation is constituted frequently when there is no obvious and clear convenient answer to a situation set up by a lived set of circumstances. In this way, a crisis compels people to face some truth of life about themselves. In other words, a tragic experience can become a blessing which offers people new and liberating perspectives on life. As a vehicle for discernment and a means of differentiation, a crisis tends to confront us with our own identity question that may begin with the experience of doubt, uncertainty and anguish. This questioning experience turns into joy when we discover and celebrate a certain disclosure or new expression of some reality which redefine us in a new way with a sense of significance. So, a crisis comes to have value only when it constitutes a birth and dwelling place for celebrating and re-creating our humanity. Fundamentally, this recreation of humanity consists in re-discovering and joyfully being oneself in freedom and that letting others also be themselves as much as they are able to do so.

Fundamentally, a crisis disrupts, disturbs and upsets a living equilibrium, which cannot be fully reconstituted yet has to be restored from the moment of its occurrence in relation to changing conditions which inhere in every organic work of life. Put differently, amidst a crisis the manifestation of transcendence becomes unmistakable and profound through imaginative and creative encounters and shifts in perspectives and reflective awareness. To speak this way is to imply a certain germination of transcendence within a context of ultimate situations: "it is in the ultimate situations, in the confrontation with death, suffering, and sin, for example, that the mysterious transition from existence to transcendence is seen to take place."[78] An ultimate situation confronts us radically with the ques-

---

76. Marcel, *Searchings*, 66.
77. Marcel, *Man Against Mass Society*, 25.
78. Marcel, *Creative Fidelity*, 234.

tions and issues of our mortality. In an ultimate situation, we re-prioritize our needs and wants, plans and desires, that is to say, we give them new proportions and perceptions. In an extreme circumstance or ultimate situation which constitutes a crisis[79] personal identity is subjected to trial or test. In fact, the test implies a challenge to immediate experience, that is, a conditional challenge that makes reflective judgment possible so that we may modify our attitude towards some reality.[80] A test or trial provides a response to the question of some reality identified with value in a given context of life.[81] What is more, the proper function of the trial is to make a reflective judgment possible so that people are able to modify to its reality the affirmation of immediacy. And in this context everything becomes a function of freedom and freedom alone. It is further an essential characteristic of the test that it is possible to be unaware of itself as such.[82]

The extreme circumstance, *par excellence*, involves the immediate nearness of death and nobody can really be sure that his or her death is not imminent. We can view this world in the light of this threat so that the normal state may, in a sense, be regarded as an extreme state.[83] The normal state always remains precarious. Every moment of our lives holds no unassailable guarantee; in it, the worst always remains possible. In other words, the normal state of a human being, a state which implies some minimum of comfort and security or safety, is by no means the most favorable to inward alertness.[84] Concrete life is fraught with manifestations of ultimate situations and perhaps most of life may require responses whose character requires this awareness. Within a context of ultimate situation destruction and chaos terrify the human being. Suffering is particularly terrifying when it introduces the possibility of pointless extinction. The metaproblematic of *no longer being* exemplifies a systematic of despair which abolishes itself when realized in suicide, an act of complete disenfranchisement, an absolute desertion.[85]

---

79. A crisis takes place in a network of relations in that every person lives personal life in a structural context. A crisis begins when a new situation shows up or enters into a person's living relational locus so that a person's structural context needs dismantling and reconfiguring or abandoning in order to take into account the new element.

80. Marcel, *Creative Fidelity*, 74.

81. Ibid., 73.

82. Ibid.

83. Ibid., 76–77.

84. Marcel, *Being and Having*, 39.

85. Ibid., 142.

Communion and Transcendence

A transcendent response to a crisis situation involves a commitment to some spiritual adventure.[86] In such response we discover that an individual, say, Nelson Mandela, is capable of sacrificing his life or of running the risk of losing his life. In an ultimate situation the transcendent act takes place when a person affirms his or her humanity in ways that transcend physical existence or survival. Through an act of transcendence a person accomplishes some goals that relate to others and the world. In this way, the person tends to create the self as he or she opens up and gives of self.[87]

By and large, human beings live in the name of some basic values as embodied in things they take to heart and with which they identify. These values influence self-perception, what people do and what people have. Some of these values may include or are symbolized by freedom and health, honor and property, loyalty and power, friendship and enjoyment, commitment and work, success and prestige, art and recreation. Spiritual existence proper to the human being accomplishes the transcendent act through fundamental bonding with intrinsic values, for where there is intrinsic value there is also being. A certain identity exists between being and intrinsic value.[88] That is why transcendence is "only conceivable in terms of a participation in a reality which overflows and envelopes me, without my being able to view it in any way as external to what I am."[89] A person defines him or herself—or people identify their sense of significance—through realities that represent values which overflow and envelop who they are. Often, then, an ultimate situation threaten people's opportunities to live for values. That is to say, in a situation of value vacuum life becomes meaningless. Such a circumstance tends to obfuscate or problematize being. Questioningly, "Are not our extreme possibilities of self-destruction inversely proportional to a certain positive power which ceases to be conscious of itself the moment it breaks its ties with being and challenges or problematizes it?"[90]

For example, a person who is compelled by circumstances to abandon his or her religious faith is placed in a situation of crisis. The crisis is constituted by the contradiction of the need for respect and freedom of religious belief *vis-à-vis* victimization on the grounds of such a belief. In such circumstances, contradiction as felt and suffered becomes necessary

---

86. Marcel, *The Mystery of Being Vol.I: Reflection and Mystery*, 42.
87. Marcel, *Creative Fidelity*, 53.
88. Marcel, "Reply to Paul Ricoeur," 498; *Tragic Wisdom and Beyond*, 183.
89. Marcel, *Creative Fidelity*, 144.
90. Ibid., 143.

for sustaining one's integral existence. Otherwise, a person breaks down or succumbs to passive resignation and the transcendent act does not take place. The transcendent act involves focusing on, exploring and finding possibilities of a new embodiment for the selfsame value or its equivalent. It would be much more accurate to say that the issue is how to constitute a certain mode of experience for other modes that are fuller in that they are rooted in the security of plenitude.[91] When a person experiences captivity, exile, persecution or a context that compels him or her to live in a framework of values that he or she actually abhors, transcendence comes to consist in an appeal to a level of being, an order of spirit, which is also the level and order of grace, of mercy, of charity. In this appeal, people proclaim that they repudiate *in advance* the deeds and the acts that may be obtained from them by any sort of constraints whatsoever.[92]

Transcendence and History

Also, the transcendent act as a witnessing is often charged with a historical and social variety. There always exists a historical datum in every witnessing (i.e., testimony).[93] In fact, the struggle implied in every historical and social variety does not exclude the possibility and opportunities for negotiations, pacts and agreements or peaceful resolutions of contentious issues. However, as noted earlier, every act remains transcendent when we proclaim that we do *not* belong entirely to the world of objects to which men and women or circumstances may seek to assimilate us or in which they are straining to imprison us. This is also to say, "We must maintain that in so far as we are not things, we belong to an entirely different world-dimension, and it is this dimension which can and must be called supra-temporal."[94]

Moreover, an onset of a crisis situation may begin when a person starts to cast doubt over the validity of a chosen or lived commitment, say marriage, in light of other values, say, friendship and business, a new relationship or job, wealth or religion, esteem of others or status, that have come to light. In such a circumstance, a crisis sets in because a person questions or gives up or betrays, for example, a marital commitment and its orientation for the uncertainty of assessing, pondering and searching for fulfillment in a different value. Here, then, the need for transcendence

---

91. Marcel, *The Mystery of Being Vol.I: Reflection and Mystery*, 48.
92. Marcel, *Man Against Mass Society*, 22.
93. Marcel, *The Mystery of Being Vol.II: Faith and Reality*, 130.
94. Ibid., 186.

presents itself and is deeply experienced, above all, as a kind of dissatisfaction. Every kind of dissatisfaction which is not part of a depression implies an aspiration towards transcendence.[95] Of course, the casting of doubt over marriage that is mentioned earlier may arise from dissatisfaction and uncertainty towards a marital commitment, without perceiving as yet an alternative value. It may also arise from being at a crossroad, that is, in trying to make a choice in the face of some experience of betrayal. In the circumstances, the exercise of secondary reflection becomes crucial for transcending the spontaneous course of life. A person capable of communing with himself or himself and, so, of renewing contact with an invisible and limitless reality reveals himself or herself as capable of transcending the spontaneous course of life.[96]

As noted earlier, the act of transcendence is frequently characterized by the fact that it is oriented; it entails intentionality. It is an exigency and an appeal, it is not a claim because every claim is autocentric. But we may also add that the transcendence of the One to whom I appeal is transcendence of all possible extrinsic experience as well as of all rational conception, which is but experience anticipated and schematized.[97] Such transcendence implies a certain experience of plenitude that exceeds all experience of conditional values. The reference to plenitude grasps us and we intimately experience it in our concrete and wondrous performance in the world.[98] The encounter with plenitude wakes us up to personal significance, warm-heartedness and the joy of living. In this light, the question "What am I?" cannot be confronted the way in which a problem can be confronted because the question encroaches on those same conditions which make it possible for us to raise it: who am I to question myself on what I am? And at this point I perceive the question imperceptibly changing into an appeal.[99] Frequently enough, in the contexts of trials, acts of transcendence constitute antidotes to the exigencies of self-complacency or the drying up of vital energies of the self-quest.

A transcendent resolution to a crisis could still come about by endorsing the same commitment questioned or some other value whose unsuspected importance was only glimpsed fleetingly over time but to which a person becomes more fully alert. The main temptation in a crisis

---

95. Marcel, *The Mystery of Being Vol.I: Reflection and Mystery*, 42.
96. Marcel, *The Existential Background of Human Dignity*, 94.
97. Marcel, *Creative Fidelity*, 145.
98. Marcel, *The Mystery of Being Vol.I: Reflection and Mystery*, 45.
99. Marcel, *Creative Fidelity*, 145.

situation is that of regarding the practical as meaningful and nonpractical as meaningless. In this way, many people can threaten the notion of significance with deprivation: the genuine sense of significance is that of being a regulating vehicle independent of situation because significance involves participation in being, the unconditional.

Transcendence, Love, and God

In an act of transcendence, I recognize myself as freedom that expresses an availability which exists beyond the sphere of the finite and contingent world. In the face of every temptation to despondency and dissolution or death transcendence constitutes the ontological counterweight to despair and death. This counterweight can be neither life itself, always disposed to compromise itself with the forces that destroy it, nor an objective truth. The ontological counterweight can only lie in the positive use of a freedom which becomes adhesion (union, bond), that is, love.[100] Certainly, love is comprehensible ultimately in terms of transcendence as inseparable from communion which entails wakefulness to wondrous life. This life cannot be separated from a certain participation in the "absolute Thou" as its absolute justification. Where the thou is absolute, then it can only be present to invocation or prayer; it ceases to be merely accessible. And the self-transcendence of presence grounds all invocation. Certainly:

> ... there is no human love worthy of the name which does not represent for him who exercises it both a pledge and a seed of immortality ... it is not possible to exercise this love without discovering that ... it passes beyond itself in every direction, that it really demands for its complete realisation a universal communion outside of which it cannot be satisfied and destined to be corrupted and lost in the end. Moreover, this universal communion itself can only be centred on an absolute Thou.[101]

Conversely, human love lies to itself if it is not charged with infinite possibilities. If human love is centered on itself, if it sinks into a mutually shared narcissism, it turns into an idolatry and pronounces its own death sentence.[102] Love is rooted in being; it is an identifiable marker of a value that is not commensurate with anything that can be set or with what can simply be regarded as *marketable*. In transcendence, even loss of external freedom awakens inner life. And in an act of betrayal love strengthens a

---

100. Ibid., 143.
101. Marcel, *Homo Viator*, 152.
102. Marcel, *The Mystery of Being Vol.II: Faith and Reality*, 157.

sense of faithfulness. Amidst uncertainty about values and a felt sense of emptiness love leads to new ways of valuing possibilities and opportunities for understanding, compassion and growth.[103] Within this perspective, it may be set forth also that transcendence "is for the indecisive mind a permanent stimulus to judge oneself and to hope."[104] "To hope" is to ground oneself in the spiritual reality that is the Absolute Thou: "The act of transcendence, probably the highest act of which the human mind is capable, might well consist of precisely [the] conversion where the visible becomes the actual symbol of a particular spiritual reality, and hence appears to be suspended from it."[105]

Indeed, it becomes important at this juncture to attempt to understand the divinity of God as Absolute Thou. In the first place it must be noted that God and goodness[106] are coextensive and inseparable. In this sense, God refers to the supreme symbol and wellspring of life and freedom in their fullest experience and expressions. For God, then, much about us matters in relation to our filial relationships or fellowship among ourselves. As a result, things which pertain to human beings have worth primarily in constituting dwelling places for celebrating the intrinsic worth of persons and human relations. When things awaken people to recognize and celebrate their identities, the experience simultaneously unravels and reveals the mystery that is God. God begets us into being in which we live and move. Through being God shares Godself as fullness of being with people and their living ties with one another. God shares God's own life with us: God begets us in His or Her own Image. God shares God's own life with us. Persons and living ties among people are from the same stuff or stock of God. Persons are part and parcel of God.

103. Jolana Poláková, *The Possibilities of Transcendence: Human Destructiveness and the Universality of Constructive Relations* (Lewiston: The Edwin Mellen Press, 1995), 23.

104. Marcel, *Creative Fidelity*, 146.

105. Marcel, *Searchings*, 66.

106. It may be noted that a good reality answers a natural appetite, tendency, exigency or internal demand of an existent. Within this perspective, the good can be that which we desire to have, to do, and, ultimately, genuinely be. In this light, the good participates in the fullness of being as intrinsic value and plenitude, which is ultimately and consistently desired for its own sake. The good may give pleasure, afford satisfaction, fulfillment, provide requisite proper use, serve an end or purpose or may tally with proper human fullness. God as goodness, then, is that at which or towards which human beings liberatively aim or tend and from which human beings and relationships achieve fulfillment. In effect, God as goodness prescribes and proscribes our ways of being and the means which we employ in determining the choices, actions, directions and quality of life. God as goodness symbolizes and concretizes fullness or plenitude. In this sense, God actuates the supremely desirable freedom and expansive joy which enhance human agency, wellbeing, welfare and delight.

In a concrete way, to know and celebrate the unconditional identity and dignity of persons and human kinship is to celebrate a vital flowering from the wellspring and groundswell of divinity. Within this perspective, forgiveness, gentleness and patience, for example, become very crucial values in the enterprise of bringing forth and celebrating divinity in ways that *re-gather* and *realize* people's deep desire for harmony. *Divinity, then, consists truly in the experience, realization and awakening of the all in all, where each person becomes himself or herself in fullness of human kinship, freedom and joy.* The vehicles or means for awakening and realizing concrete divinity are appeals, goodness, reconciliation, exemplariness and positive presence that gradually and continually disclose and deepen the consciousness of who persons truly are, that is, as of unconditional worth. This is an ongoing awakening and disclosure that reveal each person and living tie among people as intrinsically and unconditionally admirable, desirable, attractive and lovable. Such revelation not only expands self-perception, it also liberates the attitude, the sense of initiative and responsibility as well as the actions of people with vibrancy and warm-heartedness.

Consequently, liberative truth of persons positively molds them, their relationships and the opportunities they offer one another. When people are molded positively the results are vibrancy and light-heartedness of brotherhood, sisterhood and human fraternity or fellowship as criteria for distinguishing what is good and bad for human living, for judging what needs to be done and for processing new forms of human living or arrangements. Accordingly, God as divinity has no power, no honor and no glory, except that which God has with people who live as brothers and sisters, sons and daughters of the same quality directed towards the full life. The main thing about God, then, has to do with what God is with persons in all their ways towards plenitude. God's love has to do with God *being with* people in their needs, aspirations, demands and strivings for transcendence in communion. This is also to assert that there are continual aspects and fermentation of trust, faith, charity and hope in all persons and human relationships. In the final analysis, divinity is essentially *being with-in-through-for-all*. This divinity implies developing the urgency, agency and responsibility for begetting and giving life, patiently. Divinity infuses self-giving with fervor for life and *being with* others in a spirit and experience of *liberative familyhood*. Divinity entails further that, for the sake of who we are and our shared origin and destiny of the full life, we learn to live together, in contexts and with a spirit that cherish a culture of freedom, inclusive unity and peace.

In this light, the mystery of God as the parent or begetter and goal of our full life defines positively and symbolically the meaning of our whole life (that is, our self-perception and self-definition as sons and daughters, brothers and sisters of the same quality), our relationships, our values and our existence in ways and terms that make possible true, proper and highest possible experience, expression and quality of expansive freedom and joy.

Accordingly, there is communion in blood and life between divinity and human beings when people are bonded together with an interior unity that embraces all people, time and places. In this way and uninterruptedly, divinity becomes present and contemporaneous with us. Simultaneously, we become contemporaries of divinity. "We" here does not represent an isolated or intramural group. It represents, rather, an entire and an ever-expanding and living community of the human family, comprising the living and dead, which renews itself as such. Where divinity lives and dwells, fellowship and warm-heartedness among people merge into the experience and realization of divinity. Of course, divinity is here to be understood truly as a mystery and not as some easy slogan, which would, in fact, devalue and distort it. In the last analysis, authentic conviction about divinity, awakens people to co-responsibility, collaborations and relationships of multiplicity and unity in personal and relational living. Enlivening and concrete co-presence is at the heart of all divinity.

Availability, Communion, and Transcendence

As noted earlier, both communion and transcendence manifest forms of human openness and spiritual availability or *disponibilité*[107] that is love. The relationship of openness that typifies communion and transcendence initiates a bonding by means of which we go beyond ourselves in the very heart of *our* love. In this experience, the doubt which threatens to infiltrate each of us is abolished to make room for a superior certainty, that is, assurance based on being, which transcends us.[108] This availability truly expresses hope which is not simply for oneself but always *for us*. This hope cannot be separated from spreading and keeping its flame burning by including others.[109]

Both communion and transcendence imply thinking ahead, acting, confronting, and straining unceasingly towards greater justice, truth, compassion and freedom. This perspective is significant because "to hope

107. Marcel, *Tragic Wisdom and Beyond*, 255.
108. Marcel, *Creative Fidelity*, 99.
109. Marcel, *The Mystery of Being Vol.II: Faith and Reality*, 160.

cannot but be to hope for us—for all of us. It is an act which in some way embraces in itself the community which I constitute with all those who have been sharers of my own venture."[110] Communion and transcendence also imply surmounting the limits of selfishness, unbridled pursuit of wealth and prevailing over personal and social barriers which impede human relations. The spirit of communion and transcendence implies being mobile and adaptable with courage and vitality that surpass and transform obscurantism and anachronism. This spirit itself implies a recognition of captivity. After all, we are capable of hoping only insofar as we start by realizing that we are captives. At the back of hope lies some incompleteness or some sort of tragedy.[111] Additionally, "to hope is to carry within me the private assurance that however black things may seem, my present intolerable situation cannot be final; there must be some way out."[112]

In order to underscore communion and transcendence as realms of hope it is important to recall that hope essentially consists in the availability of a soul which has entered intimately enough into the experience of communion to accomplish the transcendent act—the act establishing the vital regeneration of which this experience affords both the pledge and the first fruits.[113] Communion and transcendence as realms of hope also imply the humility and tentativeness of waiting. All this means, "what we must keep before our minds with all our strength, is that we are surrounded by possible sources of despair. These possibilities springing up beneath our feet like the riotous and malignant growth of a bewitched jungle."[114]

Availability and Admiration

Communion and transcendence lie at the heart of human availability, which may be understood negatively as not being nondisponible or nondisposable. To be nondisponible or nondisposable is to be occupied with oneself; it is to be encumbered from within. It is to be occupied with one's health, one's fortune, one's mistress, one's boyfriend, one's girlfriend or one's temporal success. To be occupied with oneself is not to be occupied with a determinate object. Rather it is to be occupied in a certain manner which remains to be defined. It is to be invaded by an anxiety that is itself essentially indeterminate. Self-preoccupation fixes a person anxiously within a

---

110. Ibid., 171.
111. Ibid., 160.
112. Ibid.
113. Marcel, *Homo Viator*, 10.
114. Marcel, *The Mystery of Being Vol.II: Faith and Reality*, 147.

zone or determinate scale. In fact, an indeterminate anxiety remains at the heart of the fixation; it gives the character of *exasperation* which causes it to remain compatible with the agitation constantly going on at the center of a limited zone. This anxiety constitutes an agony of a creature living in time, that is, as making one feel that one is at the mercy of time.[115] The more that a person is nondisponible the more that God also appears to him or her as "someone who." This very situation constitutes a denial of co-presence.[116] Nondisponibility and, consequently, nonpresence, is connected with self-preoccupation. When I am with a non-disposable or unavailable person, I am conscious of being with someone for whom I do not exist and as a result I am thrown back on myself and frustrated.[117]

On the other hand, to be *disponible* or available to others is to be present to and for them, to put one's material, emotional, intellectual and spiritual resources at their disposal. It is to be open and permeable to them. To be disposable to others is to believe in them, to place oneself at their disposal and to maintain the openness of *availability*. *It is really to place oneself in another person's world*. Within this perspective, availability refers to our self-possessed openness towards others. Through availability we welcome, beckon and invite others and create space for them in our lives. *In this experience, a person exposes himself or herself to the experience of another through presence, communication and a certain spiritual interconnection.*

Human availability realizes itself not only in the act of charity but also in admiration. The verb *to lift* forcefully and accurately denotes the kind of effect that admiration evokes in people, or rather realizes in persons as a function of the object which evokes it. Admiration tears people away from themselves and from the thoughts that they have of themselves. Admiration relates to the fact that something is revealed to us. In this sense, admiration makes reference to an élan, an irruption, which can only occur in a being who is not a closed or hermetic system into which nothing new can penetrate.[118]

Insofar as admiration may be rendered in the form of a judgment, however, it precisely constitutes an affirmation of a superiority which is not relative but absolute, that is, *incomparable*. The spirit of comparison, doubtless, intervenes after the event but this is relatively contingent with respect to the original datum which is the awareness of a certain absolute.

---

115. Marcel, *Being and Having*, 73.
116. Ibid., 81.
117. Ibid., 72.
118. Marcel, *Creative Fidelity*, 47–48.

If I am an admirer, I come to think of myself relative to that absolute and become uneasy about the position I occupy with respect to it, only by a reflex motion. As a consequence, there is hardly anything which is more characteristic of our present state of degradation than the tendency to view with suspicion any acknowledged mark of superiority. A burning preoccupation with the self lies at the bottom of this kind of suspicion, namely, a "but what about me, what becomes of me in that case?"[119]

Before an object of admiration I confront the choice of recognition and nonrecognition of what reveals itself before me: depending on whether I act or not I will be suspicious of that which has just risen up before me. This object of admiration can make me pale into insignificance in my own eyes or in those of others whose judgments I must consider since that judgment directly influences the judgment I tend to have of myself. However, admiration always expands our existence. In this connection, the fulfillment which admiration engenders means that the proper function of the subject is to emerge from and realize itself in the gift of self and in the various forms of creativity.[120] Within this context and in the light of admiration as enthusiasm, continuity comes to exist between the fact of feeling and creativity.[121]

It may also be set forth that the refusal to admire is not always based on jealousy or resentment. Admiration or enthusiasm can be condemned or considered suspect by critical intelligence on the ground that they abolish self-control. It is, therefore, completely meaningless to assume that critical intelligence will help persons to decide whether a piece of work is or is not worthy of admiration.[122] At the existential level, admiration implies that it may only be by submerging people suddenly in the lives of others which submersion forces them to see things through their eyes and thereby free themselves from self-obsession. Alone, a person cannot succeed in this, but the presence of another accomplishes this miracle, provided that a person assents to it and does not treat it as a simple intrusion but as a reality. Nothing is freer in the true sense of this term than this acceptance and consent.[123]

---

119. Ibid., 48.
120. Ibid., 49.
121. Ibid., 29.
122. Ibid., 49.
123. Ibid., 51.

Communion, Transcendence, and Community

Community experience touches on the issue of human bonding or kinship. Both communion and transcendence imply rising above the spontaneous course of life into the security of being. In this sense, they have a bearing on understanding community. As an outwardly expression of inward kinship and warmth, community is a locus of participation, representation and interpersonal openness. The participation characteristic of community involves assessment, review and re-imagination—of course, participation implies individuals as centers of inherence or self-conscious selves. Without communion community does not exist. Communal life requires active and mutual sharing of love and co-responsibility for life. Communion produces a community of love. Indeed, no real community exists where no real plurality exists. A community includes a variety of people and interests which enrich it. Plurality in which particularity is a needful ingredient forms the grist for the mill of community living. A community is only possible where beings acknowledge that they are mutually different while existing together by the very act of communication and conversations wherein the theme of freedom emerges clearly.[124]

The experience of co-presence and kinship ties lie at the heart of community life. This is also to say that joy, pain, respect and the struggle for humanity, justice and respect bind people together. A person's humanity and existence remain inseparably connected to and can only be expressed adequately in connection with respecting others and being respected by others. People realize their humanity through others. We become alive through active involvement with others in the course of which we also produce, write and analyze our personal and social stories. Community grows when it offers space for justice, solidarity and liberation. Consequently, community growth requires continual re-imagination, re-creation and re-construction. In this way, community enables people to live together and share their thoughts, deeds, welfare and life's directions.[125]

In a community people gather together in the name or in service of some common heritage and concerns, tasks and the shaping of mutual aspirations and growth. A multiplicity of views, critiques and contrariness do characterize community life. This means that a community accepts and respects plurality among its members by valuing and regarding its individual members as precious. And "an attempt to bring all human acts under very general rules, ceases almost entirely to be acceptable as soon

---

124. Ibid., 8.
125. Dube, 140–41, 147.

as one becomes aware of that element of the unique and the incommensurable which is the portion of every concrete being, confronted with a concrete situation."[126]

Indeed, differences, disagreements and divisions can weaken and threaten community's effectiveness, enthusiasm and sense of care and compassion. But because we always belong, our humanity always remains caught up with that of others. The urgent, passionate and compassionate human quest for cohesion in the community entails mutual love, respect and a sense of human integrity. A cathartic, accepting and worthwhile sense of life with others enhances kinship ties among people.

In fact, diversity constitutes the basis of authentic unity in a community. Community living implies respect and love of differences. Subsequently, differences enrich us. A living sense of oneness does not come from reduction of members to sameness; rather it honors individual value and uniqueness. Unification by reduction can only be at the expense of forfeiting living values; shared identities which are coerced tends to oppose intrinsic values.[127] The richness of transcendence and communion implies that in our differences we can always work together, care for each other and celebrate life by sharing what and who we are.

Community needs to be liberating (i.e., promote real affection, friendship and love), yet that liberation takes place only when human dignity and the reality of every person is properly recognized and respected.[128] The highest level of unity in a community is created when in love people recognize each other as different yet complementing each other in the itinerary of life towards a sense of wondrous togetherness.[129] In so being, people become bearers of joy and promise in a community. In fact, oppression is only sustainable when members of a community become fragmented and isolated from each other by gnawing suspicion that disrupts community cohesion or solidarity. A dictator or an oppressive regime survives by nurturing suspicion that poisons the wells of human relationships so that people begin to see others as cabals, enemies, demons or incubi.[130]

Of course, the means of poisoning the wells of human relationship is frequently propaganda as a means of de-vitalizing and manipulating the consciences of people. Propaganda advances frightening tragedies and

---

126. Marcel, *Man Against Mass Society*, 25.
127. Ibid., 166.
128. Ibid., 168.
129. Ibid., 218.
130. Ibid., 44.

crises of alienation. Through its distortions, propaganda aims at conformism which undermines the assertive character of the human personality. Of conformism the following understanding is apt:

> Conformism, whether intellectual, aesthetic, or political, implies submission to a certain order emanating not from a person but from a group which claims that it incarnates what *must* be thought, what *must* be valued, in a particular country [or community] at a specific moment in time, but a group which is careful, to be sure, not to acknowledge the stigma of relativity which affects every mode of knowledge or taste.[131]

Bonds of community grow where people know, honor and love rather than merely conform to each other. The sense of community develops through shared deeds, shared lives and shared sensitivity.

What is more, living tradition characterizes the life of a community. A living tradition renews and hands on a received way of life. This handing on involves transmitting the experience of the past to succeeding generations through the happenings of ordinary, everyday life, high drama, stories, narratives, tragedy, politics, art, dance, friendships, enmities and a host of characters. Some forms of collective or corporate interests characterize the lifeblood of every living tradition. A healthy tradition also encourages active involvement, collaboration and cooperation among the community members. Through a tradition, a community strives to transmit to its younger members its ways, assumptions and habits of thinking, living and working in order to create a life, which fits well a given expression of being human individually and communally. By means of its living tradition, a community becomes an actor and a leaven in the social order.

A living tradition is truly a spiritual heritage which imbues the hearts and lives of the community members. This heritage engages the intuition of a fuller sense of life which involves greater freedom for the common good and the service of one another. The splendor of every community requires responsible, productive and creative members. Conversely, frivolous, apathetic and irritable members can make common life painful and difficult in ways that wear and damage personal and common health.

Community establishes itself on the wonderful gift of memory and activities through which personal initiatives engage life with others. This engagement can be linear, spiral or haphazard. Even when productive, they can remain turbulent and conflictual. The itinerary of living with others is rarely tidy because it involves leaps and bounds.

---

131. Marcel, *Creative Fidelity*, 186.

Multiplicity of perspectives makes common understanding important in community life. In order to understand one another, members of a community need to appreciate, engage and embrace their various heritages. This process frequently implies conversations and negotiations about common life. A spirit of openness among the members facilitates the resulting contacts and interactions. Community living means that there ought to be exchange among the members who participate in its life. People continually need to learn to listen and compromise together. Context and current questions shape perceptions and meaning of experiences. In this regard, too, a discordant voice can help a community grow. While people who think and do things differently can be inconvenient, they can unmask real but uncomfortable concerns. Certainly, discordant voices need to be inspired by honesty and passion for common welfare. When it honors a discordant voice, a community can initiate new answers to old questions and new insights into new contexts. So, it is necessary that community constantly revisits differing opinions within it. This further implies that members cultivate open-mindedness and a willingness to be proved wrong.

In certain settings or situations, authority in the community may need to act boldly. An authority in the community may compel people from waywardness and educate them toward certain behaviors or conduct. Nevertheless, authority in a community always needs to be open to and allow for divergent interpretations, disputed opinions and continuing conversations about issues. In this light, a community truly becomes a locus of synthesis, insights and of new approach to existence.

Additionally, good accountability fosters community wellbeing and growth. It can expose realities of, for example, poor quality of leadership and disturbing relationships within a community. In fact, where social ills like discrimination, bullying and harassment prevail, a sense of frustration, distrust and fear undermine collaborative sense of commonwealth. Inertia of entrenched negativity hinders people from being their best selves. Unfettered discretion and arcane wiles of some members of the community need not dominate common life. At the same time, people can be always corrected civilly and fraternally. The paradox is also that civil conversation does not grow without trust, yet trust itself requires honest conversations. Accordingly, mechanisms for common, fair and credible accountability among members facilitate a directional flow of lives. In other words, ways of life that conceal and disregard the wellbeing of ordinary members of a community harm positive imagination. An enabling and supporting community inculcates trust, confidence and good will. A beneficent community provides for or offers possibilities, opportunities and conditions for a vibrant, purposeful and affirming life to its members.

Accountability uplifts community existence. Multiple accountability enables different people or constituents of a community to fashion a picture for themselves of what it means to live together. In the circumstances, mutual accountability inveighs against biased and intimidating approaches in dealing with problems. Familial piety within a community, promotes members' confidence in one another and a sense of responsibility.

Communication among people in a community further implies good faith and truthfulness. People need to work with the assumption that the other party acts and speaks in good faith and hold them at that. What people say in a conversation must make sense in some frame of reference which one, perhaps, may not have understood. The task is to listen and understand them. Frequently, narrow focus of attention cuts off people from the larger picture of living together.

It really requires a great human maturity to make sensible decisions and to discuss with others why one promotes certain decisions or choices and to get into conversations with others about their implications. Multiplicity of narratives will always typify some common life; community living is not a matter of mindless compliance. People will frequently take several stances on different issues, at times asserting themselves against one another. Interactive and interpretative conversations enlighten, enliven and shape character, the sense of responsibility, vision, courage and supportive participation of as many people as possible in the common life. This is a matter of lifting up the various dreams, objectives, goals and expectations. It is when diverse people work, live and strive together that they can share and realize a fullness of joy.

In the end, community refers to common and social life in which people recognize each other, can be for each other and expand their lives through partnership with others. A vital, healthy and real community experience nurtures and develops an open and trustful view of the self and others. A good community respects diversity among its members. It expands presence, the sense of care, mutual acceptance and affective listening. A healthy community recognizes that persons are more alike than different, even though they are more unique than identical. At the same time, they remain deeply relational. The solace of shared rhythm, warmth and embrace enliven community.

Death of a Beloved and the Trajectory of Hope

We consider some deaths routine, but the death of a beloved counts in that it deeply affects us. Because it heralds the breaking of a bond, the profound pain that we experience shocks us into awareness. When the death of a beloved takes place, it shifts horizons of human care and sharing. The shifts in human relations, which the death of our beloved brings, can undermine everything we think about life. In this respect, the death of our beloved ordinarily stands in negative relation to our deepest promises, yearnings and wishes. Accordingly, as an experience of existential darkness that gives new shapes to our lives, the death of our beloved can make us feel hopeless, helpless and lost. Within the ambiance of this death, the struggle for life also becomes noticeably detailed, precise and urgent for the experience tends to touch on the conception of the past and the future. It affects how people understand life's meaning and the promise of an expanded good life because it raises the questions about the makeup of the self. In dispossessing people of their possibilities, death exposes the limits of the possible. In this regard, people tend to speak of the shadow of looming death. Death reveals itself as that which does not take place in the light; it occurs in the space of the nocturnal. Even so, the way people name and speak about death affects their expectation, sense and imagination of it.

Death is a dramatic horizon. It opens up a space from which we may get a glimpse of our lives. When the death of a beloved occurs we frequently raise questions about the quality of our own existence as well. We confront ourselves with how best we lived our lives. A dramatic horizon is one to which we become joined. When life becomes dramatic we struggle for our own roles in it. Death as a dramatic horizon comes to us precisely because there is a tragic dimension that we all live. The struggle for our own role in the drama of life consists in a tension of striving to find the character that we want to be. The authenticity and earnestness to find our roles or engage the dramatic action give each individual life its charisma and definition.

However, it must also be admitted that a technological conception of life changes the meaning of death. Death becomes the normal end of a particular piece of apparatus or what can be likened to a machine that has served its time. It becomes no more tragic whether we are talking about human beings or any other machine.[132] In addition, it is not true that I have to think of myself as destined to death. There is no such unequivocal

---

132. Marcel, *Searchings*, 34.

relationship that can be known by everyone. Such unequivocal relationship would exist only for the body as an object, that is, insofar as a person isolates it from its mysterious ties with the subject, namely, the deciding and acting self. There is no relationship between myself as subject and my body that could be defined in an unequivocal and generally valid manner. I have to establish my own relationships with my body or, more precisely, originate and invent the relationships.[133]

In fact, it is the death of the other who stands in close and intimate relationship to me that affects me deeply. The death of other people whose significance touches me personally affects me. These are people bound to me by ties of friendship, familiarity or love to such a degree that their physical death inflicts a serious wound upon my person and identity.[134] This is because love can only devote itself to a subject, namely, to a being who is able to give love in return. In this way, love exhibits an incomparable dignity which transcends mere feelings. Thus, outside intersubjectivity or the human sense of kinship or connectedness love worthy of the name does not exist. In this way, the death of someone we love interests and touches us in all the real sense of the word.[135]

Death exposes and shows human finitude; it is an intrinsic element in human existence. In this sense, death remains our constant albatross rooted in our incarnate existence. As a loss that is a deeply personal tragedy, the death of a loved one is more fundamental than my own death. While I cannot thoroughly dismiss the question of my own death, I can certainly suppress it. I can become indifferent or weary in regard to it. But the death of someone I love, who is virtually another self to me, immediately shocks me into awareness. The bond has been broken and I can hardly bear it. At the same time, it is not really broken, for even after the separation I am even more intimately united than before with the person who is no longer at my side. This tragic sense of contradiction is precisely the unbearable element. It involves a scandal that casts a disgraceful shadow of absurdity over reality. In this experience also, freedom which is identical with love and which reaches from selfishness to surrender can enter the situation through a dyadic relationship by means of which someone who has passed away inhabits the living.[136]

---

133. Ibid., 67.
134. Ibid., 63.
135. Ibid., 64–65.
136. Ibid., 68.

The previous inquiry into communion and transcendence also makes possible an understanding of some distortions that frequently attend the notion of loss associated with the death of a beloved person. Of course, it is normal that people grieve when they have lost someone they love. The tragedy of death causes much stress. When loss is real it hurts but it should not constitute the last word. Whenever people come to grips with and open up to the pain and the felt sense of loss they burst into sobs of anguish and grief. Without a doubt, grief is a devastating experience. It can become implosive as it brings deep sorrow, anger, disbelief and even a certain risk of idolizing the deceased. Grief is the felt experience, conviction and sadness that accompany a person when real love, real hate or real attachment has been disrupted and broken. The experience of grief links closely with our human attachments or living relationships. This experience is not tied to interests, diversions or entertainments but comes with the table stakes of our relationships, that is, according to the emotional capital we invest in the lives and times of others.

Grief issues forth and surges into us when those we love die or when our relationships with people we love become altered in such a way that we can no longer love them in the way we knew. In the rough jolt of grief, the human personality can easily lose self-control. The experience one feels brings with it the sense of burdens and bruises. In this way, grief becomes a deeply emotive and synthetic experience that results from an unspeakable loss. This experience tends to bring with it the sense of isolation, abandonment and a termination. Grief can generate self-revulsion and alienation, not only from others but also from the self and from the sense of purpose as well. It can also bring with it a felt recognition that one is, at a certain level, uprooted from a sense of human kinship, meaning and comfort. Imbedded in grief are also reflections on the past and the desire for a future life. In the event of a successful resolution of grief, stark realism and a persistent belief result in a re-negotiation of meaning and human kinship within a new context of some felt presence and absence. In this regard, the rhetorical quality to grieving assumes great importance. Like every human experience, grief comes to its fulfillment when it is accepted and understood, that is, when its significance is consciously or ritually appropriated through understanding.

A breakthrough with grief begins to occur when there is an acceptance and a certain realistic appreciation of a deceased's influence and significance on one's life. Yet it is always easy to become entangled with grief by holding onto a tactile historical dispensation. People can remain caged in the experience of past life, even though the process of living needs to continue even amidst the pain. In the circumstances of the death of a beloved, a person will always be confronted with the sense of void and inadequacy which may also get re-enforced by an already problematic sense of self-worth or relational desirability. During an experience of grief, a person can come to an awareness that there is nothing left for him or her to engage his or her loyalty and attention. In failing to move on, a person stagnates and basically begins to live in the past. In other words, petrifying attachments can hold and enslave people to the past. It can withhold them from moving into the future so that they fail to live in the present with all its promises and beauty. Paradoxically, people will not make space for new relational space in their lives, after the death of a beloved, unless they truly redefine and transform clutches of attachments to a past relationship. At the same time, though, relational awakening, not in a self-serving but in imaginative and expansive understanding, tends to take place only after emotional exhaustion.

Additionally, love continues even after death; it never ends. This love is only possible where there is hope. The concept of loss is overwhelmed with the darkness of grief when there is no hope. This is particularly so where the exigencies of the *ego* dominate a set up of life. Within the framework of the *ego*, relationships are apprehended predominantly in terms of *having* which provides little room for hope. Within the framework of having, death becomes truly a dramatic and pointless fact of the cessation of all vital activities and operations. In such a case, losing someone represents destruction and dissolution as supreme tragedies of existence. Death symbolizes ultimate chaos. In this respect, we may immediately note that we only truly lose what we have: to the degree that I think that I possessed the other I can truly be aware of having lost him or her irrevocably. For, "what I do not possess is by definition alien to me and I cannot really lose what has never been mine."[137] Having is a typical mode of existence by which the *ego* relates with the world. Within this perspective, many relationships are often degraded to the level of having, that is, to something one has instead of being something which comprehends one who participates in it. Whatever a person possesses can always be contested or disputed.

Because the pervasive *ego* tends to define human relations in terms of possession or having, it implies that when another person dies, there always lies the danger of being hypnotized, that is, of being fixated on an image of the deceased in an obsessional way. The personal relation to a deceased ought, however, to triumph over this kind of obsession. After all, we are concerned primarily with *the life of this relation*, a living communication,

137. Marcel, *Presence and Immortality*, 86.

a living relation to another.[138] The notion of a living relation signifies that the being that remains present to my thought, to my heart, to my inner vision, has not at all been dissolved. Inasmuch as a person is regarded as a being, he or she participates in a mysterious permanence.[139] The fact of the egoistical self in the structure of our persons implies, at least in part, that there exists in each of us an almost invincible tendency to equate memories which I have retained of the deceased with photographs that I have kept in my possession and which I could glance over. From this point of view, the idea of a living relation to another loses all significance.[140]

When a relationship has been lived merely in terms of having, a person easily remains stuck to the last image of the dead. Persons become attached to the relational dispensation of physicality and empirical data instead of presence. Whenever I let myself, as a grieving person, to be obsessed by the last state or the last image of the other I transform the being I love into a thing which in effect turns out to be lost.[141] Inexorably, then, the response to death can only be in terms of seeing it as one supreme dread and catastrophe. Conversely:

> ... the more the missing being is really conceived as being ... the less will it be grasped as a possession; the less, consequently, will its disappearance be felt as a loss ... Unfortunately ... our affections are possessive ... my inner attitude with respect to the one who is no longer there has an effect upon him (in as much as he stands in relation to me, but this relation has a constitutive and not an exterior quality ...).[142]

The dead loved ones whom we have known and loved remain a being for us insofar as they are not reduced to simple ideas we may have of them. They remain attached to our own personal reality and continue to live in us.[143] Admittedly, the being whom I love is not only a *"thou," that is, a person with whom I relate through living presence and reverential respect.* In the first place, he or she can be viewed as an object which comes within my view and towards whom I can effect all the operations whose possibility is included in my condition as a physical agent. We can remain fixated or chained to images of our beloved dead and exchange places with them

---

138. Ibid., 78–79.
139. Ibid., 78.
140. Ibid., 79.
141. Ibid., 86.
142. Ibid., 87.
143. Marcel, *Creative Fidelity*, 149.

in our fantasies. Secondly, a beloved dead is also a *that* and precisely so in the measure in which he or she can be regarded as a thing. But insofar as he or she is a *thou*, he or she is freed from the nature of things and nothing that I can say about things can concern him or her, that is, can concern the *thou*.[144]

When faced with the death of a beloved I run the risk of being obsessed with him or her as someone whom I had possessed and, so, objectify him or her. When we become fascinated with the other or the past we cling to them. As we do so, we immobilize them. In turn, they immobilize us and paralyze our inward growth.[145] So, to all intents and purposes, "it is really out of love for the other that I must free myself from this obsession. I owe it to him not to immobilize him, not to deny him as it were being and life."[146] One thing is certain: "The other is present in the act by which I liberate myself not from him, but from the idol I substituted for him in making him static."[147] Indeed:

> The other, in so far as he is other, only exists for me in so far as I am open to him, in so far as he is a Thou. But I am only open to him in so far as I cease to form a circle with myself, inside which I somehow place the other, or rather his idea; for inside this circle the other becomes the idea of the other, and the idea of the other is no longer the other *qua* other, but the other *qua* related to me; and in this condition he is uprooted and taken to bits, or at least in process of being taken to bits.[148]

Additionally, "In fact if I treat the Thou as a He, I reduce the other to being only nature; an animated object which works in some ways and not in others."[149] When I treat another individual as *him* or *her*, I treat them as essentially absent. It is this absence which allows me to objectify them, that is, to reason about them as though they were a nature or given essence. Or again, I become external to myself inasmuch as I see another person who is with me as external to me. In confronting a Mr. So-and-So I also become another Mr. So-and-So.[150] To treat another as a thou, on the other hand, is to apprehend him or her in his or her being; this also implies

---

144. Marcel, *The Mystery of Being Vol.II: Faith and Reality*, 154.
145. Marcel, *Homo Viator*, 255.
146. Marcel, *Presence and Immortality*, 88.
147. Ibid., 89.
148. Marcel, *Being and Having*, 107.
149. Ibid., 106.
150. Marcel, *Creative Fidelity*, 32–33.

address, discursive recognition and affirmative respect due to others and human relationships.

The dramatic context of the moment in which our existence truly takes shape draws us to life which overflows with warmth and prodigal compassion and which quicken the building up of the whole. We find ourselves caught up in the experience and radiance of fullness shared in love. As a consequence, that which summons us to aliveness and presence actually sustains us with freshness, spontaneity and kenosis (self-transcendence). This reality is the plenitude of being which urges us towards an ever-expansive relationship of unconditional availability and self-realization. Clearly:

> ... that which summons us to survive ... is actually what sustains us ... And those whom we have never stopped loving with the best in ourselves become like an immense skyscape, invisible yet somehow felt, under which we move forward ... toward the instant where everything will be enveloped in love.[151]

In the light of being, it cannot be seriously maintained that survival after death is purely and simply unthinkable.[152] Intersubjectivity is the key to the question of our survival because the idea of solitary and narcissistic existence loses all meaning.[153] This is also to say, "a really coherent and meaningful theory of survival cannot be carried out except in connection with a philosophy of love."[154] To love another person intensely involves the experience and expression of unreserved closeness, assurance and devotion as though he or she can never die. The pivot of survival after death lies with oblative love. This is the love that is directed towards the other person and is characterized by presence.[155] A relationship of presence partakes of the unconditional, that is, a certain plenitude or fullness of life. As long as love is free from possessive desire, it appears to be on the level of the dyad, that is, on the level of where a "you" can *never* be converted into a "he" or "she." It is here that someone who has passed away can inhabit the living.[156] The quality of presence which characterizes oblative love puts forward an invincible assurance of immortality. Oblative love is supra-hypothetical: it

---

151. Marcel, *Tragic Wisdom and Beyond*, 130.

152. Marcel, *The Existential Background of Human Dignity*, 141.

153. Gabriel Marcel, *The Influence of Psychic Phenomena on My Philosophy* (London: Society for Psychical Research, 1955), 17.

154. Ibid., 19.

155. Marcel, *Presence and Immortality*, 235.

156. Marcel, *Searchings*, 69.

gives rise to an invincible assurance which is connected with the joy of living together. It manifests and expresses itself in the presence of one person to another. The people whom we love deeply become part of who we are. Through oblative love other people live in and through us. The assurance of oblative love connects people with who they most deeply are through ties that they share with one another.[157]

Indeed, where love persists, where it triumphs over whatever tends to degrade it, death cannot but be vanquished definitely.[158] When it is a matter of partaking in life's fullness, death can only be explained by life. In its gratuity and superabundant measure, life transcends death. In this world we need to be "aware of the incessant interplay of light and shadow suffusing the whole of existence."[159] At death, human vitality and form is reabsorbed in its total energy of Life. Free from the inertia of extrinsic validation, human bodily form reintegrates with life-source in an experience of transcendent communion. In the end, what death designates can only be a certain conjunction of reason and love under the precarious conditions of our existence.[160] Within this point of view, death realizes self-accomplishment.[161]

Piety towards the dead is a refusal to betray a person who has existed by treating him or her just as no longer existing. It is an active protest against a kind of trick of appearances, a refusal to yield to it or to lend one's self wholeheartedly to the game.[162] The dead man or woman is someone who is no longer even elsewhere, no longer anywhere. The very thought about him or her is the active denial of his or her extinction. When we think of someone, it is himself or herself that we are thinking of. There is an active denying of space, that is, of the most material and also most illusory character of the experience of *being with*. In fact, to deny space is to deny death—death being, in a sense, the triumph and the deepest expression, of such separation as can be realized in space. When I think of a finite being, I restore a community and an intimacy, between the person and myself, an intimacy which might seem to have been broken.[163]

---

157. Marcel, *Presence and Immortality*, 242.
158. Ibid., 231.
159. Marcel, *The Existential Background of Human Dignity*, 93.
160. Marcel, *Awakenings*, 79.
161. Ibid., 80.
162. Marcel, *Being and Having*, 97.
163. Ibid., 31–32.

Further, the thought of our own death, that is, of the only future event we can acknowledge as certain, can exercise a fascination over us in a way that somehow invades our whole field experience, extinguishing all our joys and paralyzing all our efforts. This meta-problem of death and of non-being is possible. Suicide is possible. It is the temptation-type, the betrayal type to which all other temptations and betrayals refer. As an existent being, it is not sufficient to say that I am subject to death. If this were so, I would be subject to the feeling of being swallowed up by death and also to a view of the world as a place of illusions where death ultimately has the last word. Such a view holds only if I were wholly my life. But it is not entirely true that I am my life. I can sometimes judge my life. I can fail to recognize myself in my life. This judgment is possible on the basis of what I am.[164]

The fact of living can appear to me as consisting in maintaining as best as possible a complicated set of mechanisms subordinated to ends which are themselves problematic. When this happens, I become naturally inclined to admit that death is reducible to the rupture of these very mechanisms, that is, to the casting aside of an apparatus. In effect, a person who proclaims that there is no life after death will be inevitably led to depreciate or devaluate this existence insofar as it is seen as bound to eventuate in the absolutely meaningless fact of dissolution. This life literally comes to be seen as entirely at the mercy of total meaninglessness of pure chance.[165] It seems, then, that what warrants the most scrupulous reflection on our condition is that of constantly making ourselves more actively permeable to the light by which we are in the world. We can always hope that death tears us from ourselves in order to ground us in being.[166]

The preceding considerations make clear the fact that there is no privileged state which allows people to transcend time. The only possible victory over time must have fidelity as one of its factors. At the same time, in order to transcend time we do not need to raise ourselves, as we do sometimes, to the actually empty idea of *totum simul*, namely, the knowledge of the whole at once—a total simultaneity of all reality, time and space. *Totum simul* is empty because it remains outside us and thereby becomes, in some way, devitalized. We do not have any central observatory or perspective from which we can contemplate the universe in its totality. We apprehend the universe only partially and obliquely. We transcend

---

164. Marcel, *Creative Fidelity*, 173.
165. Ibid., 93–94.
166. Ibid., 173.

Communion and Transcendence

time by participating more and more actively in the creative intention that quickens the whole. In the process we also raise ourselves to levels from which succession seems less *given*, i.e., levels from which a cinematic representation of events looks more and more inadequate and ceases in the long run to be even possible.[167]

The death of a beloved always confronts us with the seriousness of life. The accompanying grief is a painful, difficult, agonizing and profound experience that also calls for redefinition and re-perception of the self and the world. While grief may disclose the fact that life is precarious, the responsibility to live life more fully that grief engenders must be acknowledged and recognized. Within this perspective, grief can also motivate us to take charge of life courageously. To confront life with freedom and responsibility places its charge into our own hands. We become agents of responses and actions; we make changes in life. This also means however that we are free to do with our lives whatever we want but we also are responsible for the consequences of our choices and decisions.

It is necessary to resist the mesmeric power which death exerts over the man or woman who looks on death as the final word. To look on death as the decisive reality on human existence is to reach a certain identity of death and evil, which is at the same time to recognize death as presenting a certain tragic reality. To admit this is to consign the world to a glaringly terrifying and monstrous reality. Of course, there is an appalling error in denying death its gravity which easily gives to human life a quality of tragedy without which it is nothing more than a puppet-show. In this regard, death has an apparent final value. But it is more serious and weightier to have a dogmatic affirmation that death bears the final seal on human existence.[168] Undoubtedly, every human being can dwindle into a condition which is akin to the vegetable: this implies that biologically a person can be alive yet be spiritually dead. On the other hand, we have many cases in hospitals, war fronts, schools and homes of people who have remained alive in the spiritual sense until the verge of death, when their spiritual strength seemed utterly exhausted.[169] In effect, in the face of suffering or a concrete expression of evil which may be in the form of death, it is the task and responsibility of every man and woman to recognize that there is another dimension which is too easily inclined to give up the struggle and to despair rather than to hope. It is within the *interior citadel* that every

---

167. Marcel, *Being and Having*, 18.
168. Marcel, *The Mystery of Being Vol.II: Faith and Reality*, 146.
169. Ibid., 163.

human being needs to exert the same efforts as in the exterior zones in which he or she communicates with his or her neighbor.[170]

Conclusion

We define ourselves to a significant degree in the context of others' presence to us. The presence of others in our lives is an unquestionable experience. Touch and gestures, encounters and significant memories, intonation and voice inflexion are incommunicable qualities which announce the presence of other people. Neighborhood and schools, market places and playgrounds, things and words, biographies and creative works, gifts and relationships, also relate us to the presence of others with whom we enter the experience of communion and transcendence.

In existence, persons are called to be with one another and share in a plenitude of being that bears witness to an inclusive humanity which consists of enlivening human identity, expansive responsibility and positive relationships. Human participation into being as intrinsic value and plenitude constitutes the ultimate treasure of human life. In it paradoxes, light and darkness, life and death, love and hate, openness and vulnerability converge, harmonize and give birth to new life and expansive truth of who we are. This rebirth also engenders a certain mature and authentic peace and joy.

In communion and transcendence, we are invited to go beyond ourselves so that our personal thrust in life comes to be that of a call of justice in situations of oppression, cultivating dialogue in a context of discord and offering collaboration and support in circumstances of marginalization. We are also invited to let go of bondages in the forms of fears, prejudices and covetous desires which encumber us so that we become freer. Communion and transcendence invite people to a life of hope. This is a life that is centered on openness and "a passionate interest in individual beings and an irresistible attraction toward reality in its inexhaustible mystery."[171]

Indeed, to be a subject of hope is to be a subject of communion and transcendence. In this way, the human subject who hopes always remains spiritual and responsive. Whenever the human subject lives life itself assumes an enduring significance; life has a point that cannot be annihilated. In other words, communion and transcendence find and justify their meaning and purpose in being as intrinsic value and plenitude and as the

---

170. Ibid., 161.
171. Marcel, *The Existential Background of Human Dignity*, 21.

nexus of genuine kinship among people. Therefore, the key thing for the human subject is leading a humanized life.

In the final analysis, to be a human being means not only to possess the biological characteristics of a given species but also to live in a human way. To live humanly means to live in such material conditions that the human being is not crushed under the weight of self-preoccupation and self-care.[172] A humanized life is a life in which the exigencies of survival, of flourishing, of living together and of meaning are recognized, integrated, fulfilled and celebrated. This is a materially healthy life, a life centered in positive relations of human kinship and, ultimately, in an enlivening and empowering relationship with the Absolute Thou. Signified here is the experience of being charged with an indwelling presence and a sense of life's excellence, significance and plenitude which ground human language and the exigencies, responsibilities and rights, which make up the subject-matter of the forthcoming chapter.

---

172. Marcel, *The Decline of Wisdom*, 34.

6

Human Existentiality[1]

Preamble

As we have seen, the human subject is a profoundly relational being who establishes his or her true character in a relationship of interactive, imaginative and compassionate love with others, where love implies the act of a free human self affirming another free self and which is free only by this very affirmation. Love cannot be separated from pure freedom insofar as it incarnates creative interpretation. In this regard, love validates us with the sense and experience of security and comfort, which come with self-worth and self-esteem. The energy of love also expands human communal consciousness. There is, at the root of love, the belief in the inexhaustible richness and the unpredictable spontaneity of the being who is loved.[2] The order of love is beyond the relative world of merit and demerit; it is the order of free gift.[3] The order of love is an order in the present and concrete relational world of creative significance.

Earlier chapters give a good impression of the multi-dimensional aspects of life of the human subject who hopes, because such a being is also a subject of communion and transcendence. Accordingly, the human subject who hopes may be specified as a self-conscious human being, spiritually interconnected, actively oriented towards others and responsive intellectually and emotionally to the whole of life.[4] A human subject who hopes continually strives to increase his or her opportunities in life and to make use of the opportunities of living and acting in a given circumstance, place

---

1. Human existentiality points to the relationality of concrete experience which opens out to the quality of the unconditional in human existence. Existentiality involves a participation which transcends subjectivity and objectivity.

2. Marcel, *Philosophical Fragments*, 109–10.

3. Ibid., 112.

4. The whole of life is here regarded from the point of view of decisions and self-definition, freedom and responsibility, and the sense of significance.

and time. The human subject who hopes as a concrete person must not be dissociated from his or her existential milieu. And it is in light of the concrete milieu of hoping that this chapter considers linguistic character and human exigencies as the basis for correlating rights with responsibilities. Even though every existential context provides room for discontent, the characteristic discontent of the one who hopes remains imaginative and creative of value. This is because for one who hopes life in this ambivalent world can be made better under conditions where exigencies, responsibilities and rights are duly recognized and promoted and not merely foisted on others through language which the next section discusses.

The Linguistic Character of the Human Subject

People live incessantly with the common concerns for values, human relations and the responsible exercise of freedom even as they organize their lives intelligently and seek expressions of human fullness. A felt sense of life's unity and relatedness affect human understanding and groundedness in existence. Human consciousness exists, in spite of its plural expressions, as a unitary reality. In all existence, understanding remains pivotal. Human understanding occurs through linguistic experience and expression by means of which people grasp situations and master existence. Actually, language refers to human awareness and its expressions. Through silence, gestures, metaphors, speech forms, words and grammar language relates people with life and reality. As deeply rooted in human beings, language enables human beings to speak scientifically, sapientially and morally.

As a matter of fact, human experience demands language that frames it. An unexpressed or unspoken experience remains incomplete. As the vessel and stuff of life and human connections, language supplies the human currency for conveying information and sentiments. Language and its interpretation create and structure reality. Language offers possibilities; it is a fountain for human understanding, growth and change as it shapes imaginations, beliefs, self-perceptions, character of persons, and their relationships. Through language people can conceal and reveal, uplift or injure, protect and hide, expand and recover realities of human existence in vivid ways. The experience and expression of a language can wound and hurt as much as it can inspire, vivify or console. Words in a language, for example, can help people understand their experiences of loss, or quicken and stir their imaginations with the wonder and spectacle of existence. Paradoxically, only in speaking and/or expressing experience into some language form may people awaken fully to what meaning or significance underlies it. In fact, life is solidified by the experience and fact of framing it into language forms or words.

Of course, human experience precedes language which expresses it. Language puts names to our experiences. Through concrete forms language expresses and arranges, compares and determines, defines and designates, demarcates and distinguishes the realities of particular experiences. When situated within the framework of truth and love, language utters a whole network of meanings that constitute the intelligible background of human existence. Through language multiple dimensions to experience also come into play. Language helps people to penetrate their experiences. Language embodies life and locates the human spirit which dwells within. In this regard, significant words, as words that evoke transcendence or through which people rise beyond the immediacy of personal experiences, become efficacious; they delimit and illuminate, gather and unite. Significant words are not merely disembodied thoughts. They make present people's ways of being in and understanding the world. Such words gather and condense lived exigencies, realities or polarities of life that may fascinate, encumber or set free. In this respect, language mirrors the inner kinship between people's self-definition and existential insecurity. Language may also disclose how persons may be imbued with love, delight and reverential spirit towards life. Of course, human self-realization in language tends to remain, frequently enough, shrouded in ambiguity. Nonetheless, the bursting forth of great human illuminations in language can pervade life with joy, serenity or utter sense of peace.

In language, significant words incarnate realities in imagination and thoughts, by means of which a kind of vitality may be produced in and among persons. In a sense, our embodied thought makes up our world. In significant words or language forms pieces of reality are presented and signified. Words or language forms make reality present by placing them before human consciousness through understanding. In consequence, human experience reaches its fulfillment in being known, unveiled, recognized and embraced through language. As experience renders its positive freshness through words or language forms, it tends to unmask and produce effects in people's lives. Every grasp of experience through language opens up the human possibility for communication, dialogue, effective judgments and transcendence. Language captures and expresses the way people are. Language offers the means by which people negotiate their ways in existence and bring imaginative and concrete reality into expression. Language allows people to discover and organically shape their world.

Through language, human beings in diverse ways participate in a self-sharing. The varied forms of language prompt personal, interactive and communal realizations of humanity. Because it is personal and incarnational, internal and external, language becomes credible and effective when it also gives people the interior power to realize themselves. The historicity of language implies that it is akin to a terrain that changes its contours in many areas of personal and existential areas of life. Language is wrapped in contextual reality; it is responsible to contextual reality. The construction of reality that takes place through language nourishes the birthing forth of insight and newness in life and existence. In taking place within the human community, language is also a public human activity that affects the sense of self, how others are imagined and the meaning of reality as well as the acknowledgement of diverse needs, demands and service. In history, language becomes constitutive of human existence as a vehicle that makes possible the realization of convictions, order and effectiveness through naming and describing, creating and rearranging. Language brings newness and antiquity, gain and loss of good and bad experiences in life. As it pervades human existence, language constitutes a basic human way of being explicit in the world, and becomes a disclosive vehicle of some truth. Furthermore, contexts and situations of human knowing and acting establish the historicity of all linguistic expression and construal of meaning.

Existentially, when I hope, I do not bear myself as though I have no neighbors, as if I am only concerned with myself and have no responsibility towards others. My responsibility to actively foster and establish possibilities of living together with others is as much a challenge as an obligation. Yet to understand another person, I have to use a language common to both of us which will allow both of us to understand each other. Also, I must somehow, at least, be willing to make room for the other in myself. It will be obviously impossible for me to receive, to incorporate in myself the message of the other while concentrated on my sensations, feelings, or anxieties.[5] Here it may be noted at once that receptivity can only be considered in connection with a readiness or pre-ordination to receive. A person receives others in a room, in a house, or if necessary in a garden, and not merely on some unknown ground or in a forest.[6] To receive is to admit someone from the outside into one's own home, that is, to introduce him or her into a qualified (prepared) area and to admit him or her to participate in it. In fact, for a person involved in the act of hospitality, receptivity usually refers to the gift of self, of having another person participate

---

5. Marcel, *Creative Fidelity*, 88.
6. Ibid., 89.

in some form of plenitude. To provide hospitality is truly to communicate something of oneself to the other.[7]

Thus far, it is recognizable that language exemplifies a mode of self-giving. Language offers the most radical medium for entering into and receiving another through mutual interiority achieved in true communication. Language is the locus and vehicle for the self-disclosure of being. Language makes the encounter with the real possible. In being so bound up intimately with being, language expresses the sense of self; it brings the self to light. Language can even become transparent to the divine being; it can lead to the encounter with God. Language reveals; it is the primary instance of human symbolic activity.[8]

Through language we receive people into our lives and interpret or influence the situations and processes around us. Within this framework, the one who hopes, in as much as his or her hope is real, seems to be involved in a kind of a process directed towards realizing noble specifiable goals.[9] Realizing the specific requires that a person be well-informed. To be well-informed requires interactive communication and dialogue with others through language. A well-informed person recognizes that human contexts are multi-formed and differentiated in a complexity of needs, claims and aspirations. And "Reflective analysis will no doubt here suggest the idea of a relationship between the immediate, the anticipated and also the remembered which, we might say, back the operation."[10]

Being aware of one's own existential circumstances positively constitutes and fosters the growth of the creative spirit.[11] A response to a situation that is informed by hope acknowledges the historical pre-formation

---

7. Ibid., 90–91.

8. A symbol is that by means of which something makes itself present and known. A symbol makes present something that cannot be present otherwise. A symbol renders something other than itself actual. The symbolized cannot be encountered in any other way. In this way, a symbol participates directly in the presence and power of that which it symbolizes without exhausting the reality. A symbol symbolizes through interaction with an interpreter who thereby encounters the reality it embodies. While it brings into expression the reality symbolized, every interpretation remains incomplete, inadequate or limited. Unlike a symbol, a sign stands in or substitute for or indicates something other than itself. No intrinsic or internal relation exists between a sign and the reality it represents. A sign points away from itself. See, Roger Haight, *Dynamics of Theology* (New York: Paulist Press, 1990), 130, 133; Sandra Schneiders, *The Revelatory Text: Interpreting the New Testament as Sacred Scripture* (Collegeville, Minnesota: Liturgical Press, 1990), 35–36.

9. Marcel, *Homo Viator*, 35.

10. Ibid., 43.

11. Marcel, *The Mystery of Being Vol.I: Reflection and Mystery*, 135.

of the situation. This acknowledgement requires language that recognizes and welcomes whatever positive contribution others can make to personal and common life. This aspect of language further implies the openness and readiness to modify one's attitudes and understanding.[12] This is also where a reflective person:

> ... preserves in himself a paradoxical equilibrium between the spirit of universality on the one hand, inasmuch as this is embodied in values which must be recognized as unalterable, and on the other hand his personal experience which he neither can nor should ignore, for it will be the source of whatever individual contribution he might make.[13]

It is in the very process of working on facts, relationships and personal attitudes in a specific situation that a human being who hopes actually needs to use language with care so that words do not become dangerous, and are not depreciated or emptied of their authentic significance.[14] People need to use language to utter and express what they mean, and they need to stand for or imply what they communicate through language. This is important because when I speak sincerely or truthfully, I do not only serve the supra-personal community which I form with my interlocutor, I help to make human faith in humanity grow in this world; I help to strengthen the bonds which make a universal community possible.[15]

When an individual hopes, he or she also stimulates his or her imagination or creative spirit. He or she conceives ideals, draws images, delineates wishes, characterizes criticisms and takes into account practical considerations. All these expressions of human reflective power ordinarily involve language. In order to use language I need to be aware of what I am thinking; I need to reflect. Human beings do reflect when they use language, because "our consciousness is essentially a consciousness *of,* or more precisely a consciousness *directed towards,* something. It is directed towards a reality..."[16] At any rate:

> ... the human creature under normal conditions finds his bearing in relation to other people, and also to physical objects, that are not only close to him in space but linked to him by a feeling of intimacy... One might go further and speak of a kind of

12. Marcel, *The Mystery of Being Vol.II: Faith and Reality*, 114.
13. Marcel, *Tragic Wisdom and Beyond*, 31.
14. Marcel, *The Mystery of Being Vol.I: Reflection and Mystery*, 33–34.
15. Marcel, *Homo Viator*, 156.
16. Marcel, *Man Against Mass Society*, 134.

constellation, at once material and spiritual, which under normal conditions assembles itself around each human being.[17]

As an activity of human reflective awareness, reflection enables people to soar above a perfunctory perception of life. As reflection focuses, enlightens and raises people up to a realm of the spirit it preserves and expands vitality. It also spreads warmth around life. "In speculation and reflection we soar above every possible kind of mechanical operation; we are, in the strict sense of the phrase, in the realm of the spirit."[18]

Furthermore, hope requires language because human language has a peculiar dimension of presence that distinguishes it from animal sounds. This presence coextends with the very notion of the person as subject: "While the animal can call—and this is common to both man and animal—only man can address, and this implies a recognition of the other person as a subject."[19]

However, the importance of language for hope need not blind one to its limits. Language at a certain level cannot say everything about human existence and life; "ontology [that is, the regions of being] transcends all logical predication; it is here more than anywhere else that speech reaches a deadlock."[20] Being cannot be reduced to thought; the experience of being is the experience of fullness, the experience of the inexhaustible. Language remains an inadequate vehicle for expressing fullness. Nevertheless, language has a creative character to it. Of the creative character of language the following may be noted: to the extent that a child, for example, learns to speak (where conditions are positive), the child participates in a kind of re-creation of the world in a sense far more intimate and difficult to express. This remains so inasmuch as the world becomes a home—that is, a dwelling place of value.[21]

Nonetheless, the creation of a humane world through language takes place when language operates at the level of encounter, presence and openness—that is, at levels that partake of some plenitude. At such levels language becomes the dwelling place of intrinsic value and vitality, a quality which confers upon language a certain sacredness.[22] In encounter, presence and openness, language becomes truly a medium by which we

17. Ibid., 147.
18. Marcel, *The Mystery of Being Vol.I: Reflection and Mystery*, 215.
19. Marcel, *Searchings*, 81.
20. Marcel, *The Mystery of Being Vol.II: Faith and Reality*, 154.
21. Marcel, *Problematic Man*, 49.
22. Marcel, *Man Against Mass Society*, 114.

understand, interpret and re-create worthwhile possibilities of human living. There exists a relationship—so intimate that we can scarcely conceive it—between the blossoming of language and the conditions, human or otherwise, in which this blossoming is realized. "Human or otherwise" implies "being penetrated or not with love."[23]

The inner logic and concrete operations of thought express themselves through language. At the same time, language as an experience and a conceptual vehicle alters the powers of thought by giving thought the means of representing and explicating the world. Through language people construct, control and relate with reality in this world. In expressing the inner life of people language enables them to grasp and understand the salient features of human intentions and of the human condition. As a tool kit of human existence, language regulates, sorts out and clarifies people's thoughts about themselves, their relations and the world. As a historical reality, language expresses a culture's symbolisms in their dynamic postures and forms. As a vehicle for transmitting cultural history, language raises and expands consciousness. Within the cultural milieu, language enables people to acknowledge and recognize, name, claim, and express human exigencies.

In fact, language makes it possible for people to continually reconstruct life's sense of purpose and meaning. Within a given set of circumstances, people are able to read, interpret and evaluate experiences through the heritage and condition of the interpretative community of which they are a part. Of course, to interpret is to judge; and an excess preoccupation with fear and vanity distorts interpretation. People construct reality out of the myriad forms in which they structure the experience of the senses, the deeply symbolic experiences of being in a social environment as well as various forms of intentionality and conception. Language carries its function of reconstructing life's sense of significance by illuminating its forms of narrative sensibility, responsibility and selfhood.

The pluralities of language forms as well as their flexibility make language adaptable to the ruggedness, irregularity, vulnerability and persuasion of life's itinerary. Language is able to trace, fit, adopt and capture particularity, localness of contexts, historical opportunities and embarrassments that accompany human experiences. The flexibility of language enables it to establish, modify and replace old meanings and also to reconstruct new meanings with encapsulating knowledge, imaginative understanding and generalizing judgments. Through language, people construct meanings with which individuals can regulate their relations with themselves, others

23. Marcel, *Problematic Man*, 49.

and the physical environment, and, in doing so, inherit, recreate and reinvent culture. In this way, language enables people to impose their points of view about the world on others as they renegotiate their placement and meaning in life. By means of language, people can open up and plumb the depths of unsuspected possibilities of interpenetration and directive meanings. Such meanings could also become the guide to a reconstruction of reality and psychological realities. Language transmits and re-constitutes a way of understanding life.

In the concrete, a proper use of language needs to be alert to human exigencies, which constitute the focus of the next section.

On the Vital Exigencies[24] of the Human Subject

The task of the current consideration is to specify the existential aspects of the human subject because the living home of the human subject is this world. The human subject is not only in this world, he or she is also of and with this world in the vital construction of relations, decisions and power as an active presence.[25] At the same time, life cannot be lived without some form of risk, which involves the division between what concerns me and what does not concern me, a division rational enough in the making.[26] Effectively, the person who hopes is always involved in some kind of venture and also a struggle, because "our own world harbours seemingly inexhaustible possibilities of waste and destruction."[27] In our deeply ambivalent world, startling beauty exists together with revolting

---

24. In this and the following chapter as well as in the main considerations of the preceding chapters vital exigencies refer the psychic, psychological, social and productive exigencies. The vital exigencies embody fundamental in-built demands, drives and aspirations that point to, uncover and identify living fountains of human vitality. They signify and symbolize the organic, energetic and dynamic urges and flows of life in their basic degrees and circumstances of equilibriums, motivations and self-giving expansiveness and orientation. In fact, the realization of the liberative aims of the vital exigencies unleashes energies that integrate, and fulfill the experience and expression of human flourishing. The life-giving push and trajectories of the vital exigencies foreshadow and marvelously connect with meaning, beauty and becoming. These living human energies inform, inspire, enlighten and organize perceptions, perspectives and the imagination of life and the horizon of common living. The self-involving and self-grasping nature of the vital exigencies clarify, direct and unify life's possibilities and directions. It also awakens people to their inner reasons for being within contexts of particular experiences.

25. Gabriel Marcel, "Introduction," in *Fresh Hope for the World: Moral Rearmament in Action*, Gabriel Marcel, ed. (London: Longmans, 1960), 6.

26. Marcel, *Being and Having*, 70.

27. Marcel, *The Mystery of Being Vol.II: Faith and Reality*, 144.

brutality, emancipation coexists with entrapment. Liberating and peaceful possibilities remain marred by propensities of unconscious distortions and disturbance. Conflicting arguments, conversations and interpretations remain part and parcel of human existence. Historically speaking, conflict, fear and guilt exist in tensions, on the one hand, with the exigencies of joys, hopes and celebrations, on the other.

That is also to say, the acting human subject is vulnerable and open to being threatened in his or her existential exigencies. An exigency[28] is a need, demand and aspiration to living a fuller human life that a human subject has an incumbent responsibility to meet as well as a right to satisfy. An exigency is not only a need but also something that is *demanded*.[29] In fact, "what defines man are exigencies."[30] This further implies that "there are realms of experience which possess a particular order or intelligibility subject to conditions which cannot be properly specified; if they are specifiable, it is because they inhere in the subject himself insofar as he is identified with a living experience which cannot by its nature mirror itself."[31] The exigencies mean that many demands, needs, roles and stories shape human agency. The individual always remains a wonderfully complex reality. Pre-discursive and interior relationships structure individual lives. This also means that the human individual cannot be a closed subjectivity. Relationships with others and performance in the world make people into who they are and what they can become. Furthermore, the exigencies imply that human beings have concrete concerns, anxieties and aspirations or demands, such as decent living conditions and relationships. Human beings also desire access to veritable spiritual experiences, or experiences that would constitute a certain fullness of life. At the same time, however, the exigencies can be smothered or stymied either by despair or temptations to despair.

Indeed, the personality always implies some relationality; the person is profoundly relational. The person is transubjective and intersubjectively available. There are four distinguishable vital exigencies that are identifiable with a human subject as he or she participates liberatively in this world. These are the psychic, psychological, social and productive exigencies; they may also be considered organic, psychological, productive or social functions experienced within the framework of vitality and the value

---

28. In his writings, Marcel frequently uses the word *exigence* instead of exigency.
29. Marcel, *The Mystery of Being Vol.II: Faith and Reality*, 37.
30. Marcel, *Tragic Wisdom and Beyond*, 34.
31. Marcel, *Creative Fidelity*, 7.

of intrinsic significance.³² The exigencies signify that I, as a human subject, am active within the world in the sense that I cannot really stand aside from the universe, even in thought. Only by a meaningless pretence can I place myself at some vague point outside of the universe. Nor can I place myself outside myself (a revealing parallel).³³ The rise and ascendancy, or the fall and disgrace, for the human subject are rooted in the exigencies which presuppose, shape and condition each other. The exigencies interpenetrate and interconnect; each exigency requires the undertone and the animation of the others.

Worldly Situatedness of the Vital Exigencies

The exigencies imply a certain nexus of human presence to the world. As noted earlier, the self seems to endue with a certain quality of its surroundings which it makes its own: hence, a kind of harmony between the two renders the surroundings habitable to it. The more I emphasize the objectivity of things, thus cutting the umbilical cords which bind them to existence and to psycho-organic presence to myself, the more I affirm the independence of the world from me and its radical indifference to my destiny and goals. The more, too, will this world, proclaimed as the only real one, be converted into an illusory spectacle, a great documentary film presented for my curiosity, but ultimately abolished simply because it disregards me. But the act of trying to break the nexus uniting me to the universe, my body being this nexus manifested, can only be an act of pure abstraction.³⁴ This is impossible from an existential point of view. In the absence of such abstraction, there is a *feeling at home* with respect to a self and that self can be the self of another person, that is, a being capable of asserting I. Home refers not merely to a building; more importantly it refers to the living space and environment that feel and smell right. Subsequently, "I cannot refer to *my feeling at home* unless I grant or imply that the self does or can seem to itself to impregnate its environment with its own quality, thereby recognizing itself in its surrounding and entering into an intimate relationship with it."³⁵

What is more, *being at home* is only relative to a *self* which, moreover, can be that of another person. Someone who says or who presumably can say, *I*, who can posit himself or herself or be posited as an *I* must not only

---

32. Marcel, *Problematic Man*, 139.
33. Marcel, *Being and Having*, 19.
34. Ibid., 20–21.
35. Ibid., 27–28.

possess in the sense of legal ownership a certain domain, but must also experience it as his or her own. Besides, it may very well be the case that in living among objects which belong to me, in a house I have bought or inherited, I do not have the feeling of "being at home." This means that the framework within which I live becomes alien to me. I do not comprehend myself in it. I seem to be placed there. It can also occur that one of my relations or fellow-boarders, because of the fact that he or she is living with me, dispossesses me of that awareness of *being at home* which I apparently should have. In the circumstances, the other intervenes between me and my possessions. When a belonging separates me from others, it breaks the vital connections or living ties between me and them.[36]

Now, the object shares in the nature of my body, that is, insofar as the body is not thought of as an object. My body, insofar as it is mine, frees itself from the hold of concepts and representations. But the body always remains this worldly; as a nexus it connects me to the world. In other words, we establish the existence of the world through our pre-deliberative contact with it by means of our bodies. In this regard, the more we treat the world as a spectacle, the more it becomes unintelligible, because the relation then established between us and the world becomes intrinsically absurd. In proportion to how much a person treats the universe as an object, he or she cannot help asking how this object was formed, how this "set-up" was stated. This questioning implies the mental reconstruction of a series of operations which has unfolded successfully. But this further presupposes the initial action by which persons separate themselves from the world, as they separate themselves from the object which they consider in its different aspect. Noteworthy is the fact that in this interrogation lies the understanding that the genesis of the I and of the world constitutes one and the same problem. The insolubility of the problem is bound up with my very position, my existence and the radical fact of that existence.

What is more, the universe as such, not being thought of or able to be thought of as object, has, strictly speaking, no past: it entirely transcends a "cinematographic" representation. At a certain level I cannot fail to appear to myself as contemporary with the universe that is eternal, i.e., a temporal and spatial whole.[37] My own reality then is only intelligible as a mystery. That is also to say, thought cannot go beyond existence; it can only in some degree abstract from it. Thought is *inside* existence which is a mode of being. That is, it is a privileged mode of existence that can make abstrac-

---

36. Ibid., 90.
37. Marcel, *Being and Having*, 18–20.

tion from itself *qua* existence, and this only for strictly limited purposes.[38] In this sense, thought, far from being a relation with itself, is essentially a self-transcendence.[39]

The principle of identity accompanies the exercise of thought throughout but thought can, without leaving the determinate, rise to the notion of positive infinite. The principle of identity only ceases to apply at the point where thought itself can no longer work.[40] In short, thought is made for being. There is a sense in which I only think insofar as there is a kind of space between me and being. All thought transcends the immediate. The pure immediate excludes thought as it also excludes desire. But the transcendence of thought implies a magnetization and even a teleology.[41]

Now, there are two modes of detachment possible in the world: that of the spectator and of the saint. The detachment of the saint springs from the very core of reality. This detachment reflects the highest form of participation. The detachment of the spectator is just the opposite; it is a desertion, not only in thought but in act. The attitude of the spectator corresponds to a certain form of lust and to the act by which the human subject appropriates the world to himself or herself.

It also needs to be granted that the human activity of thinking operates at two levels: *thinking* (a thought) and *thinking of* (an object). *Thinking* entails recognizing (or building or isolating) a structure. *Thinking of* is something quite different: one thinks *of a being* or even an *event*, past or to come. *Thinking* does not come to bear on anything but essences or depersonalized entities, perfectly allowable on its own terms. However, in the order of *thinking of* a certain person can think of a particular being or thing. The more we fill in or supply contexts, the more we slide from just *thinking* to *thinking of*.[42] Persons could not deny the principle of identity without denying that thought can have a bearing on anything at all. A person ceases to think when his or her thought becomes the slave of a content which inhibits or even annuls it.[43] Both *thinking* and *thinking of* are involved in understanding the vitality of exigencies. The awareness of this world is originally given to people according to the perspectives which are theirs and no one else's. The apprehension of the exigencies takes place

38. Ibid., 26–27.
39. Ibid., 30.
40. Ibid., 33–34.
41. Ibid., 38.
42. Ibid., 31.
43. Ibid., 30.

through the contexts and contents of personal and shared experiences. Nonetheless, a person exists in the world only insofar as the world is not a representation, but something shaping him or her as in a womb.[44]

The moment a person is involved in the order of the living being, he or she is exposed to influences, both internal and external, that become internalized and qualified in ways which modify him or her. In fact, to be a human being, at all, is to be in a situation, namely, in a juncture of internality and externality. If a person is exposed to influences because he or she is in a certain situation, it means that he or she, to some degree, becomes permeable to them. Permeability relates to a lack of cohesion, or of density. A being is more exposed to influences insofar as he or she has less density. These possible influences become all the more numerous or diverse insofar as the nature of a relatively incohesive being itself implies a greater multiplicity of elements. Of course, cohesion assumes or expresses itself in the form of disposability or availability. A person's condition as a living being admittedly subjects him or her to objectively describable properties, but also exposes him or her to, or, even better, opens him or her up to a reality which he or she communicates.[45] As pointed out earlier, four basic exigencies define the human subject and, subsequently, his or her being in a situation.

The Psychic Exigency

What may be called the psychic exigency signifies that I am possessed of intuition, a sense of personal freedom, subjectivity and individual history. It implies that it is my responsibility to maintain and deepen my personal sense of identity. This exigency, which entails being in touch with oneself with warmth and a sense of pursuit of authentic care and life, actuates itself whenever a person affirms himself or herself as a free and thinking being who transcends the static snapshots of states. Within this perspective, freedom becomes the ground for the very thought itself which tries to understand or conceive it. Psychic exigency means that in the deepest sense, I am my freedom. It also means that I must realize myself for I fulfill my freedom in my self-realization. Human dignity lies in human freedom.

In fact, freedom constitutes the being and existence of a human subject. Thus, fundamentally, psychic exigency refers to the fact that I am a subject: I am an I, a self-present being. And I do not have being, or at any rate, I can only grasp myself as being on condition that I feel, and to feel is

44. Marcel, *Creative Fidelity*, 29.
45. Ibid., 88.

to receive, to open myself to, and hence, to give myself.[46] In being, an ultimate identification of receiving and giving realizes itself. In other words, when I identify my deepest self with my freedom it manifests itself in positive self-affirmation and in self-giving and generous living. Furthermore, there is only a difference in power, and not in nature, between the ability to feel and the ability to create; both presuppose the existence not only of a self but also of a world where the self can act, expand and realize itself. This is a world that is intermediate between the closed and the open, between being and having, of which my body necessarily seems the materialized nucleus or symbol.[47]

When imbued with the psychic exigency, the human subject becomes aware of himself or herself as experiencing and perhaps attending and intending some goal, evaluation and decision. This exigency urges a person to see himself or herself as a locus of inherence, that is, as a being who is aware of being a conscious subject, however fragmentary or incoherent this awareness may be. To treat myself as a subject is really to treat myself as somebody with whom I am intimate, that is, to be in touch with myself.[48] So, psychic exigency involves that feeling of a certain sacred reality in the self which cannot be separated from an apprehension of the self in its subjectivity.[49] Subjectivity then means that I can meaningfully say "I" as my unique prerogative as a personal being. In my subjectivity I become inwardly present to myself, a presence that is manifest in my deepest attachments, spontaneous tastes and sense of engagement in this life. In light of deeply held human attachments, tastes and a sense of personal engagement, it is notable that the definite characteristics that constitute the self insofar as I grasp it as a particular individual, or somebody, have a contingent character. This is also to say, it is in relation to myself as a subject that these definite characteristics of my particular individuality are felt and acknowledged to be contingent.[50] Of course, our biography, history and self-understanding constitute our individuality which implies our participation in the world.

My psychic exigency connects with the *certainty which I am as a living being*. In the midst of multiple relations or connectedness that characterizes my life, I always remain the same unique, self-governing and inward being.

---

46. Ibid., 91.
47. Ibid., 92.
48. Marcel, *The Mystery of Being Vol. I: Reflection and Mystery*, 87.
49. Ibid.
50. Ibid., 86–87.

That is also to say, I am not just anybody. I am a particular somebody. I am named. To be given a name is to be conferred with an identity in an act of consecration with a personal resonance; it is to be affixed with a seal of care, responsibility and relationship.[51] The surname or the family name of a person is not simply a sign. It is the individual being's inalienable property. The name lies at the intersection between being and having. The name signals the unique place which belongs to the individual in relation to the social whole in which he or she has to find his or her place and discover the type of creative activity, however limited, which is his or her own.[52]

As conventional signs, names give us identities in addition to locating us in space and relationships. Thus, a name reconfigures and enriches common life. A name entitles a person to ask questions about life and experiences. It points to and concretizes history and drama so that a name memorializes people. It cries out and expresses presence that can be touched. In this sense, a name concretizes. A name also reflects a sizeable ambiguity; it suggests solidarity as well as one's participation in the tragic drama of life. In a name resides the judgment of personhood that makes possible the process of human communication, reconciliation, consolation and conflict. Subsequently, a name leads us from the external to the internal space or from public to private space at which people interact and connect with one another. In a word, the whole humanity is caught up in a name.

In fact, naming manifests an affirmative response to and appreciation of an experience that continues to unfold and develop in the midst of our existence. To name is to recognize and acknowledge another. A name focuses the experience and uniqueness of persons. Naming initiates and actuates the beginning of both relationship and commitment to the continuity of the human communal living. In sharing or participating in identity, naming involves, affirms and legitimizes an assumption of responsibility for the other. Naming brings people into a relationship in that it makes them a part of the human community. This relationship leads further to a fuller integration into the larger human community. Accordingly, while the act or process of naming promotes distinctiveness, it also advances a sense of human commonality by ordering or organizing relationships.

A name makes a person present by setting him or her in relational space and the totality of human life in the world. As it articulates the hidden nexus of human kinship ties, a name also brings out the truth of persons that establishes them in being. As a relational symbol, a name

---

51. Marcel, *Problematic Man*, 48.
52. Marcel, *The Mystery of Being Vol.I: Faith and Reality*, 55.

plays a crucial role in bringing out the potentials of a person for being. In articulating identity and significance of a person, a name further embeds a person in self-awareness and a symbiotic relation to life.

In effect, to name a being effects a sort of subtle transposition of the *thou* into a *he or she*. Naming closely links with knowing how a being needs to be called. The designation which comes with naming guarantees this act. To name a person is to recall, to *remember* that the being of whom we are speaking can become the object of invocation.[53] Naming implies being; it cherishes and acknowledges the other's intrinsic desirability, attractiveness and worth or lovableness. The intrinsic reality of being implies that "the more a man becomes dependent on the gadgets whose smooth functioning assures him a tolerable life at the material level, the more estranged he becomes from an awareness of his inner reality."[54] The reality of being also signifies that *we are also what we are not*. There is a counter-reality to ourselves, that is, our lives which are not embodied directly in our acts, but which may hover over them like a shadow that may become the source of creation itself.[55] Where technical knowledge begins to claim primacy in existence in relation to modes of thinking, the human concentration comes to be more on doing than on being as people begin to lose awareness of themselves.[56] We are not our lives, that is, our lives cannot be reduced to techniques. In a world taken over by techniques, technical achievements tend to seem more and more the chief, if not the only, mark of a human being's superiority to the animals. In this exaltation of techniques there might be Promethean defiance, not without its own greatness and nobility.[57]

It must also be recognized that the reality that I am consists in the unity and continuity of always coming to be. We continually need to become more of our being.[58] However, the unifying of my life and my being is subject to wide-ranging adventures and varied fortunes. That is to say, each one of us is called upon to become aware that our personal life can be disrupted from top to bottom following events which take place in a part of the world where we have never set foot and of which we perhaps only formed the vaguest of images.[59] The consciousness implied refers to the pervasive char-

---

53. Marcel, *Metaphysical Journal*, 160.
54. Marcel, *Man Against Mass Society*, 55.
55. Marcel, *The Existential Background of Human Dignity*, 61.
56. Marcel, *Man Against Mass Society*, 71.
57. Ibid., 58.
58. Marcel, *The Existential Background of Human Dignity*, 88.
59. Marcel, *Problematic Man*, 132.

acter of human existential uneasiness and its wide-ranging repercussions for individuals and communities. Existential uneasiness cannot be eluded: it can only be faced. However existential uneasiness "should be transmuted into an active disposition which partakes of faith."[60] For, "uneasiness and the aspiration to being are today closely interdependent."[61]

What is more, who I am touches on my self-perception. A human being depends, to a very great degree, on the idea he or she has of himself or herself and that this idea cannot be degraded without at the same time degrading the person.[62] What is presupposed here is an understanding that personal life is always subject to the dialectics of experience, something that is foreign to the state of innocence. Thus, innocence is not about losing ignorance or moral status. Of innocence the following may be stated:

> . . . state of innocence taken in itself already contains the possibility of fault or, if you will, of the fall. "Innocence is ignorance . . . man is not yet determined as mind, but only in his psychism, in unity with what constitutes his nature . . . there does not yet exist anything which is contested, any dialectic, the mind is not yet dialectic . . ."[63]

Innocence is a way of loving which arises from participating in the milieu of the unconditional presence and value. This is an atmosphere of love. The real loss of innocence comes with betrayal of love which needs to be reaffirmed in its original intention if the lost innocence is to be regained. Loss of innocence refers to love betrayed. That innocence can be lost also implies a deep ambiguity within human existence. We regain our innocence when we regain our love. In this light, innocence is deeply about the glory of humanity.

In a sense, to be human is to be in conflict. It is to live through and also harmonize internal conflicting tendencies by means of liberty and spontaneity. To gain one's lost innocence then is to confront oneself historically and from the perspective of vulnerability. When one confronts or wakes up to the data of one's own life and narrative from the perspective of vulnerability, one ceases inescapably to be the same again. One opens up to and gains a whole new way of life. A re-balancing of the will and

---

60. Ibid., 141. In faith we participate in being; faith is a relationship of recognizing and understanding that we are of intrinsic unconditional worth and oriented towards fullness of life.

61. Ibid., 139.

62. Marcel, *Man Against Mass Society*, 20.

63. Marcel, *Problematic Man*, 103.

wish occurs. Vulnerability transforms the deciding self into a vehicle of expansive love. When a person becomes vulnerable to another, the experience also becomes a matter of dependence on life's providence. One gains further freedom of being in touch with oneself that enables one to grow to be one's authentic self.

Back to the question of psychic exigency, it may be added that who I am also embraces my measure of self-acceptance and personal wrestling with limits. The fact of wrestling with limits implies that:

> The human being who denies his nature as a created being ends up by claiming for himself attributes which are a sort of caricature of those that belong to the Uncreated . . . this pretended or parodic human autarchy . . . [tends to] degenerate into a resentment turned back on the very self for which such absurd claims are made . . .[64]

Because of psychic exigency, then, as a human subject I do not belong to the world of objects.[65] I am a personal being. My dignity consists in my being, that is, in my *I am*. My being constitutes the ground for personal mastery and remaking of life. My being is my ideal self by which I construct my functional identity and evaluate and master the world, and in so doing continually reconstitute my life. But this task of self-governance and transformation necessitates the "daily effort to sustain one's own moral integrity."[66] The existent being that I am at any given moment is something that I also construct through the events, experiences, tragedies, joys and sorrows of my existence and life. The existent being that I am is defined by the multiplicity of possibilities or of possible actions which constitute a network or gridiron which confers a meaning upon things and which places them in a certain totality that is the world.[67] Furthermore, in the midst of a trying situation I can always grow inwardly, that is, I can always live significantly with demanding life situations. Consequently, the psychic exigency constantly challenges persons to struggle against things that humiliate their dignity or which fill them with horror and contempt for themselves and for their fellow-sufferers.[68]

With psychic exigency also comes the power of animating, the ability of prompting initiatives and issues. What is even more:

---

64. Marcel, *Man Against Mass Society*, 75.
65. Ibid., 22.
66. Ibid., 42.
67. Marcel, *Problematic Man*, 111.
68. Marcel, *Man Against Mass Society*, 43.

... the power of animating is the power of using to the full, or, to go more deeply, of lending ourselves, that is to say of allowing ourselves to be used to the full, of offering ourselves in some way to those *karoi*, or life-giving opportunities which the being, who is available (*disponible*), discovers all around him like so many switches controlling the inexhaustible current flowing through our universe.[69]

Accordingly, psychic exigency is a human personal calling to respond and clarify one's situatedness in the world. The existential datum of psychic exigency suggests a world in which the individual is the bearer of mysterious energies, cosmic or spiritual, and whose nature he or she vaguely feels.[70] At the same time, who a human subject is remains significantly intersubjective and relational in its character. This is because, as a human subject, certain people make up, for example, my environment (my family, my profession and so on) and this environment in turn constantly supports me; without it I would be literally lost. Other people keep up "everyday" relations with me (sales attendants, the taxi or bus driver, the police officer and the milk or postal man, for instance). Also, there are those who are only passers-by, people whom I meet occasionally and who, as far as I am concerned, might just as well be non-existent.[71]

Moreover, the intersubjective is really within the subject himself or herself, that each one is for himself or herself a "we," that he or she can be himself or himself only in being many, and that value is only possible on this condition. This interior or intersubjective plurality maintains the closest and least easily explorable relations with the extra-subjective plurality. I am neither *alone*, nor *one*.[72] In the real world, who I am in my subjectivity is not a cloistered affair. No one lives in this world without having been transfixed by his or her social and cultural roots. We each carry with us social, historical and cultural fabrics. We are persons who are drenched by our own history and culture: a memory sometimes scattered, other times sharp and clear. From this perspective, psychic exigency signifies that beyond inner sense of who they are, communication and understanding persons are also constituted deeply, genuinely and spontaneously by the network of personal, social and cultural strengths, weaknesses, fears, desires, triumphs and tragedies.

69. Marcel, *Homo Viator*, 146.
70. Marcel, *Creative Fidelity*, 95.
71. Marcel, *Searchings*, 62.
72. Marcel, *Presence and Immortality*, 201.

Yet there is a dark side of the psychic exigency which shows itself in a prevailing sense of self-doubt. Under such circumstance, persons tend to conceive of themselves as pure pieces of mechanism and make it their chief businesses to control the machine as well as possible, and they regard the problem of their life purely as a problem of tangible results.[73] Self-doubt takes over as persons fail to control their lives and become devoid of interior support.[74] Descriptively, such persons are usually aware of themselves far less as beings than as desires to rise above everything which they are or are not, above the actuality in which they really feel involved and have a part to play, but which does not satisfy them, for it falls short of the aspiration with which they identify themselves. Their motto is not *sum* (I am) but *sursum* (upwardness as an existential contraction)—in which case reality is depreciated and viewed as something to be conquered.[75]

In the last analysis, my psychic impulse involves my sense of my life, a personal sense of self-identity and an acceptance of who I am. Because psychic exigency is an ongoing personal demand and energy for actuating a sense of the self that is unconditional, the thrust of psychic exigency primarily gives rise to a unifying philosophy of life: a directness of life and its definitions in terms of values and responsibilities. Needlessly, idealism always threatens the integrity of psychic exigency. In its modern versions idealism contributes to the acceptance of the complete divorce between myself and my life where my life appears as a group of phenomena falling within the province of the natural sciences, perhaps of sociology too, but deprived of its characteristic intelligibility. The self comes to identify itself with the very act of thought. In fact, what is common to both idealism and materialism is their rejection of the pivotal datum of the incarnation.[76]

The Psychological Exigency

The psychological exigency refers to the human psychosomatic and cognitive responsiveness that is habitually pre-reflective, yet expressive of human motivations which shape interactive and functional behaviors. The psychological exigency arises from the fact that we are interpretatively conscious beings. This is partly because an intrinsic quality of consciousness is that it cannot be detached or contemplated; consciousness is above

---

73. Marcel, *Homo Viator*, 24.
74. Marcel, *The Philosophy of Existentialism*, 31.
75. Marcel, *Homo Viator*, 25–26; *Creative Fidelity*, 144.
76. Marcel, *Creative Fidelity*, 93.

all consciousness of something which is other than itself.[77] Events of consciousness do not all occur indifferently or vacuously. As they occur they also carry with them some propositional content. Accordingly, "There is no sense in saying that I know my states of consciousness; to the extent that they are mine, I live them, I do not know them. If I convert them into objects, I liken them to external objects."[78] The milieu of other persons specifies human interpretation and responsiveness. Indeed, "if I am somebody, a particular individual (though not merely that), I am only so in connection with and in opposition to an indefinite number of other somebodies"[79] so that the assertion "I exist" is valid only if it signifies an original datum which is not "I think" nor even "I am alive," but rather "I experience."[80] "I cannot think of myself as existing save in so far as I am a datum for other consciousnesses, that is to say in so far as I am a datum in space."[81] And because we are mindful of persons other than ourselves, our human consciousness undergirds our need and aspiration to respond to situatedness, that is, be responsive beings.

The psychological exigency is our responsive demand to be recognized by others and to recognize others within an existential space. We experience our need and aspiration to be acknowledged and responded to in the very process of being in the world. The consciousness of existing links up with the urge to make ourselves *recognized* by some other person, some witness, helper, rival or adversary who is needed to integrate the self.[82] The psychological sphere is a milieu of responsive living and vital interactions with others. The need and demand to be recognized by others shape and involve ways of thinking and manners of acting, specific to contexts of living and action, which arise from self-reflection. One could say that the psychological exigency depends on the irreducible and vague experience of presence which remains inseparable from the sense of being in the world.[83] Frequently, this experience also involves wrestling with feelings and desires and protesting against a world which fails to offer love.

Now, the need and demand to be acknowledged elicit feelings which touch on or connect us to our operative sense of ourselves: self-concept

77. Marcel, *The Mystery of Being Vol.I: Reflection and Mystery*, 51–52.
78. Marcel, *Presence and Immortality*, 132.
79. Marcel, *The Mystery of Being Vol.I: Reflection and Mystery*, 86.
80. Marcel, *Creative Fidelity*, 16.
81. Marcel, *Metaphysical Journal*, 18.
82. Marcel, *Homo Viator*, 15.
83. Ibid.

or self-definition. That is to say, feelings are affection. Accordingly, the affective character of psychological exigency connects us to the mystery of our concrete persons, the profundity of our human subjectivity. It is also from the perspective of feelings relating us to the core of our subjectivity, that is, rootedness in a certain self-definition, that we are able to further appreciate that the human body-subject defies complete control. The body is not simply an object for gratifying feelings.

> To understand this, one can take as an example the emaciated [skinny] girl who tells her parents that her body belongs to her, that she can do what she pleases with it. But in this case we should not overlook the fact that it is actually for herself that she wants her freedom, her body being for herself a kind of materialized equivalent of herself. Experience may show her—and in many ways—that this freedom has limits she did not suspect, that the body can be only imperfectly controlled, if, for example, she finds herself pregnant.[84]

Besides, psychological exigency has a significant bearing on patience that we need to cultivate towards our own selves. It is clear in everyday living that:

> . . . a harshness or an excessive malice towards oneself can . . . be paralyzing . . . hence there is need for patience towards oneself, a patience that may be reconciled with complete lucidity . . . However, this is possible and meaningful only when the distance from and nearness to the self which define the act of charity, are realized in and relative to, oneself.[85]

The psychological exigency further calls for attentiveness to our feelings as a way of maintaining loyalty to who and where we deeply and existentially are. Feelings relate us to who we are. They manifest and express our deep loyalty to ourselves in this life. Remaking and re-creating ourselves through feelings is an opportunity that may present itself in certain moments, say, of anger, frustrations and/or in moments of contrasts and contradictions. So, an efficacious handling of feelings is not only good and right but also emotionally healthy. For to recognize one's own nature, at any level whatsoever, is possible only for a being who is effectively acting. But this activity may be exercised within extremely narrow limits not perceptible to the outside observer.[86]

---

84. Marcel, *The Existential Background of Human Dignity*, 98–99.
85. Marcel, *Creative Fidelity*, 46–47.
86. Marcel, *The Mystery of Being Vol. I: Reflection and Mystery*, 143.

The psychological exigency expresses a felt existential need and demand to grow in wisdom that embraces affection and passion. And here we may observe that wisdom which does not include passion, which does not acknowledge the subterranean justifications of exaltation and sacrifice is not worthy of being called wisdom. For passions ought to be a fact as fundamental as life or death.[87] In the human vista of psychological exigency, the human subject is a deeply affected and relational being who gets "there" by starting from "here" motivationally and compassionately. In the end, it may be noted that in our psychology lies our sociology: when persons enter deeply into their interior lives that shape their behaviors and responses, they expand their capacities to transform their social lives.

The Social Exigency

Living in a society, and in communities, implies that we have to share existence with people whose ways, attitudes and values may differ and disagree with ours. Working out and finding peaceful terms for mutual co-existence within boundaries of communication, dignity, civility and tolerance is what the social exigency is about. The social exigency refers to the public give-and-take exchange of interacting and interpretative relationships within broadly pre-existing and structured patterns and possibilities of human relations. This exigency grounds healthy give-and-take in our broader interactive and communal relationship or coexistence with other persons without whom our lives would be different. In this regard, the words *mystery of being* translate in a very schematic, and therefore inevitably inadequate, way the fact that as a thinking being I am involved in a vast communion, a vast *co-esse* of which I can only have a fragmentary awareness through key experiences.[88] In other words:

> I find myself in strictly determined circumstances regarding my birth, the milieu in which I live, the people I have met, and so on . . . It would be altogether inadequate to maintain that these conditions are due to pure chance and for that reason, insignificant. It is in relation to them that I have to assert my freedom, and in the course of doing so I am led to appreciate my circumstances as having been—in the strongest sense of the word—given. In this way I come to think of a will which is giving and at the same time free.[89]

---

87. Marcel, *Tragic Wisdom and Beyond*, 198.
88. Marcel, "Reply to Gene Reeves," 274.
89. Marcel, *The Existential Background of Human Dignity*, 30.

Social exigency undergirds and informs the human experience of being a subject of a certain thrust of connectedness and vast relations with others that make a person into who and what he or she is: "to exist is to co-exist."[90] Co-existence with others informs the sense of being relevant and particular in interactive life. In reality:

> A secret voice which I cannot silence assures me in fact that if others are not there, I am not there either. I cannot grant to myself an existence of which I suppose the others are deprived; and here "I cannot" does not mean "I have not the right" but rather "It is impossible for me." If others vanish from me, I vanish from myself.[91]

Social identity implies a consciousness which acknowledges and recognizes people as having some common cultural codes of representations within a social context that gives them common language to define themselves. In this light, food, territorial land, race, ethnicity and creedal affiliations become significant and vital categories. Social self-understanding defines the way people see and accept themselves and interact with their neighbors. Within this backdrop, social exigency signifies that a particular culture always remains an authentic way of expressing how particular people vary and adopt, incorporate and celebrate human life, human relations and human flourishing. A given culture gives people permission to open and inhabit the world and discover themselves through the horizons that it offers. A given culture also makes its members open to some changes by offering them meanings and symbols that make it possible to expand their perspectives, identities, decisions and claims in existence. Every culture reaches out, claims its own domains and establishes influences over its members or, even, at times, on its neighbors. In a culture, then, persons realize that they are part of whole communities with memories, hopes and creativity.

Concretely, as we grow up and live in a given historical cultural context, we make and unmake and remake ourselves. Frequently, the family becomes the locus and context from where people gain knowledge of the sacredness of and respect for life, of compassion and love, and of common courtesies and hospitality. The social contexts in which people grow up and/or live normally constitute a close-knit environment with strong bonds of affection and loyalty. Such contexts also create and establish a strong sense of individuated identity and psychological possibilities that obtain to an individual. This is also to say, "our itinerant condition is in no sense separable from the given circumstances, which in the case of each

90. Marcel, *Presence and Immortality*, 205.
91. Marcel, *Homo Viator*, 138.

of us that condition borrows its special character."[92] Or again, "our condition in this world does remain, in the last analysis, that of a wanderer, an itinerant being, who cannot come to absolute rest except by a fiction."[93] The noncontingency of the situation is affirmed by the subject itself in the very process of creating itself *qua* subject.[94]

In fact, we develop common sense, namely, the ability for shared perceptions and patterns of thinking and acting, within social contexts. There is and there can be no common sense where there is no common life or common notions. That is also to say, where there no longer exist any organic groups such as the family, the village, the neighborhood and clans.[95] As we live with others we affect social life by our own views, as that life is also affected by the views and judgments of others, and these relations create "a primordial bond, a kind of umbilical cord, which unites the human being to a particular, determined, and concrete [physical and social] environment."[96] In the social milieu we also develop our own thinking and feelings, likes and dislikes, aspirations and set of possibilities by which we define ourselves through living with others so that *to be among others* evidently belongs to what we are.[97] Accordingly, our identities tend to remain more familial and communal than individual and private so that care for the family unit tends to be very important in our upbringing.

Persons cannot credibly deny their common humanity with others. The social condition is part of being human. The concrete man or woman is forever being shaped by his or her society. And any attempt at separating the self from society, be it out self-interest or otherwise, will constitute a point of self-destruction. People's perspectives, self-knowledge and skills are forever embedded into the deeply felt vitality of social bonds. Also, how people respond to their social and cultural environments affects their likes or dislikes, what actions they take or do not take, and what art they value or practice and what kind of appreciation or expressions they enact. Consequently, judgments affect social living: there is no such thing as a social plateau.

Human social situatedness gives every individual human being a sense of rootedness and a starting point for judgments. "There is a sense in

---

92. Marcel, *The Mystery of Being Vol.I: Reflection and Mystery*, 133–34.
93. Ibid., 133.
94. Ibid., 134.
95. Marcel, *The Decline of Wisdom*, 46.
96. Marcel, *Tragic Wisdom and Beyond*, 38.
97. Marcel, *Searchings*, 62.

which we are all historical beings; that is to say, that we come after beings from whom we have received a great deal, and this in a way which gives us something by which we are differentiated from them."[98] Frequently, social rootedness provides a person with a framework for living and interpreting life in ways that define appropriate behavior and conduct. Social situatedness establishes a life history and modes of relationships and growth because *to be in a situation* and *to be on the move* are modes of being that cannot be dissociated from each other; they are, in fact, two complementary aspects of our condition.[99] For example, there are always people who influence and shape my life and "I am bound to [them] by ties of friendship, familiarity and love to such a degree that their disappearance would inflict a serious wound upon my person."[100] As an individual I am a center and a product of a bonding process with certain other persons so that "existence is not separable from communication, i.e., from a certain *coesse* which is spiritually apprehended, any more than it is able to be grasped outside of its rootedness in time."[101] An inescapable interpersonal relatedness marks us. Thus, personhood is characterized precisely by an openness to and involvement with others.[102]

So, social rootedness means that no success I can achieve will be valid if it is not also the success of the community to which I essentially belong in virtue of the real relations which bind me to the whole of the universe.[103] The social exigency implies that persons long to love, connect and communicate with other persons: in effect, people imbue others with influence and a sense of identity and purpose. Naturally many people like to relate to and relax with others. Yet contexts of sharing with others also bring with them bruises and bumps of life as well as concerns and interests, grief and rejection. Life with others may also generate much fear, frustration, misunderstanding, miscommunication and misunderstanding. Of course, the social exigency does not negate the personal demand to maintain respectful individuality.

Social exigency signifies that individual persons need to be respected and affirmed because as a being the human person is gifted with a value of intrinsic significance. In fact, when individual persons are genuinely

98. Marcel, *The Mystery of Being Vol.II: Faith and Reality*, 5.
99. Marcel, *The Mystery of Being Vol.I: Reflection and Mystery*, 134.
100. Marcel, *Searchings*, 63.
101. Marcel, *Creative Fidelity*, 230.
102. Marcel, *Tragic Wisdom and Beyond*, xxvii.
103. Marcel, *Homo Viator*, 155.

affirmed they cease to be anonymous. The duty of a social being then is to multiply as much as possible bonds between beings, and also to fight as actively as possible against the kind of devouring anonymity that proliferates around us like a cancerous tissue.[104] The crowd, the mass, stifles personal originality and a sense of freedom and responsibility. And the mass is always inimical to and nonsupportive of psychic exigency. Anonymity tends to thrive in the excitement or boredom of the moment.

Social exigency also touches on the questions of gender in certain contexts and the sense of human equality and fraternity. Equality and fraternity also include an understanding that as social beings we are male and female in sexual diversity and relatedness. Our sexuality puts us in a relational space of bonding with others. As male and female, we exist in mutual belongingness and correlation to one another. And here it is important to recognize, with Olsen, that men and women are biologically, anatomically and psychologically different.[105] A healthy relatedness between man and woman needs to consist in representativeness, responsibility and charity which do not admit of subordination and superiority but only functional differentiation.[106] Healthy relatedness implies fraternity where the other is a sibling or a neighbor or companion. In lived fraternity, a person is not unnecessarily anxious about the superiority or inferiority of another because one's thought is not clenched or bound to the question of what one is or what one is worth.[107] The feeling of resentment towards one's neighbor tends to develop step by step with the increasing importance of the administrative function in the world. This is also to say, it develops with the multiplication of parasitical and purely functional relationships or functionary activities which are not only unimaginative but also destined to cripple and finally paralyze every possible sort of really creative activity. Such a situation inevitably develops as soon as activities consisting essentially of control and restraint begin to gain the day over activities which have to be controlled and restrained.[108]

A healthy realization of the social exigency makes possible mutual assent, exchanges and conversations which honor people's strengths and abilities, demands and limitations so that they may work together and

---

104. Marcel, *Man Against Mass Society*, 206.

105. V. Norskov Olsen, *The New Relatedness for Man and Woman in Christ: A Mirror of the Divine* (Loma Linda, California: Loma Linda University Center for Christian Bioethics, 1993), 130.

106. Ibid., 110

107. Marcel, *Man Against Mass Society*, 207.

108. Ibid., 29.

acknowledge each other complementarily. In this way, the expansion and the interdependence of common life can be comforting and encouraging, supportive and flexible. Where people try to act together, they edge themselves around with some form of ceremony or good manners and the observance of this can be an act of reverence for life and for the intrinsic significance of human kinship. This fundamental attitude lies at the root of civility, relational warmth and pleasant social living.

In the final analysis, the social exigency aims at justice and fairness and harmony among persons. Our very nature calls for the satisfaction of our need for the intrinsic value and plenitude of living ties among people. Additionally, this living relation requires that a person recognizes, respects and upholds the dignity of others as well. Interpersonal connectedness is at the heart of living, normally beginning with the humble and intimate levels of human life where persons are exalted or crushed by others in dialectics of struggle and competition. In other words, sociology or anthropology strikes on something deeper than itself, something that constitutes us in our very selfhood.[109] That is also to say, a man's or a woman's given circumstances, when he or she becomes inwardly aware of them, can become *constitutive* of his or her new self.[110]

People have a deep and an entirely natural foundation in and share in the primordial quality of the structure of the world.[111] As a person lives in a place, participates in what it contains or offers which remains inexpressible and inexhaustible, a certain living relationship grows between the person and the place, that is, a creative interchange takes place. And wherever there is a creative interchange between a human subject and the environment, a genuine rootedness takes place and the sphere of the problematic is at the same time transcended.[112] The self seems to endow with a certain quality of its own surroundings which it makes its own. This endowment renders the surroundings habitable to it.[113] In this sense, people's circumstances do not have real, embodied and independent existence outside of the self and its activities. Further, the self's free activities can constitute either an encouragement or an obstacle to the environments.[114]

---

109. Marcel, *The Mystery of Being Vol.I: Reflection and Mystery*, 181.
110. Ibid., 134.
111. Marcel, *Creative Fidelity*, 83.
112. Ibid., 70–71.
113. Ibid., 90.
114. Marcel, *The Mystery of Being Vol.I: Reflection and Mystery*, 134.

The Productive Exigency

This exigency urges us to use responsibly our gifts of imagination, intelligence and freedom to bring about a better society contextually and worldwide. This is the exigency of productivity and creativity of human spirit and labor derived from an understanding of this life as a gift and a task, a challenge and a responsibility. At the same time, production needs to be distinguished from creation. While any production depends on a technique, creation belongs to the meta-technical order. Every creation is a response to a call received.[115] Creation is never a production. Accordingly, it is not without profound significance that:

> We go wrong when we confuse creating with producing. That which is essential in the creator is the act by which he places himself at the disposal of something which, no doubt in one sense depends upon him for its existence, but which at the same time appears to him to be beyond what he is and what he judged himself to be capable of drawing directly and immediately from himself . . . the creative process . . . is none the less effective wherever there is personal development of any kind.[116]

To create is not, essentially, to produce. Creation implies an active receptivity.[117] Freedom exists wherever and whenever creation obtains, even at the humblest levels.[118] Doubtlessly, then, fulfillment takes on positive meaning from the point of view of creation.[119] Moreover, creation is not necessarily the creation of something outside the person who creates. There can be production without creation and there can be creation without any identifiable object remaining to bear witness to the creation. In the course of our lives we probably already know some persons who were essentially creators. The radiance of charity and love shining from their being simply add a positive contribution to the invisible work which gives the human adventure the only meaning which justifies it.[120] In fact:

> Creation is essentially a germination, and it is very difficult not only to know to what extent I can contribute to the initial germ, but also what this question precisely means. It does not seem indeed that I am able to make precise the relation that links the "I"

---

115. Marcel, *The Existential Background of Human Dignity*, 126.
116. Marcel, *Homo Viator*, 25.
117. Marcel, *The Mystery of Being Vol.II: Faith and Reality*, 139.
118. Marcel, *The Existential Background of Human Dignity*, 160.
119. Marcel, *The Mystery of Being Vol.II: Faith and Reality*, 45.
120. Ibid.

to this germ which is present to me. This whole process organizes itself in relation to a work which will have to possess a certain form. What counts is to produce this work which will have to exist by itself and impose itself not only on me but on others.[121]

This fact explains why aesthetic value appears only with the creative process which establishes the intersubjective communion, which offers itself to the appreciation of the artist as well as other possible viewers or listeners.[122] In other words:

> ... it would be a complete mistake to construe the essence of creation as a *making* or as a productive activity whose source is in the agent itself. The same presence and the same appeal to the soul by the Being within it can be found in any creative act whether visible or not; the act the same with itself despite the inexhaustibility of its manifestations, testifies to this same presence, and the soul can challenge or annul it insofar as it is a soul endowed with freedom.[123]

Or again, when I create, I can say neither that I *know* nor that I am purely and simply ignorant of where I am going. "My creation cannot be effected on the basis of a pure and simple desire to create. The desire is in itself sterile; it is only an *I would like*. But it is necessary that something be *present* to me: a character, a situation, a relation, but nothing that can be reduced to an abstract idea."[124] In this respect, invention belongs to the category of what in itself is not invention but creation.[125] Wherever there is creativity, that is to say, liberative affirmation of the human spirit, there is to some degree participation in being.[126] This participation is a demand of free thought.[127] This is to say, *there is being only for me* in the sense that the affirmation of being only has value insofar as it is not the position or the idea of an object but, rather, true participation, a creation.[128] A man or woman is a being who lives and therefore needs to contribute to the realization of *our* end through meaningful personal tasks at which he or she may actually fail.

121. Marcel, *Presence and Immortality*, 169.
122. Marcel, *Tragic Wisdom and Beyond*, 5.
123. Marcel, *Creative Fidelity*, 10.
124. Marcel, *Presence and Immortality*, 168–69.
125. Ibid.
126. Marcel, *Philosophical Fragments*, 84.
127. Ibid., 106.
128. Ibid., 84.

In fact, creativity and productivity relate to human availability in different ways. The state of gestation of the creative individual, who is concentrated on a work he or she wants to bring to fruition and to which he or she gives his or her entire substance, say a piece of art, is the embodiment of his or her vocation and that vocation is related to others and to the world. It is the person's way of giving of himself or herself. Such a person treats himself or herself as at the disposal of or available to others.[129] On the other hand:

> From the moment that I constrict my interest to the form of my finished work and it becomes the center of the world for me; from the moment I judge the words of others in terms of it or judge others according to whether I approve or disapprove of their mode of appreciation of it, it is transformed into a having on which my thought anxiously dotes, something clutched into a dead hand. Thus I pass into a state of radical indisposability. This state must be shattered if I am to be freed.[130]

Consequently, the corrosive and paralyzing element of anxiety and self-enclosing concern can constitute a state of inner inertia wherein the world becomes experienced as stagnation or putrescence. Of course, a human response to experience is free if it is liberative. In a certain sense, we all carry a burden which at critical moments may become unsupportable. The load we carry is the weight of our past, what we wanted to do and did not do, what we wanted to be but are not.[131]

In light of the above, work refers to a specific human activity by which means-ends relations are grasped so that "[t]echnology is something which [man] is obliged from now on to bear, to assume under pain of denying himself. It is not a burden which he can set down in order to lighten his step."[132] Work is an activity of service and care, which when undertaken cooperatively with others, brings whole-hearted joy, admirable growth and a felt sense of fulfillment. At the same time, it may be said that:

> The span of work is . . . no bigger than that of man's movements in their technical capacity. The tools which *homo faber* uses in his natural environment . . . humanise production further since they make it possible to manufacture something to which the craftsman, who completes the work himself, brings greater continuity

---

129. Marcel, *Creative Fidelity*, 53.
130. Ibid.
131. Ibid., 52.
132. Marcel, *Problematic Man*, 53.

and precision, carrying out his plan and giving it harmony of a finished whole.[133]

In working, a person exercises and develops his or her potential for innovation and distinction as well as identity. At the same time, however, work can become problematic and unappealing when it is reduced to merely a function or a task or a role. Work only fosters an enlivening and enduring sense of significance in a context that promotes relish for life.[134] When work is nonproblematic it affirms human subjectivity and kinship with others and there will be joy in such a work. And such joy, understood as warm-heartedness, will be joy which is not only innocent, but even noble. It is a joy which becomes bound up with the consciousness of power over inanimate things, that is to say, over a reality which is subordinate and is in a sense meant to be controlled by man and woman.[135] Beyond the positive value of technical progress, technique serves higher ends of human existence if it is directed ultimately by needs, demands and aspirations that go beyond mere utility. In fact, it is yet to be shown that advancement in social techniques as such induces, or leads to, increases in human contentedness with life or that it leads to growth in the quality of spiritual life. Still, the meaning of every endeavor consists in the work itself and also in the sense of balance between work time and nonwork time, in the joy of knowing and the joy of contemplating.[136]

Whatever a person does or does not do bears deeply upon the person's understanding of life, and living. What a person does shapes the person's attitudes towards self and towards others as well as towards personal values, perspectives and goals. By my work, for example, I become a maker of my own story, in the making of which I also lay myself open to the stories of others and, in the process, remake myself as well. Assessing personal interests at a job is thus not only worthwhile but also essential because:

133. Marcel, *The Decline of Wisdom*, 3.

134. Marcel, *Homo Viator*, 116.

135. Marcel, *The Decline of Wisdom*, 8. Here it must also be pointed out that the physical environment is important and significant for human life and common wellbeing. The technical mastery of the physical environment can go a long way in helping people provide remedial responses to problems that attend life in multiple ways. In fact, a technical approach to the physical environment is needful. At the same time, it must be emphasized that the physical environment is not simply a field for working out and exploiting technical possibilities without turning the process of technical inquiry into, perhaps, a catastrophic venture which adversely affects human life and ways of living. What is more, sustained care for the environment is tied up with the question of existential captivity which propels greed, fear and all kinds of covetous desires.

136. Marcel, *Searchings*, 39.

> From the moment in which my own job, which I nevertheless do not want to lose, ceases to interest me, my interest will tend to be obliquely towards the other man's job. And in the other man and his job, I shall hardly see . . . anything more than a threat to myself . . . the person . . . who damages my self-esteem . . .[137]

Work is a task, an office and service we do or an enterprise we undertake, not only for ourselves but also for others and the community. This means that an individual at work cannot ignore the wellbeing of others. Concern for and solidarity with others in our work is very important because in every living context "the more exclusively it is I who exist, the less do I exist; and conversely, the more I free myself from the prison of ego-centrism, the more do I exist."[138] When we work in partnership and solidarity with others, our work fulfills us. As a milieu of encounter, solidarity is a wellspring for often-inconceivable actions that involve others positively.[139]

The foregoing consideration on solidarity signifies that an over-emphasis, or an exclusive emphasis, on fame and achievement at work that ignores or mischaracterizes the well-being of others, degenerates into the idol-making of the genius, star, or celebrity. This attitude easily debases persons in the name of efficiency, for a man or woman is instrumentalized as he or she becomes a mere instrument for production and profit-making. This is why it must be laid down that *the less men and women are thought of as beings the stronger will be the temptation to use them as machines which are capable of a given output.*[140] This further implies that a person becomes worth as much as he or she produces. When people are conceived as mere units of production and their feelings lose all importance, devaluation of the sacredness and subjectivity of people occurs.[141]

In a context where people fail to uphold the sacredness of human life, the weak, the sick and the old correspondingly lose their social and personal significance. Loss of appreciation for the sacredness of life impoverishes people's reverence for and duties towards neighbors and those in need and at the margins of society. In such circumstance, employees may stay in their places of work out of the fear of being sacked or of sanctions which may range from fines to deportation; or become merely stimulated to work

---

137. Marcel, *Man Against Mass Society*, 30.
138. Marcel, *The Mystery of Being Vol. II: Faith and Reality*, 34.
139. Marcel, *Fresh Hope for the World*, 5.
140. Marcel, *The Mystery of Being Vol. II: Faith and Reality*, 148.
141. Marcel, *The Decline of Wisdom*, 17.

out of the expectation of some reward, promotion or a bonus.[142] This is a functionalized world in which people get through a task simply because it is a task or because it brings favor or income. No interior identification with one's work takes place nor do relationships which obtain at work truly come to bear any sense of intrinsic significance. Even others' success, which should be a cause for celebration of the gift and identity of the other, can only generate jealousy, envy and resentment of that other. The blessings of another can only be a curse for me. In such a milieu, people easily stab each other's backs and step on each other's toes without any qualms. Suspicion, competition, paranoia and neurosis become common staples of existence. What should bring joy ends up bringing sorrow and as dividedness comes to rule human relations, liveliness is sucked out of people lives. Certainly, it becomes difficult to realize and foster the common good: "an anthropology with a functionalist commitment has no place for anything in the nature of dignity."[143] Within this framework, technical skills easily become dangerous as they cannot be put at the service of meta-technical ends. And while science may not disavow these ends outright it tends to simply ignore them.[144] Technological advancement can blind people to true human values.

However, as a working being a person can transcend a functionalized world in that the functionalized world can exist only insofar as it is willed and accepted. A person may be involved in that world and yet retain the power to redefine, modify or reject it. He or she modifies, redefines and rejects it in the degree to which he or she succeeds in humanizing the relations uniting him or her to superiors, relations and, most of all, to his or her inferiors (people below one in social standing, one way or the other).[145] Further, insofar as power and authority are part and parcel of the understanding of work, the danger of domination and exploitation will always remain real for many people. Subsequently, the exercise of offices or authority at work requires a certain professional sense of care and sensitivity as well as fairness and justice. After all, values hang together.[146]

Material satisfaction is important in work. In fact, it is a necessary condition for human living. At the same time, the notion of human life cannot be reduced to that of the harmonious functioning of a number of

---

142. Marcel, *Man Against Mass Society*, 203.
143. Marcel, *The Existential Background of Human Dignity*, 164.
144. Marcel, *Searchings*, 38.
145. Marcel, *The Mystery of Being Vol.II: Faith and Reality*, 43.
146. Ibid., 165.

organs, although that is presupposed in the notion of human life.[147] That is, material satisfaction is not the sole content of the sort of wondrous human life for which people incessantly yearn. The material reward of work does not exhaust a person's totality and possibilities of self-fulfillment. However financially rewarding my work, for example, is, it remains inadequate before the question of who I am which relates to the question of my life as a whole. Who I am depends on my relation to myself, to the world, to fellow men and women and to the circumstances in which I find myself. It also includes being in this or that way of life, this or that field of values. Human life is not biological functioning pure and simple, rather everything human truly hinges on spiritual life.[148] In fact, every meaningful activity needs to embrace the spiritual, mental and bodily aspects of a person's life; when that embrace takes place creativity and productivity follow.

In the final analysis, productive exigency embraces the personal sense of respect as well as accomplishment and achievements. And it is in the light of the significance of productive exigency that we are able to appreciate and understand the poignancy of unemployment.

> Unemployment is first seen from outside as a fact. It tends to become boredom or tedium as it becomes more conscious. The unemployed appears to himself to be unattached and even cast away by what is real, as it were to some desert shore; it seems to him that life has no more use for him . . . What eats into him is the more or less distinct sense of life's almost inconceivable cruelty . . . Here unemployment borders on despair; despair is nothing but unemployment which has attained the most acute self-consciousness . . . it is the breaking of an engagement, the desertion of conscience which has no further part in reality . . . The unemployed or the man without hope . . . is not only someone who no longer gives anything, he is someone who has lost the power of animating the world in which he feels he has been thrown, and where he is superfluous.[149]

When linked and connected appropriately with one another the vital exigencies lead to healthy living and human relations. They balance individuals with one another and with the community and the wider society. In consequence, a person learns proper life skills, and develops both better capacities for judgments and a better sense of their motivation. With a healthy degree of self-awareness and sense of self informed by good judgments, an individual becomes open to learning, is willing to adapt

147. Marcel, *The Mystery of Being Vol.I: Reflection and Mystery*, 81–82.
148. Marcel, *Searchings*, 33.
149. Marcel, *Homo Viator*, 145–46.

to situations and grow in generous and imaginative attitudes toward life. Moreover, such a person's responsible sense of initiative will also promote an appreciation of ready and reflective service and common courtesies.

As a person strives to grow in self-understanding and self-knowledge, he or she also develops a searching and learning attitude towards life. This further entails an acceptance of life's invitations to grow, through positive presence and filial participation in community life and activities in terms of thoughtfulness, charity, appreciation, interdependence, openness, personal hygiene and dependability. A person with a healthy sense of the vital exigencies practices appropriate manners in dealing with people, and exercises, through conversations and attitudes, personal sacrifices and love, familial concern for their wellbeing in contexts of dedication and joyful availability. Of course, genuine interior silence also permeates the person who understands and appreciates the creativity, self-acceptance, self-criticism and evaluation that the vital exigencies necessitate in the forging of a wise, responsible and coherent view of life.

The Vital Exigencies and Liberative Morality

While morality requires the elements of freedom, truth, significance, commitment and a sense of self for it to be actuated, it gains a concrete foothold in existence through these exigencies. The dimensions or realms of the vital exigencies play practical roles in the choices and decisions that enable people to act with fairness, honesty and truth telling through those various levels of interpersonal relations and dealings which foster human coexistence. In so acting in accordance with the positive energies of the exigencies, people recognize, respect and cultivate liberating morality. Morality does not take place in a vacuum; it takes place in situations which call for judgments and particular choices of conduct. Whatever kinds of vital exigencies come into play or make alliance in moral considerations give particular shape to the choices that people make.

The vital exigencies imply that within a given set of circumstances, particular norms cannot claim absolute validity in all contexts of interpersonal relations. Within a given set of circumstances, norms pertaining to specific exigencies exert relative validity. In all relational and contextual situations, relative values which come with specific exigencies must be balanced against the relative values of other exigencies in order to determine what response a moral situation may demand. Within a given situation that involves several cultural factors, variables and information, what is morally good, right or obligatory truly becomes what is the most appropriate thing to do. In such a case, a person will be absolutely obliged to actuate a particular course of action or response. The exigencies offer an interpretative framework for bringing demands, feelings and inclinations into play and for insisting on the struggle or tension which is necessary for every significant decision.

Coming to grips with the exigencies particularizes choices and decisions in specific kinds of positive morality within given contexts. The narratives, logic and interior momentum of morality which take into account, harness, interpret and reconstitute the relative values which spring from the exigencies, promote a healthy sense of self and of life with others. Such morality not only partakes of expansive and creative consciousness, it also moves life in the world towards greater compassion, harmony and peace, symbolically and actually. Such a perfomative morality, insofar as it is creative (shaping), maintains, renews and expands self-experience and a commitment to live in certain positive and appropriate ways. In its milieu, a person does not experience life merely through the veil of the chattering and self-conscious ego. In its resulting re-creation, the ego also diminishes as it gradually begins to cease to interpose itself between the acting human subject and the lifeworld. A person then experiences himself or herself as part of a larger spiritual heritage. Further, such morality manifests an experiential, imaginative and creative sense of wholeness that connects and actively restores persons to others and to the experience of their depths. Persons become committed to others and to encouraging and embodying liberative paths of living. This experience also shifts people's attitudes to responsibility, service, light-heartedness, meaningfulness and re-creation, all of which are different ways of affirming personal identity and the sense of community. In the end, liberative morality works within the framework of hope, which allows people to experience themselves as part of an inward and relational significance that transcends them, expressing itself differently according to circumstance, time and place.

It is in light of the exigencies that it also becomes significant to speak of heroic acts like giving one's life for one's friends. Such acts are noble precisely because they transcendently manifest and express the demands of particular exigencies. Acting according to the excellences of the exigencies qualifies acts as heroic or of great moral worth. What is more, the exigencies are also a sign that a person's self-transcendence need not undermine their capacities for continual wellbeing and a reasonable degree of self-reliance and self-determination or interdependence. In this regard, to be deficient in self-respect through neglect or timidity, for example, in ways that allow oneself to be abused, manipulated, controlled, emotionally blackmailed, or taken advantage of by another, is to be undermine the healthy promotion of psychic exigency. On the other hand, an excessive concern with profitability, control, efficiency and effectiveness of one's work fails to foster a healthy social exigency. In the business world, if a firm, for example, does not pay attention to the welfare of its environing society and other business partners, the firm will fail at building needed trust which makes possible and strengthens business security, good public image and workers' productivity. In this regard, it may also fail to offer existential incentives against bribery, espionage and workers' theft. In other words, even productive exigency demands the support and tenor of psychological and social exigencies.

Implications of the Vital Exigencies

The mutual participation of the exigencies in each other makes each of them complex, dynamic and self-transcending. There is a certain movement of convergence and divergence of the different types of exigencies. The appreciation of the exigencies this way implies that the more fixedly the reduction of living to subsisting becomes for persons, the less persons shall be tempted to assign, no need to say dignity, but merely a positive meaning to the expression: *my life*. For everything comes to occur as though an anonymous quality of social life has progressively invaded persons to the point where it abolishes in them any temptation to see in their destiny a line of development, particular characteristics or visage. In the final analysis, people come to acknowledge little more than pleasure and pain, and lose the vitality to resist this internally collectivized existence.[150]

The exigencies require a certain minimum of their realization for a man or woman to survive, live and flourish. They signify that a human subject has original and specific abilities and duties to discover as well as a need to establish how his or her life as an individual and as a member of the community can flourish. "The existent being which I am is defined by the multiplicity of possibilities or of possible actions which are in me; they constitute a network or gridiron which confers a meaning upon things or places them in a certain totality which we call the world"[151] Personal destiny is by no means a solitary affair; it involves participating in the vicissitudes of life that engage others. The "existent subject is such only in his relation to the world."[152] Stated differently, a being has value in the

---

150. Marcel, *Creative Fidelity*, 94.
151. Marcel, *Problematic Man*, 111.
152. Ibid., 112.

precise measure in which, through his or her example and work, he or she will have developed and renewed our human reasons for loving. But this power can be turned against being, that is, against love.[153] The exigencies point to the decisiveness of personal and interpersonal connectedness at the heart of both the human subject and of human existence.

Also, the exigencies establish the dynamic character of hope in persons and human relations. If in the search for riches, pleasure, power and security a person undermines the quest for identity, dignity, justice, or truth, that is, values of being, then a person becomes less human as he or she gives himself over to the world of functions that ultimately have no continuing reference to intrinsic significance. It is precisely for this reason that life in a world centered upon the idea of function is exposed to despair, because in reality it rings hollow.[154] A person need not shrink from sacrificing material ends if the being of the human person and human kinship demands such sacrifice, because there is an unfuntionalizable and mysterious element, a human unconditional preciousness or dignity, in every human being and every living relationship.[155] The notions of personal dignity and the intrinsic worth of living ties among people imply that every person and every human community has intrinsic value that cannot be relativized.

The personal distinguishes itself by self-consciousness and awareness of others, intelligence, will, appreciation of values, relationships with others, ability to choose between possibilities, capacity to respond to situations and responsibility for what is decided and done. Conscious purpose awareness of value lies at the heart of the personal reality. In effect, personal being may be described as a unity in continuity of knowing, willing and caring. To be a human mind connects profoundly with the essence of personal being. With the foregoing affirmations, suffering connects closely with the human mode of life which says not only *no* to poverty, death and misery in our world but also *yes* to life, love of freedom, justice and peace and their glories. Suffering expresses our lived *yes* and *no* with regard to the joy of living and loving what is of human worth in this world.

The exigencies are grounded in the aspiration and demand for intrinsic value. Within this framework, a certain revolutionary fervor expressed by *I belong to this or that cause* does not seem separable from a feeling, both acute and intense, of the opposing forces which threaten to destroy the work one has dedicated oneself to. This *I belong to* implies the awareness of

---

153. Marcel, *Presence and Immortality*, 128.
154. Marcel, *Problematic Man*, 139.
155. Ibid., 47.

a contest which is engaged, which can therefore be lost, and for the sake of which one completely exposes oneself, rather than an attitude of detachment or reserve. Conversely, *I belong to* is degraded just to the extent that the reality to which it subordinates itself is consolidated and stabilized, hence becoming like a machine of which I am a gear.[156] *I belong to* means that the more I identify myself with a certain closed system of determinate interests, the more hollow and illusory this formula is shown to be. Basically, it can be reduced to a protest against certain intrusions which are disturbing my peace. It is quite different, however, when the self affirms itself as a creative power, as freedom or as a thinking being. In the end, I can validly assert that *I belong to myself* only insofar as I create myself, that is, where it must be admitted that I do not belong to myself.[157]

The Vital Exigencies, Responsibilities, Rights

The exigencies, being inseparably linked to the fact of existing, constitute basic requirements and demands for self-determination, judgment and accepting responsibility for *this life* in order to come to grips with participating in *this world*. And *this world* refers to the global sense in which my possibilities are projected upon the background, obscure and devoid of meaning, of raw realities.[158] The person who finds himself or herself engaged in this world of the demands of the exigencies experiences deep within himself or herself the call that there be *being*, that is to say, that everything not be reduced to a game of successive and inconsistent appearances. This life is not of no intrinsic significance or merely "a tale told by an idiot."[159] The unity of being constitutes the original font out of which springs, develops and grows the multiplicity of human exigencies and experiences. In fact, it must also be stated clearly as a consequence that the exigency of being gives depth, direction and unity to all the other exigencies and, with them, to the whole human personality and community.

The significance of the exigencies lies in the conviction that human beings and human kinship or living ties among persons bear an unconditional value that grounds and catalyzes the capacities for moral sense, sensitivity and reverential respect for the integrity and health of human existence. In short, a human being deserves respect and moral consideration. In moral

---

156. Marcel, *Creative Fidelity*, 96.
157. Ibid.
158. Marcel, *Problematic Man*, 111.

159. Ibid., 139. Here it may be pointed out also that "a tale told by an idiot" is a phrase that Gabriel Marcel takes from William Shakespeare's *Macbeth, Act V, scene v.*

decision making or in discerning wise counsels, it becomes important to recognize others' welfare, respect their rights and, as far as reasonable, further their interests and wellbeing. Furthermore, a person's considered judgments cannot ignore his or her personal concerns and needs and the liberty to act on those judgments. Besides, the exigencies imply that it is impermissible for persons to use their powers to humiliate or degrade others, as it violates their dignity and sense of relational trust, self-esteem, self-respect and relational wholesomeness. In effect, the exigencies impose upon people the inherent sense, demand and obligation to recognize that their own and others' wellbeing hang together: they rise and fall at the same time.

Persons need something of permanent value and significance, namely, not merely of functional value. So, because the exigencies are grounded in intrinsic value and significance, they entitle us as human subjects to rights and responsibilities which interpenetrate and reinforce one another. In other words, because human persons and human kinships are gifted with intrinsic value, that is, dignity, then they have the rights and responsibilities to care for and protect, sustain and promote their worth, desirability and attractiveness as persons. Yet to merely emphasize *my* rights, *my* life and *my* freedom distorts my pursuit of wellbeing and to distort the fact of being a human person. The human subject is constituted not only by inward relatedness but also by a recognition and commitment towards the well-being of others, that is, a milieu of responsibilities understood as supra-functional.[160] Because bonding is a fundamental tissue of human living both inwardly and interpersonally, what must be postulated as equal are rights and duties or responsibilities which people must reciprocally recognize; for if that recognition is lacking, we have chaos or the primacy of the most vile over the most noble.[161] Of course, because existential insecurity characterizes social and contextual living, rights of people remain continually exposed to all kinds of infringements and violations. Rights can be rendered nugatory through the ways people behave and act towards and relate with one another. Hope constitutes and expresses the context within which rights arise and from which their expansive meaning gain sense, is understood and engaged. In addition, it is within the perspective of hope that the sensibility of rights emerges and identifies itself from the employment of vital exigencies.

Rights and responsibilities are necessary and inseparable; their stimuli, demands and enveloping meanings have grips on history so that they feed and correct each other. When rights and responsibilities go together they

---

160. Ibid., 47.
161. Marcel, *Man Against Mass Society*, 161.

lead to an ongoing transformation of histories. When combined and they become increasingly integrated, rights and responsibilities build expressive and awesome realities and situations of human life. Subsequently, to pursue only *my rights* without acknowledging *my responsibilities* in personal and social spheres can lead to hostility, conflicts and chaos. Without a sense of responsibility on my part, my freedom can deteriorate into domination over people weaker than me. In a relationship of friendship, it could mean subordinating the other to my demands and, in fact, making my relationship conditional upon exclusive personal ends or needs.

Correlation of rights and responsibilities implies that every individual acknowledges sincerely not only his or her rights, but also his or her own duties towards others and the common good. Endowment with, bestowal of and sensibility towards rights go hand in hand with, touch on and imply consciousness of duties or sensitivity towards responsibilities. In this light, the right to freedom of speech, for example, coexists intimately with the sensibility of press responsibility. Rights and responsibilities correlate:

> Democracy, considered not in its principles but in its actual achievements, has helped in the most baleful manner to encourage *claiming* in all its aspects, the demanding of rights—and indeed to bring a mercenary spirit into all human relationships . . . Each individual claims from the start to enjoy the same consideration and the same advantages as his neighbour; and, in fact, his self-respect tends to resolve into an attitude which is not only defensive but ever claiming rights from others. Thus he considers it beneath his dignity to do anything whatsoever for nothing.[162]

A social atmosphere that is only rooted in the claim for rights always sows mistrust, not only of others but of life itself that makes a person less and less a vital milieu of hope and joy.[163] Freedom of rights implies and requires freedom for responsibilities. The fundamental rights of and responsibilities for subsistence, security and participatory liberties make possible the enforcement of human accountability, appreciation of social ills and human promotion. Basic civil freedoms and responsibilities must not be squelched and become subordinated to selfish or sectarian economic and political interests.

In fact, to recognize that responsibilities and rights correlate is to accept that pain and sacrifice are necessary constituents of this life. Rights require a sense of responsibility. It is in fact ludicrous for a person to claim

---

162. Marcel, *Homo Viator*, 56.
163. Ibid., 57.

rights while he or she ignores his or her responsibilities to family, community, society or self. As a citizen, for instance, it is not enough that I have a right to defend myself against the dictatorship of my local district officer, I need to see how I also meet my civic responsibilities in terms of whether I relate with others in good faith, with respect for personal or property rights or with respect towards the reputation of others.

> If we look at . . . a citizen of a free country, we notice that he is subjected to all kinds of obligations—taxes, the military, and so forth. These obligations are part of what it means to be a citizen, and . . . if a man tried to evade them he would do so only in the name of a false or at least childish notion of freedom. It must be added that a country can remain free only if its citizens live up to their obligations . . . a citizen, to the extent that he is conscious of what his citizenship implies, tends . . . to recognize that he cannot flee [an] obligation, however painful it is, without endangering the community to which he belongs and which, after all, lets him be what he is.[164]

Responsibilities and rights cannot be separated in the light of human exigencies; they are the fruitful sides of every human exigency. A right in a given context entails a responsibility to that context in terms of duty. For example, a right to life entails the responsibility, for instance, that when an illness impinges on the being of the person, he or she has to define his attitude towards it.[165] That is to say, the comportment of a person suffering illness may manifest and teach others their own sense of responsibility before adversity.

Responsibilities and rights are inalienable because they are deeply rooted in the exigencies and manifest who a human subject is and his or her privilege as a being. Rights and responsibilities flow directly and simultaneously from the being of the human subject. The human subject as a being, for instance, explains why "I cannot delegate to the political party of which I am a member the right to decide what I am and what I am worth, without becoming guilty of a total alienation of my rights and my privileges which is really equivalent to suicide."[166] What is more:

> . . . it may in fact be maintained that party membership threatens either to sustain a continuous division between the words or gestures of a man and his true thoughts or feelings, or, what is

---

164. Marcel, *Tragic Wisdom and Beyond*, 84.
165. Marcel, *The Mystery of Being Vol.I: Reflection and Mystery*, 209.
166. Ibid., 152.

no less fortunate, to culminate in the enlistment of the soul itself, discipline becoming internalized to the point where all inner spontaneity is eliminated. The more organized the part, the more it encourages either hypocrisy or spiritual subservience.[167]

We also need to acknowledge that a fraternal world requires that we recognize the character and complementarities of responsibilities and rights as prerequisites for peaceful co-existence. This understanding has a bearing, for example, on global disarmament so that "I do not accept for myself the right to advocate unilateral disarmament which, circumstances permitting could deliver the free world, without possible recourse, to the attacks of an opponent to whom conscience is merely a word without a content."[168] Mutual disarmament requires mutual trust which comes through peaceful adjustments of human relations, sincerity in negotiations and fulfillments of promises and obligations. In consequence, responsibilities and rights are linked inseparably to living although they are also continually exposed to infringements, assaults or abdication. In any case, there is little doubt that today men or women systematically infringe upon principles which they are perfectly well aware of; even more, with an unparalleled impudence, the very men or women who are trampling these principles underfoot do not cease to invoke them and to lend their own authority to the underlying ideas (democracy, liberty and so on).[169]

The correlation of responsibilities with rights is sustained by vigilance—staying awake, fighting against the sleep of indifference or non-wakefulness to the milieu of intrinsic value.[170] Nonetheless, it needs to be underscored that responsibilities establish the limits of rights. In short, rights embody participatory ways of exercising the authority of intrinsic value. Rights also regulate relations of the individual and communities with one another. Besides, rights preserve the individuality of the human subject while responsibilities authenticate bonds of human freedom and commitments. Responsibilities spring from the intrinsic worth of persons and a deep sense of human kinship.

Conclusion

Being realistic about the experience and expression of hope involves language that influences the way we see the world, and articulates the require-

167. Marcel, *Creative Fidelity*, 157.
168. Marcel, *Philosophical Fragments*, 15.
169. Marcel, *Man Against Mass Society*, 224.
170. Marcel, *Philosophical Fragments*, 12–13.

ments and demands of life in a given set of circumstances or context. The articulation of the requirements and demands of life arising from the exigencies is necessary. Such articulation not only re-creates the world but also the human subject, human kinship and the sense of life's intrinsic significance. Language and the promptings of the exigencies concretely make possible the description and explanation of strivings and critiques in human life that people bring to bear on particular situations. Understanding the exigencies throws some light on how to grasp the sense of achievement and frustration, self-regard and self-doubt people experience and live with in many situations. The quest for opportunity and a decent life, comfort and joy are grounded in the demands for the full life.

Subsequently, the relational character of the human subject who is able to nurture and promote hope is tied up with the vital demands of the exigencies without which the human subject loses the sense of value of intrinsic significance. And because the exigencies are rooted in the urge for being, they ground and tie together rights and responsibilities.

When the exigencies are actualized in rights and responsibilities, they bring about qualities of attention and focus that integrate the lives of persons, social interactions and human relationships. Because they have the same grounding in the exigencies, rights and responsibilities together form an inextricable network of mutuality for an ever-fuller living. Also, they allow all persons to express themselves actively and resourcefully in lives of commitment that hold promises and that urge people towards a future of hope. The focus of the next chapter is on the character and élan of commitment in life.

7

The Meaning of Commitment

The Complex Issue of Commitment

A SOCIETY that fails to keep promises, disregards contracts, breaks oaths or violates and abandons commitments at will simply falls apart. The fact of people keeping their commitments is one of the cohesive forces of society. When people keep their commitments they help keep social interactions and society from falling into chaos. Commitment is as human a question as health, love, mortality and security. Even people who want to be free of commitments count on the fact that there will be others who will remain committed in their lives while they exercise their right to be free of everyone. People commit themselves to causes, to things and persons in a variety of ways, with a variety of motivations or complexity of intentions. People benefit and suffer, rise and fall, are honored and broken on the basis of commitments that touch on their lives. A commitment can be successful and rewarding. But when people become overly focused on their commitments it could indicate that something is wrong or that there is tension or that their commitments are in jeopardy. Moreover, when a person becomes over-committed, their personality merges into and is consumed by the object of their commitments. As a result, their personality fails to develop as they oversubscribe to the object of their commitments. Nonetheless, people commit themselves to either values or persons. In this regard:

> . . . is it not quite evident that the judgment of value, or, more precisely, the metaphysical appreciation which is called for by the ontological demand itself, cannot possibly depend in any way on the empirical conditions in which our experience, analysed more or less carefully, allows us to recognise the insistence and nature of this demand?[1]

---

1. Marcel, *Being and Having*, 39.

People do not simply commit themselves to the continued experiences of wishes and cravings or to the trivial attractions of life. Commitment pertains to matters of personal significance.

In her book, *The Creative Communication: 399 Tools to Communicate Commitment Without Boring People to Death,* Barbara A. Glanz quotes Albert Schweitzer thus: "The power of ideals is incalculable. We see no power in a drop of water. But let it get into a crack in the rock and be turned into ice, and it splits the rock; turned into steam, it drives the pistons of the most powerful engines. Something happened to it, which makes active and effective power that is latent in it."[2] Glanz adds that "Commitment is a lot like that. If commitment to an organization's beliefs and values is communicated sincerely, powerfully and creatively, members of that organization will be inspired in a new way to take action to make those beliefs and values a reality."[3]

Cameron Thompson makes the point that, in the past, the word "dedication" was more commonly used to suggest the same absorption of one's self in a cause or principle.[4] However, we may ask:

> What, then, [makes] commitment itself worth examination as a significant value? A list of names taken from this century alone suggests an answer: Gandhi, Schweitzer, Lenin, Madame Curie, Picasso, Martin Luther King, [Mandela, Nyerere]. Such people (and, of course, many others) evidence a superior capacity to identify themselves with a purpose fully believed . . .[5]

From the above citations, we notice that commitment is linked with beliefs, values, purposes and reality. Also, the question of commitment precedes that of fidelity which derives its meaning and significance in its light. Fidelity is never to oneself; it refers to the hold that another being has over us.[6] Further, there can be no question of commitment unless some identity has been posited. The identity question cannot be simply abstract; it is the identity of a particular directed will. The more abstract this will is, the more a person becomes a prisoner of form and builds up a wall between himself or herself and life. It is quite different where there is

---

2. Barbara A. Glanz, *The Creative Communicator: 399 Tools to Communicate Commitment without Boring People to Death* (Homewood, Il.: Business One Irwin, 1993), 2.

3. Ibid.

4. Cameron Thompson, *Philosophy and Literature: Truth/Beauty/Goodness/Commitment* (New York: Harcourt Brace Jovanovich, 1969), 391.

5. Ibid.

6. Marcel, *Being and Having,* 46.

at the root of commitment a fundamental apprehension directed towards Being or towards a human being.[7]

No act of commitment is possible except for beings who can be distinguished from their own momentary situations and who *recognize* this difference between themselves and their situation. Such beings treat themselves as somehow transcending their own life-process and capable of answering for themselves. The less twisted the life-process the easier will be the task of making a commitment.[8] All commitment is partly unconditional, that is to say, it is of its essence to imply that we shall disregard some variable elements of the situation which form the basis of our entering commitment.[9] What is more, there is not commitment purely from my own side; commitment always implies that some value or another being has a hold over me. All commitment is a response. A one-sided commitment would not only be rash but also could be blamed as an act of pride.[10]

Furthermore, commitment is not motivated simply by results; at its core lies the question of faithfulness or fidelity. Besides, I have no right to enter upon a commitment which it will be materially impossible for me to keep or rather which I should know to be so, if I were perfectly sincere. In other words, in matters of commitment I have no right to frivolity.[11] In the end:

> there must be absolute commitment, entered upon by the whole of myself, or at least by something real in myself which could not be repudiated without repudiated by the whole—and which would be addressed to the whole of Being and would be made in the presence of that whole. That is faith. Obviously repudiation is still a possibility here, but cannot be justified by a change in the subject or object; it can only be explained by a *fall*.[12]

Commitment to God needs to be seen as an act of transcendence that has its ontological counterpart in the hold that God has over a person. This hold is the term in relation to which even a person's freedom is ordered and defined.[13] So, to ask oneself how one can think of God is to enquire in

---

7. Ibid., 43.
8. Ibid., 42.
9. Ibid., 41.
10. Ibid., 46.
11. Ibid., 45.
12. Ibid., 45–46.
13. Ibid., 54.

which sense one can be with Him or Her.[14] In fact, the gap between Truth and Being fills up, in a manner, *of itself,* the moment we really experience the presence of God.[15] Socially, a person lays himself or herself open to painful sanctions if they fail in their commitments.[16]

A Concrete Approach to Understanding Commitment

It is common to hear people saying for example, Caroline is committed to her studies, Duffy is committed to his Jesuit life, Maureen is committed to her marriage, Catherine is a committed friend.[17] Do these assertions mean the same thing? That is, is being committed to studies the same as being committed to Jesuit life as well as being committed to a marriage or being a committed friend? In any case, what makes all these commitments?

In the above assertions, each claim has the word commitment and the usage of this word is in the same sense in every claim. However, the objects of this word are different. The object of commitment in the first claim is studies, in the second, Jesuit life, in the third, marriage and in the fourth, friendship. This analysis raises the question: before whom does a person make a commitment? What is the underlying ground of commitment from which all other objects of commitment take their character? In other words, what is the essence or the constantly abiding element in a commitment?

From the above observations, we recognize that commitment can have different objects. These objects are better conceived as values. Values capture and posit authentic possibilities which people work to actuate and achieve. Thus, a value is something worth living or dying for. People find meaning in striving to incarnate values in their lives. The quest for values is tied up with the quest for meaning in life as that which engages our ultimate attention and loyalty. In fact:

14. Ibid., 32.
15. Ibid., 22.
16. Ibid., 45.
17. It is of decisive importance to note at the outset that there are different levels of commitments so that commitments to friendship or studies, for instance, do not exist at par with marital commitment or the commitment to a vowed religious life. Honoring pledges in the latter forms of commitment tend to involve a person more fully than the former—in a profound way, they affect a person's self-perception, self-definition and life's direction. In so being, they also tend to take priority over other competing concerns. In a sense, then, the profound significance of a given commitment needs to be appraised in relation to its object. Whatever the case may be, a commitment translates dedication to simple truths of action and parallels between commitments need to be understood analogically.

The Meaning of Commitment

> The quest for meaning in life is not a search for an answer to the question, What is *the* meaning of life? That is not an intelligible question. The quest for meaning in life is a quest for something worth living for, something that will redeem our lives from the superficiality and pointlessness of mere temporality. That quest is satisfied when we are grasped by the inherent worthwhileness of some task—any task—that engages our efforts and our loyalty. Meaning in life is a dividend that is bestowed upon those who invest some portion of their lives in something they believe to be worthy of that investment.[18]

As such, values confer meaning and put an effective term upon our lives, demand our loyalty and confront us along the pathway of life. Consequently:

> Life is experienced as meaningful insofar as it is lived in the service of values that impress us as being worthy of our efforts. If one is grasped by the terrible spectacle of human suffering caused by disease, and in response devotes one's life to the prevention and cure of disease and its consequence, one finds meaning in so doing. If one is moved to action by an awareness of the awful human consequences of ignorance, and in response spends one's best efforts in the overcoming of ignorance, one experiences a sense of meaning in the process.[19]

To some extent, commitment, it seems, always pertains to some value that confers meaning on our lives, demands personal allegiance and confronts us with particular choices along life's path.

Undoubtedly, commitment is always either to something or somebody. But this something or somebody must be conceived in terms of a value or as a dwelling place of value. Duffy is formally committed to Jesuit life, Caroline to studies, Maureen to marriage and Catherine to friendship. The object of commitment is always believed to be valuable, worthwhile. Duffy cannot commit himself to Jesuit life if he believed that Jesuit life was trivial or terrible or bland; nor could Caroline or Maureen or Catherine be respectively committed to studies, marriage and friendship.

Apart from the objects of commitment, let us look at the subjects of commitment. Who makes a commitment? As already pointed out, Caroline is the one who is committed to her studies, Duffy to his Jesuit life, Maureen to her marriage and Catherine to her friendship. This question, however, will be answered adequately when we examine the meta-

18. Halverson, 467.
19. Ibid., 466.

physical character of commitment, though at the outset it may be set forth that the subject of commitment is a person, that is, a person capable of perceiving or conceiving values. And these values engage personally the one who commits himself or herself. That is, Caroline is committed to her studies because she values them; her studies constitute a value. This too applies to Duffy, Maureen and Catherine. They, too, value the objects of their commitment. For, in a commitment, it is a value that a person dedicates himself or herself towards. So, it is not simply on the basis of tastes or liking that people are led to the pledge of commitment. A person can like something and still fail to be committed to it. For example, I may like jokes but I am not committed to them. But how do we know that so-and-so is committed to his or her object of commitment? Of course, one way to ascertain an answer to this question is by means of careful observation of the consistency or the focus that a person gives in lived experience or their personal reflections towards some embodied value.

Apart from the external observation in which the subjects' character concurs with our understanding of these subjects' objects of commitment, there is no other way we can judge whether a person is committed or not. A person may challenge the conclusions of observation by asking: how do we ascertain truly that a certain person is committed to this and not that? Even then, how do we know that the person may not be lying or pretending? Consider the following dilemma:

> I am visiting an invalid; I notice that my visit has given him more pleasure than I expected; on the other hand, I understand his solitude better, his suffering, succumbing to an irresistible impulse, I commit myself to come to see him regularly. It is quite clear that when I make this promise to him, my mind definitely does not dwell on the fact that my present disposition is capable of changing ... Let us assume that I have been invited to a play which I want to see and that the performance takes place precisely at the time that the invalid is expecting my visit. But I have promised, I have to keep my promise; what helps me to do so is of course the thought of the disappointment inflicted on the invalid if I break my word, and also the idea that I could not give him the real reason for doing so because it would hurt him. Nevertheless, I go to his bedside unwillingly; at the same time I reflect that if he knew the mood in which I kept my engagement, my visit would not bring him any pleasure; it would even be painful to him. Therefore, I have to act a part. Hence the paradox ... that fidelity—or at any rate the appearance of fidelity—in the eyes of the other, and a lie in my own eyes, mutually imply one another and cannot be separated.

> The truth is that in this situation there is something, which does not depend on me; it does not rest with me to prefer the play to the visit, which has become an irksome duty.[20]

So, from a spectator's perspective, there appears to be some routine in the behavior of a committed person. This behavior may appear as a habitual conformity, that is, an act of mere adherence. Could we say, then, that to be constant in one's behavior or to conform to a particular routine or habit is equivalent to or, rather, is commitment?

On the other hand, to say that so-and-so is committed to someone or something is to implicate a certain sense of faithfulness. Unmistakably, to be committed to some person or something is at the same time to make a claim of faithfulness to them. That is, Caroline is faithful to her studies, Duffy to his Jesuit life, Maureen to her marriage and Catherine to her friendship. At the same time, however, it needs to be pointed out that faithfulness stands in contrast with constancy and conformism. To be faithful implies taking one's past into account and accepting in freedom and choosing it again as one's own, particularly regarding one's commitment. Faithful persons resituate and reconstitute themselves in the experience of kinship and communion; this is a process that remains an ongoing process.

Yet to the external observer, commitment may veritably be appreciated as an experience of conformity or constancy. However, to the subject who makes a commitment, it remains an act and experience of fidelity associated with some particularized exigency that makes access to the experience and expression of the full life a real possibility. If commitment were merely the act of constancy or conformity, then, commitment is, perhaps, deprived of an energizing element that justifies it. Subsequently, it does not seem easy to understand the notion of commitment at face value. A question inevitably arises: how do constancy, conformity and fidelity relate to commitment? This questioning leads to the examination of commitment in the next sections.

Commitment vis-à-vis Constancy, and Conformism

A person may ask the question: Is being committed equivalent to being constant? Thus, when we say Duffy is committed to his Jesuit life, is it equivalent to saying that he is persevering in his Jesuit life? Does this apply to Caroline's, Maureen's and Catherine's respective commitments to studies, marriage and friendship?

20. Marcel, *Creative Fidelity*, 159–60.

Constancy may be viewed as the rational skeleton of fidelity. In this regard, constancy could be defined simply as perseverance in the pursuit of a certain goal.[21] When we say Duffy is constant in his Jesuit life, we actually mean that he is persevering in his Jesuit life as a value or way of life. In this vein, commitment becomes simply a steadfast act of the will from which the breath of life and spirit may be absent. What is more, constancy in the pure state, with respect to interpersonal relations, always remains in danger of being replaced by a struggle, at first internal, then external, which can culminate in hatred and in mutual aversion.[22]

Commitment as perseverance implies steadfastness and persistence. Steadfastness conjures up the signature and a sense of endurance. As an act of firmness, steadfastness does not belong to the same species as making U-turns or hesitant softness.[23] One can know empirically whether a person is constant or not. Constancy is observable. But, when we say Duffy is committed to his Jesuit life, is it the same thing as to say Duffy is constant in his Jesuit life? What is more, constancy seems incompatible with the renewal, multiple adaptability and flexibility which characterize commitment. Constancy does not truly belong to the nature of commitment. Constancy is more an outward or external or observable trait while commitment belongs, in fact, to the domain of the inward or the interior experience:

> It should be noted that a being who is constant can make me see that he simply forces himself not to change, that he makes it a duty not to exhibit indifference on a certain occasion when he knows that I am counting on him; he can make it a point of honor to fulfill his obligations to me down to the last detail; and in such case . . . his constancy is quite clearly based on an idea he has formed of himself and which he does not wish to be unworthy of.[24]

From the citation above we see that constancy implies a rigid sense of obligation which a person makes to himself or herself. Constancy is somewhat akin to a merely legalistic sense of existence. Within this perspective, constancy belongs truly to the realm of ideology or doctrine that controls and drives behaviors. In this sense, constancy is easily objectifiable.

---

21. Ibid., 153.
22. Ibid., 156.
23. Hans Küng, *Global Responsibility: In Search of a New World Ethic* (New York: Crossroad, 1991), 95.
24. Marcel, *Creative Fidelity*, 154.

Subsequently, to say someone is constant in their marriage is not the same as saying that the person is committed to their marriage.

Thus far, it is recognizable that constancy does not capture the enduring meaning of commitment. Furthermore, commitment can be confused easily with conformism. Here is a case of conformism which Jean Vanier recounts:

> A few years ago, a number of people from our Communities went on a pilgrimage to Rome. We had an audience with Pope John Paul II. While we were waiting for him to arrive, Fabio, a young man with disabilities, walked up and sat down in the Pope's chair. It was obviously the best chair in the room, which is why Fabio felt so attracted to it. Bishops who were close by did not know what to do. An assistant however helped Fabio find another chair that was quite good too![25]

In the above case, everybody else conformed to the norm, while Fabio broke it by sitting on the Pope's chair. In effect, "I tend to conform to what is expected of me and am fearful of going against the norm or of what my 'Superiors' want of me."[26]

Conformism has to do, unambiguously, with abiding by the norm or rule, which dictates what is expected of one. Thus:

> Conformism, whether intellectual, aesthetic, or political, implies submission to a certain order emanating not from a person but from a group which claims that it incarnates what must be thought, what must be valued, in a particular country at a specific moment in time, but a group which is careful, to be sure, not to acknowledge the stigma of relativity which affects every mode of knowledge or taste.[27]

True, there is a sense in which a committed person has to fulfill some expectations but commitment is not just fulfilling some expectation, or abiding by the norm; it goes beyond the requirements of expectations and laws and touches on a much more fundamental sense of intrinsic value and plenitude. In fact, the lifeblood and lifeline of commitment lie in *creative fidelity*.[28] When we make commitments in life it is normally meant to *last*. Every commitment intends to be all-embracing; in its interior momentum and logic it strives to be readily unconditional. Such a commitment

25. Jean Vanier, *Becoming Human* (Toronto: House of Anansi Press Limited, 1998), 93.
26. Ibid.
27. Marcel, *Creative Fidelity*, 186.
28. Ibid., 162.

is justified by the object of commitment being consonant with fulfilling the transcendent end each person is capable of attaining through self-donation. The most congenial way people show that their commitment is unconditional is by saying *forever*, which also expresses an aspiration for permanence. A permanent commitment is more likely to be successful if it is an unconditional choice, or, better, a principle of choice so that every conscious re-choosing is a renewal of the original commitment. All things being equal, permanence is the property of every commitment that flows from love and continues in love.[29]

The Metaphysical Character of Commitment

The preceding considerations make manifest the understanding that commitment "is inextricably a part of the mystery of the person."[30] A person could say that commitment constitutes who one is. Duffy, Caroline, Maureen and Catherine's commitments are part and parcel of who they are. In this light, every commitment envisions, anticipates and assists in bringing about the fullness of some human truth.

The moment I commit myself, someone else registers my promise and henceforth counts on me and I know it.[31] Or again:

> The fact is that when I commit myself, I grant in principle that the commitment will not again be put into question. And it is clear that this volition not to question something again, intervenes as an essential element in the determination of what in fact will be the case. It is at once a certain number of possibilities; it bids me invent a certain *modus vivendi* which I would otherwise be precluded from envisaging... My behavior will be completely colored by this act embodying the decision that the commitment will not again be questioned. The possibility which has been barred or denied will thus be demoted to the rank of a temptation.[32]

In principle, then, in order to commit myself, I must first know myself. The fact is, however, that I really know myself only when I have committed myself. The dilatory attitude which involves sparing myself any trouble,

---

29. John C. Haughey, *Should Anyone Say Forever? On Making, Keeping and Breaking commitments* (Chicago: Loyola University Press, 1975), 54, 68.
30. Ibid., 41.
31. Marcel, *Creative Fidelity*, 159.
32. Ibid., 162.

keeping myself aloof, is incompatible with any self-knowledge worthy of the name.[33]

The primary purpose of explicit, expressed, interpersonal commitment is to provide some reliability of expectation regarding the actions of free persons whose wills are shakable; commitment offers persons grounds for counting on one another. As a remedy for inconsistency and uncertainty, commitment, at a certain level, implies a state of affairs in which there is doubt about our future actions. Commitment also signifies the possibility of failure to perform acts in the future that are intended, however intensely and with whatever firmness, now. Through commitment people give themselves bonds and give others power which will help them to do what they truly want to do, but might otherwise not be able to do in the future. In this sense, commitment is the human wager on the truth of their present insight and the hope of their present love. Promise is a devise and vehicle upon which personal relationships depend and which political life requires. Promise-making provides assurance to others and strength to ourselves; it undergirds the very possibility of human communication for it is the implicit guarantor of truth-telling.[34] In binding the self by a promise, a person acknowledges the presence of an inner hierarchy, consisting of a ruling principle and a life whose details remain unpredictable, but which the principle subjects to itself, or, still more accurately, which it pledges itself to keep under its yoke.[35]

A promise allows for the possibility of exterior conditions which may put one's power of keeping a promise into question. In a promise, the pledge which one makes is the continual renewal of presence, even amidst much alteration. However, it is important that people take into account, at the time of making a promise if it is to remain valid, an important factor: the state of mind of the person who enters into a promise. The mind must be *compos sui* and declares itself to be such in its own judgment, without reserving to itself the possibility of afterwards alleging that it was wrong. Here, then, we have a judgment of the deepest significance, lying at the root of commitment. But this does not at all discount the hold which a reality exercises over a person. On the contrary, this *hold* is at the base of the judgment itself; the judgment simply prolongs and sanctions an apprehension.[36]

33. Ibid., 163.
34. Margaret A. Farley, *Personal Commitments: Beginning, Keeping, Changing* (San Francisco: Harper and Row, 1986), 19.
35. Marcel, *Being and Having*, 49.
36. Ibid., 46.

Interpersonal commitment frequently initiates and sustains *consortium, companionship and love*. It also lies at the center of much of the history of religion. Of course, not all commitments people make are of equal significance, nor are they equally comprehensive in their claim upon people. Commitment which involves the whole of a person who makes it is ordinarily recognized as a fundamental life option. People set limits to the obligations that they undertake. Yet if a commitment is purely conditional, it obligates people only under certain conditions or set of circumstances. On the other hand, an unconditional commitment is one in which persons commit themselves to one another no matter what conditions prevail. While it is in the nature of commitments to refuse to count on some conditions as justifying a change in the commitment, most commitments are, at least, subject to the sheer conditions of the possibility of fulfillment. In the end, it is presence that keeps persons truly connected with and engaged in their commitments.[37]

In fact, every commitment has primary and secondary dimensions to it. In this sense, we could speak of commitment in its primary and secondary forms. A primary commitment or primordial commitment signifies the following:

> The thrust one gives one's being, the way one chooses to face reality to pursue the fullness one sees oneself capable of . . . The fullness I am referring to might be conceived of by one person in terms of meaning, by another person in terms of goodness or justice or beauty, etc. This primordial commitment is not to something nor is it to oneself; it is, however, of oneself in the direction in which one perceives a transcendent good [or value].[38]

If the notion of commitment has any meaning it must be in relation to an absolute which has first to be recognized. As soon as what is stressed is not an absolute to be recognized, but a creative act by which human freedom *gives birth* to its own values, anarchy takes the place of reason. But anarchy is untenable. As a result, people will find a roundabout road or substitute for it.[39] Primordial commitment places a person in the presence of the transcendent value. Primary commitment implies the basic trajectory of life's orientation molded by the sense that there be a value of intrinsic value and plenitude. In effect, primordial commitment refers to one's grounding belief which ultimately particularizes human ontological

37. Farley, 19–21.
38. Haughey, 39.
39. Marcel, *The Decline of Wisdom*, 48.

exigency. This exigency is the need and demand for human transcendence that is inspired by the sense that something is amiss in life. In other words, the ontological exigency is linked with the felt sense of dissatisfaction with the brokenness of the world. In the last analysis, therefore, primordial commitment gives direction, inchoately and implicitly, to a person's life; because of its grounding it also shapes and informs how a person views the world.

In the secondary sense, commitment refers to an act of making concrete choices in a promise which symbolizes and expresses the aspiration or claim to worthwhileness. The concrete choices which symbolize a given commitment at any given moment, however, do not exhaust it or fully express it.[40] Thus, "acts of conscious formal commitments symbolize for oneself and others the direction one is taking. These conscious commitments, in turn, make the primordial commitment more explicit. They bring the direction one is taking closer to consciousness."[41] Conscious commitments that people explicitly make constitute their formal commitments.

It is true that commitments involve beliefs and values that cohere with, justify and promote these beliefs. The objects of these beliefs are values. Beliefs have to do with one's judgment of the world, so that if one's judgment of the world is considered mistaken, then one's beliefs can be regarded as thus. In many ways, beliefs transcend human conceptual frameworks because they frequently precede them. Of course, beliefs assert their truth values within particular conceptual systems. More precisely, belief and conceptual systems are interdependent and reinforce one another. However, as one makes a commitment, one believes that her or his beliefs are reliable and not mistaken. As Duffy, Caroline, Maureen and Catherine made their commitments, they believed their respective commitments to be true, that is, not mistaken. In its character, commitment is felt and tendential, even if it is actuated by choices that give direction to one's life a trajectory in mundane existence.

The primordial object of Duffy's commitment is God, the ultimate being, which could also be the primordial object of Caroline's, Maureen's and Catherine's commitments. Their primordial commitments are made explicit by their formal choices or commitments: Jesuit life, studies, marriage and friendship. These formal commitments do not exhaust the primordial commitment, so they can evolve depending on one's religious, affective or intellectual conditions, which in turn affect the perceptions

---

40. Haughey, 39.
41. Ibid., 40.

and judgments about primordial commitment.[42] Formal commitments are "mediated by any number of things: a person, a special grace, a tragedy, a teacher, an ideological breakthrough, or an unexpected event in one's life or in society."[43] Thus, the formal commitment of Duffy or Caroline, or Maureen or Catherine determines the nature of their primordial commitments, of which they may not be fully aware. If their beliefs change, their commitment must change equally or, equivalently, since they could not be committed to what they recognize as false or mistaken.[44]

Noncommitment does not promote the humanity of a person; it merely leaves it meandering. In fact, without commitment, relationship relies completely on spontaneity, mutual interests and the convenience of circumstances, whereas companionship or friendship, in which there is commitment, can withstand distances and long periods of absences.[45] It may be asserted that, within the relational framework, commitment is truly the condition for the possibility of particularizing a person's life: "life will be found when a person is willing to particularize his choices in life and does so in such a way that he does not identify himself in terms of what he has or hopes to hold on to in terms of who he is and who he intends to be present to."[46] In effect, depth is the ground of commitment; liberative attentiveness is the humus that nurtures, fosters and strengthens it. Commitment gives shape to the lives of persons by offering them a sense of direction, prompting and enlarging persons. Or again, commitment involves the textures of personal and interpersonal existence.

Since belief and commitment may not be separated, it must be noted that belief not only refers to being, but it stems from being, that is, my being. In this sense, belief is, in fact, the ground of what I am.[47] Being is total plentitude, that is, intrinsically valuable and liberating. Being as such is existential or plenitudinous truth.[48] What is more, the symbolization of being in concrete circumstances realizes certain pre-conditions or pace-setters for peaceful co-existence or harmonic existence. In effect, as one truly believes, one participates in being as an intrinsic value. As Duffy believes in God, for instance, he partakes in the milieu of unconditional

42. Ibid., 45.

43. Ibid.

44. Roger Trigg, *Reason and Commitment* (London: Cambridge University Press, 1973), 46.

45. Haughey, 19–20.

46. Ibid., 21.

47. Marcel, *Creative Fidelity*, 171.

48. Marcel, *Presence and Immortality*, 18.

intrinsic value. "The strongest or most vital belief is one which brings all the powers of our being most completely into play."[49] Belief implies an interior gathering of oneself so that "the strongest belief, or more exactly the most living belief, is that which absorbs most fully all the powers of your being."[50] Such experience belongs truly to the character of commitment which implies a rallying to a certain course of life. When Maureen affirms her belief in marriage, she "cannot be satisfied with the enumeration of a certain number of propositions which [she holds] to be true; it seems clear that these propositions themselves express something far more intimate and profound."[51] Thus, predication is always insufficient in explaining beliefs as one may not even know the grounding justifications for one's own beliefs.

It may be noted further that belief, in the strongest sense of the word, is what faith is. This faith, when it is most real and most like itself, is most sure to issue from the whole being of man or woman and to involve him or her.[52] Faith partakes of the unconditional value and plenitude. What is more, faith and love cannot be separated:

> from the moment when my affirmation becomes love, it resigns in favour of that which is affirmed, of the thing which is asserted in its substantial value. This is precisely what love is; it cannot be divorced from this resignation. In other words, love is the active refusal to treat itself as subjective, and it is in this refusal that it cannot be separated from faith; in fact it is faith.[53]

When commitment is entered into with faith, it blossoms to its best form and expression: a liberative spirit infuses its élan. When we say Catherine is faithful to her friendship, we mean that she is committed to her friendship. And fidelity or faithfulness is the active perpetuation of presence which consists of a mysterious incitement to create.[54] In addition, fidelity truly exists only when it defies absence, when it triumphs over absence and, in particular, over that absence which we hold to be absolute and which we call death.[55] Such fidelity needs to be imaginative, ongoing and capable of replenishing itself. In short, this is *creative fidelity* that is touch-

49. Marcel, *Creative Fidelity*, 134.
50. Marcel, *The Mystery of Being Vol.II: Faith and Reality*, 78.
51. Marcel, *Creative Fidelity*, 134.
52. Marcel, *Being and Having*, 206.
53. Marcel, *The Mystery of Being Vol.II: Faith and Reality*, 62.
54. Marcel, *The Philosophy of Existentialism*, 36.
55. Marcel, *Creative Fidelity*, 152.

able and constantly renews itself with vivacity and freshness.[56] The pledge which typifies commitments demands constant renewal and re-creation. "Creative fidelity consists in maintaining ourselves actively in a permeable state; and there is a mysterious interchange between this free act and the gift granted in response to it."[57] It implies presence which dissipates the feeling of staleness, of rancidity, which threatens to overcome us whenever we focus our attention on a virtue, on the reliability of a certain value.[58] "Presence is something which reveals itself immediately and unmistakably in a look, a smile, an intonation or a handshake."[59] Presence is not to be construed as externally manifesting oneself to the other, but rather as involving a quality which cannot be so easily described in objective terms, of making me feel that another is with me.[60]

In an experience of presence, even if I cannot see you, even if I cannot touch you, I feel that you are with me; it would be a denial of you not to be assured of this.[61] This is what love is deeply about. The multiform perpetuation of this presence is what creative fidelity is all about. Indeed, if creative fidelity is conceivable it prolongs presence which itself corresponds to a certain kind of hold which being has upon us; it multiplies and deepens the effect of this presence almost inexhaustibly in our lives.[62] Consequently, presence is intersubjective. Presence involves communication and communion; availability is its mainstay. Presence makes one available to the object of commitment. When a person is available, he or she is at another's disposal: such a person readily makes an offer of self to another with freshness, spontaneity and creativity. Whenever presence is renewed and perpetuated, creative fidelity is actuated and enlivened with vivacity.

Perpetuation of presence typically also occurs within a context of ongoing re-evaluation and re-interpretation of events and experiences, that is, with a deepening of the quality of presence. True creative fidelity implies a return to origins, founding pledges but with a lens which creates a new posture for ongoing activity or vocation. To be creative is to make of something new or nobler. Such creativity is bound up with freedom and compassion and aliveness which aspires towards an ever-expanding or

---

56. Ibid.
57. Marcel, *The Philosophy of Existentialism*, 38.
58. Marcel, *Creative Fidelity*, 153.
59. Marcel, *The Philosophy of Existentialism*, 40.
60. Marcel, *Creative Fidelity*, 154.
61. Marcel, *The Philosophy of Existentialism*, 39.
62. Ibid., 36.

better life. This notion or conception of a better life is at the same time an activity of liberative imagination.

Constancy contrasts with fidelity. When compared to presence, constancy exhibits a characteristic which is to some extent formal. I am constant for myself, in my own regard, for my purpose. In fidelity I am *present* for the other and, more precisely, for a *thou*.[63] In effect, "fidelity as such can only be appreciated by the person to whom it is pledged if it offers an essential element of spontaneity, itself radically independent of the will."[64]

In a nutshell, commitment continues, grows and enriches life by means of creative fidelity, which perpetuates the presence of a person or symbol of value and plenitude. Of course, faithfulness to one's primordial commitment particularizes in formal commitments which persons choose and define for themselves. But the notion of commitment also implicates the notion of betrayal. A commitment is precisely so because it can be betrayed. A commitment that cannot be betrayed exists only at the larval or intermediate stage. Betrayal may arise from human contingency, fragility, fear or covetousness. These realities, when elicited by the realities of weakness, failure, rejection or nonacceptance, strike at the heart of human experience. Human fear, covetousness, fragility and contingency affect the living out of commitment. Human existence is undergirded frequently by the experience of existential dis-ease which arises from the felt sense of inner emptiness that discloses a gnawing anxiety that pervades life. The felt experience of inner emptiness also manifests itself incarnationally through the feelings of restlessness and loneliness which people will try to ward off by all means.

The Ego and Commitment

It needs to be understood that in addition to human contingency, the exigencies of the ego as the conditional sense of the self makes the living out of commitment arduous and strewn with betrayals or pitfalls. The ego depends on extrinsic validation which hangs on the judgments of other people. Enjoyment and the ego inseparably hang together. In this regard, the ego depends on the approbation of others. As a result, the ego is insecure because the judgments of people can always change. Yet the human subject, in his or her experiences and dimensions needs to recognize, apprehend and even own the sense that he or she is always of unconditional desirability and worth. The received identity or dignity of persons makes

63. Marcel, *Creative Fidelity*, 154.
64. Ibid., 155.

them of priceless worth. Intrinsic adequacy, desirability and worth come with the gift of every person. The conditional sense of identity of a person is not all that defines a person's existence.

In fact, individuated human identity will always manifest a certain lack of "wholeness," or harmony from which normally spring existential security. In a word, individuated identity reveals our existential security and insecurity in ourselves. With regard to the issue of commitment, an inevitable question is, "Can I affirm that the disposition, which I have just at the moment that I commit myself, will not alter later on?"[65] How sure is one that his or her commitment is "so total and irrevocable a disposition of one's life?"[66]

Fidelity to commitment is more grounded in the being of persons than in their egos. Our being guarantees our living out of commitments. Let's take an example of Catherine's commitment as we respond to the last questions. Catherine knows that right now she is faithful to her friend. And she has the right to affirm that it certainly seems to her that her feeling or inner disposition cannot change. It certainly seems to her. But it is sufficient for her to say *it seems to me* in order to find it necessary to add as though *sottovoce: but I can't be sure of it.*[67] However, we may observe that the being to whom Catherine swears fidelity can change in turn; if the friend is a man, for example, he can change in ways which give her the right to say: "this is not the man I committed myself to; he has changed so much that my promise is null and void."[68]

From the above considerations, we can affirm a second demand that human contingency and existential insecurity call for, namely, discernment: a process of making appropriate decisions in charity and truth within a given set of circumstances. Discernment here means that before a person makes a formal commitment, he or she does it responsibly, conscientiously and carefully, with honesty and in good faith. In other words, one needs to discern carefully before committing oneself formally. Also, a person needs to discern the state of his or her primordial commitment so that he or she chooses the most appropriate formal object of commitment that corresponds to it. Having articulated the meaning of discernment: let us, for example, assume that it is still possible for Catherine to act in the future towards X as though she still loved him, even though she no

---

65. Marcel, *Creative Fidelity*, 158.
66. Haughey, 62.
67. Marcel, *Creative Fidelity*, 158.
68. Ibid.

longer did love him; does she have the right to do so? In other words, can she consent to promise something about herself which will turn out to be a lie? And does not this future lie have repercussions by anticipation on the present itself, since she in effect speaks as though she could maintain a disposition which she really knows or should know, cannot be eternal? Must she not therefore view her commitment as conditional—introduce qualifications which conspicuously restrict its meaning?[69]

These foregoing questions demand a further consideration of creative fidelity. The questions presuppose that Catherine has already made her commitment to X. At the moment of commitment, Catherine identified herself with the state of herself which she can apprehend at this precise moment. Everything outside this state is obscure, impenetrable and, in any case, cannot be the object of any valid assertion.[70] In addition, Catherine's future state is something which will occur the way an external event occurs, for example, the weather.[71] When Catherine commits herself, she grants:

> in principle that the commitment will not again be put in question. And it is clear that this active volition not to question something again, intervenes as an essential element in the determination of what in fact will be the case . . . Here there appears in a rudimentary form what I call *creative fidelity*. [Catherine's] behavior will be completely colored by this act embodying the decision that the commitment will not again be questioned. The possibility, which has been barred or denied, will thus be demoted to the rank of a temptation.[72]

However, the only justification for one to remain in or withdraw from a commitment "relates to the presence or absence of communion."[73] For every commitment is a human act of hope as well as faith and love.[74] The stronger the bond of communion, the stronger the commitment, and vise versa. In a nutshell, the role of fear in commitment calls for and underscores the significance of deep personal knowledge before making a pledge of commitment. Yet it is all paradoxical. "In principle, to commit myself I must first know myself; the fact is, however, that I really know

---

69. Ibid., 159.
70. Ibid., 161.
71. Ibid., 162.
72. Ibid.
73. Haughey, 83.
74. Ibid., 82.

myself only when I have committed myself."[75] Because of this paradox, there always exists the possibility of betrayal in every commitment, for one could not really tell when he or she has deep personal knowledge before making a formal commitment.

Evidently, too, every commitment involves a promise that frees a person from being caged entirely by the expediency and exigencies of the present. Inevitably, it becomes important to understand what it really means to swear fidelity and how a promise can be made. Any kind of fidelity whatsoever must be defined as starting with the *I believe*. If I assent to *I believe*, I do so as an existent being.[76] In this light, the promise in fact is made on the basis of some present inner disposition.[77] Further, the promise is a particular kind of choice; a promise describes something we intend to do in the future. Through a promise one projects oneself into the future. The one making a promise is expressing his or her faith in his or her own power to do whatever he or she will do; he or she is asserting his or her firm intention, is binding himself or herself to a future.[78] Indeed, by giving his or her word a person assumes an obligation. He or she yields to another, or others, a claim over himself or herself by establishing an expectation. The person who makes a promise constitutes something in the order of being itself.[79] Or again, by making a promise, a person chooses freely to use his or her freedom to project himself or herself into the future in the specific manner which he or she determines or defines for himself or herself.[80] Promise is the way persons symbolize the deep currents and flows of the felt sense of significance of enduring value.

In light of what is granted thus far, the next section, will attempt to reflect on commitment in the light of freedom and responsibility.

Commitment, Freedom, and Responsibility

Let's assume that before marriage, Maureen's fiancé tells Maureen that he has a bank account, a house, a car and a private company. In turn, Maureen tells him that she has a doctorate in communications, an apartment, a credit card, a minibus and an advertising agency. From this assumption, we can infer that a human being incorporates two fundamental ways of being

75. Marcel, *Creative Fidelity*, 163.
76. Ibid., 168.
77. Ibid., 158.
78. Haughey, 27.
79. Ibid., 27–28.
80. Ibid., 28.

present to his or her world. A human being can be present to his or her world in the mode of having or in the mode of being. In fact, everything really comes down to the distinction between what we have and what we are.[81] From this distinction we can conceive, at least theoretically, of the inner disposition of one who, setting no condition or limit and abandoning himself in absolute confidence, would thus transcend all possible disappointment and would experience a security of his or her being, or in his or her being, which is contrary to the radical insecurity of *Having*.[82] From our example of Maureen and her fiancé, it must be pointed out that primacy belongs to their persons; who they are comes before what they have. Their persons precede what they have. They are the subjects of the things they have. When we speak this way we lift up the domain of being, the realm of *who we are*. This domain will help us articulate our understanding, for instance, marriage as an act.

Let us assume that after marriage, Maureen confesses to her husband that she lied about having an advertising agency. In turn, her husband, too, confesses to Maureen that he lied about having a private company. They disclose to each other that they are only executive employees of the respective advertising agency and private company. In such cases, we confront acts. A lie is an example of an act. A lie does not belong to the realm of having. One cannot say that he or she has a lie. Rather, one says that he or she is the one who lied. A person is present in his or her act. An act commits the whole human being. And an "act is voluntary."[83] In that case, for example, when one is asked, for instance, "did you lie?" The response is always either, yes or no. Thus, "the essence of the act is to commit the agent."[84] If I have committed a certain act, I must say: "yes, it is I who acted in this way." What is more: I acknowledge in advance that if I try to escape, I am guilty of disownment.[85] Hence, one is always present in his or her act. Every act bears with it the notions of freedom and responsibility which involve personal references.

> I claim to be a person in so far as I assume responsibility for what I do and what I say. But to whom am I responsible, to whom do I acknowledge my responsibility? We must reply that I am conjointly responsible both to myself and to everyone else, and that

---

81. Marcel, *Being and Having*, 155.
82. Marcel, *Homo Viator*, 46.
83. Marcel, *Creative Fidelity*, 106.
84. Ibid., 107.
85. Ibid.

this conjunction is precisely characteristic of an engagement of the person, that it is the mark proper to the person.[86]

Insofar as every act is subject to appraisal, an act can be either good or bad.

When one makes a formal commitment, he or she does so voluntarily. A formal commitment is an act. Thus, Duffy, Caroline, Maureen and Catherine, respectively chose voluntarily Jesuit life, studies, marriage and friendship. They are responsible for their commitments for they chose them freely. Yet freedom is not only freedom of choice but "freedom is [also] a conquest—always partial, always precarious, always challenged."[87] Personal and existential freedom speaks of and symbolizes freedom of being. Insofar as we are not yet fully who we are, we are free and not yet freed. Freedom of being also implies active indifference and relaxation, that is, my not being centered on myself. Besides, "it is in the midst of a situation of captivity that freedom can be born."[88] The more one transcends and transfigures the ego and its categories of avarice, the more does one become free. The free man or woman is one who is liberated from the ego and its categories of selfishness and self-centeredness. In the end, my freedom pertains to who I am and not something that I have. Only a free person can commit herself or himself. Commitment is an act of freedom and responsibility. Responsibility is a bond that unites a person and an act.

Since a person is always confronted by the captivity of her or his ego, he or she has to constantly renew his or her deliverance from the ego and its categories of avarice in order to become freer. Hence, freedom remains always partial, precarious and challenged. The captive nature of a person's existence always challenges the realization of freedom. The captive character of the human condition always makes the attainment of freedom precarious and unfinished. Due to the captive character of human existence, there always exists the possibility of betrayal in every commitment. And since an act of commitment is a conquest that is only maintained by creative fidelity, the multiform perpetuation of one's presence to one's chosen value always remain fraught with the possibilities of betrayal. Notwithstanding, in creative fidelity, not only is one in touch with oneself but one is also present to his or her object of commitment. This presence is measured by the quality of one's availability to himself or herself as well as to others. "In contrast to the captive person, the person [who] is at the

---

86. Marcel, *Homo Viator*, 21.
87. Marcel, *The Existential Background of Human Dignity*, 146.
88. Ibid.

disposal of others is consecrated and inwardly dedicated."[89] The available human being places himself or herself at the disposal of others. Such a person can be with me with the whole of himself or herself when I am in need.[90] The higher a person's availability to herself or himself and to others is, the stronger will his or her commitment tend.

Conclusion

The notion of commitment could be confused with the notions of constancy and conformism. However, "In principle, to commit myself I must first know myself; the fact is, however, that I really know myself only when I have committed myself."[91] Yet self-knowledge is a result of "a compound of experiencing, understanding, and judging."[92] We gain this knowledge when we have committed ourselves. For in committing ourselves, we experience and deepen our understanding of our commitments. Later on, we further re-evaluate and re-examine our previous experience and understanding of particular commitments.[93] This process always remains dynamic, cumulative, integrative and iterative. Thus the more I commit myself, the more I know myself. But since freedom is not only freedom of choice, but also a conquest of the ego and its categories of avarice, there always exists the possibility of betrayal in every commitment. This possibility is necessitated by the fact that a person remains an existentially captive being.

A conditional sense of self typifies everybody's existence. However, this possibility of betrayal in commitment can always be countered by the multiform perpetuation of presence, which is an act growing in the experience and expression of one's unconditional availability. In the context of our present considerations, one's unconditional availability grows as one strives to fulfill the demands of his or her formal commitment. For example, Duffy becomes more unconditionally available when he more fully fulfills the demands of Jesuit life with freshness and spontaneity. By fulfilling these demands, he also becomes more touchable, responsible and free.

---

89. Marcel, *The Philosophy of Existentialism*, 43.
90. Ibid., 40.
91. Marcel, *Creative Fidelity*, 163.
92. Bernard Lonergan, *Method in Theology* (New York: Herder and Herder, 1972), 181.
93. Bernard Lonergan, *Insight: A Study of Human Understanding* (New York: Philosophical Library, 1958), 280–83.

Conclusion

THE VISION of hope gives focus, energy and the willingness to integrate scientific, sapiential and moral thoughts, competencies, desires, interests, imagination, feelings and sense of life. In this way, the vision of hope draws life forward. The vision of hope draws a consistent picture of a preferred future that is possible. Within its framework, the efforts to bring together different views of life provide basic orientation in attitudes, lifestyle and manner of being in the world. The complexity of life's particularities and wholeness implies honoring and bringing together the scientific, sapiential and moral dimensions of life which simply go beyond the visible world.

The vision that guides hope grasps life's direction and the inner reasons to be. It awakens people to life in its past, future and especially present. The dreams of harmony, union and evolving togetherness thrive in this vision. As a living reality it unifies life marvelously. As a beautiful reality it expresses the open horizon of being. As light, it organizes perspectives with its luminosity and inspiration. This vision is gentle, consistent, peaceful and strong. It opens itself to test as it roots itself in concrete experience. It grows out of truth and freedom. It expands the self and the experience of order. It widens the flow of unity as the common horizon of living with others. As a reservoir of energy, the vision of hope reawakens self-investment, generous self-giving and union with others.

The praxis of hope looks forward to a happy resolution of the ambivalence that reveals itself in the reality of the human individual and collective with certain desire and reasonable confidence. In hope it is a confidence in the human reality as a whole that precedes and pervades human awareness, questioning, inferences and considerations. Hope affirms that there is a way out of issues and problems, that is, the human being can control and survive inner and external difficulties and dissolution.[1] Hope involves the perception of the possible, the new and the better, that what one really envisages is realistically possible through a process in concrete experience, though this may be difficult. Hope flows from the responsible and loving

---

1. William F. Lynch, *Images of Hope: Imagination as Healer of the Helpless* (Notre Dame: University of Notre Dame Press, 1966), 32.

levels of human consciousness to resolve the ambiguities of experience, understanding and judgment.

Hope of a better future, in contrast with the present or past, characterizes the human reality. The human spirit, in its thrust toward the human well-being, always yearns to put sense into or find a way out of contradictions. As a foretaste of happiness, hope is part of the very element vital for human life.[2] It gives us the energy to act. Without hope, practical and valuable incentives may lose their attractiveness. Hope engages the breadth and sensitivity of feeling, knowledge and decision. Hope flexibly explores and pursues discerned goals built into the concrete human conditions.[3] The expressions of hope arise out of particular contexts of living.

Hope always has an objective with which the uncertain future is faced. The objective repeatedly negates the past or present limitations. For example, the hope of one who is illegally detained under harsh solitary conditions is freedom. The illumination of this freedom opposes seclusion, impropriety, humiliation and bad taste that mark the lives of many in detention. But this freedom often has the negative reality of tacit indistinctness and concealment of how things will actually manifest themselves in it. Nonetheless, the objective of hope always bears some relationship with the past and/or present framework experienced within all cognition, feeling and actions.

Hoping re-vitalizes life. To live in hope implies seeing possibilities for improvement, have a meaningful present and expansive future or the promise of both.[4] All that we do in hope rests on the anticipation that it will get us somewhere. That there is a way out of difficulties belongs to the sense of hoping. Indeed, a man robbed of everything except his life can continue living because of hope. The belief and trust that there is a possibility of getting somewhere and attaining objectives that we propose to ourselves energizes our hope.[5] In other words, salvation always remains possible within the human order.

Hope lies somewhere between knowing and willing. Nobody can understand the future and yet in hope there is an awareness from the past, a past that might have been good and will repeat itself in a modified way to

---

2. Ladislaus Boros, *Living in Hope: Future Prospectives in Christian Thought* (London: Search Press, 1969), 10.

3. Tadd Dunne, *Lonergan and Spirituality: Towards a Spirituality of Integration* (Chicago: Loyola University Press, 1985), 24.

4. Otto H. Hentz, *The Hope of the Christian* (Collegeville, Minnesota: The Liturgical Press, 1997), 12.

5. Ibid.

avoid its previous shortcomings. Wishing and willing intervene in hope as creative acts. Wishing gives the will its lifeblood. However, wishing alone cannot redeem the will. Without the power to control one's wishes one, in fact, never grows up. Wishing proper to hoping implies direction which comes from freedom. Moreover, imagination complements hope. In emergencies, hope enables us to act according to our best and deepest inner resources. Creative imagination that influences hope constantly needs to be checked by rational criticism and perception.[6]

Hope has a connectedness with support or help. In hope we have the trust that the promise of help holds.[7] There are moments we perceive that our own internal means are insufficient, that they have to be augmented from without. The elementary sense for support or help is a consistent, abiding ingredient in hope. Only in some severe grief, pain or illness, may we become aware of this. The act of taking help from outside is an inward appropriation so typical of hoping that it also generates a collective culture of hope.

Hope is closely linked to the human being's temporality. The perceived objective of hope is often projected into the future and the hopeful person is alert to the future that can unfold from the present, the new and the likelihood of restyling and reorganization. However, hope becomes misrepresented if it leads to excessive concerns with the future. Concern with only the future can pass on distaste and insensitivity to the present. For, the future alone comes to claim genuine truth and value so that all that is in the present or past can be expended for the sake of supposed and projected good.

A person engrossed solely in the future loses touch with concrete realities and lives in a world of fantasy. One who lingers only in the past reduces life to conventional routine and habits. A person obsessed with the present subjects himself or herself to fleeting conditions. Accordingly, not to link the future to the past and present can lead to the sense of the insignificance of the present and past situations, escapism and, at worst, callousness. "Hope has its being in the tension of future and present, driving us out of the present, yet seeing the future from the present situation."[8] Hope that relates *only* to an imagined future is false and alienating. Hope's bond to the present and past grants a criterion for distinguishing it as either genuine or fanciful.

6. Macquarrie, 27.
7. Ibid., 40.
8. Ibid., 28.

Conclusion

Attitudes of hope derive from concrete involvement with life. The sense of hope pioneers a lot of initiatives, responsibility and care. There are two things to say about developing attitudes of hope.

First, one who wishes to cultivate an attitude of hope needs to be a person who participates in life's affairs and engages life's issues. It means living from the heart, namely, without dishonesty, and sharing in the experiences of the burdened and voiceless, suffering the anguish and impotence of being human. One lives the inward facts of life and experience with all the compassion and achievements, loneliness and misgivings, even urgings of despair. Only then does one come to a realization that human life is greater than anything that can be realized in it.

Secondly, to foster an attitude of hope, one needs an insertion into the experiences of a profound interpersonal relationship of love and friendship or companionship. This involves the disposition of self-giving and/or availability to others who come into one's life irrespective of the indignities that this accessibility may entail. This means that one can repeatedly yield to the destiny of others whom one is disposed to serve. It also means that one strives to answer for others, bears their frailties and misfortunes as well as their happiness. For an attitude of hope to evolve, one needs to take seriously the well-being of others. In this stance, one witnesses to unreserved risks, persistence and accomplishment. Also, openness to misery that others suffer tends to precipitate trustworthiness, solidarity and open-heartedness as needful ingredients of hope.

Hope qualifies human existence with a sense of assurance. Hope aims at desirable, accessible, elusive good whose attainment is strenuous yet deeply fulfilling and enlivening. In this regard, expectations often constitute the building blocks of hope itself. "Never to be satisfied when presented with a happiness whose attainment is so arduous is itself one of the greatest resources and surest riches of human existence."[9] As a universal phenomenon, hope appears in many forms and has goals from the most trivial to the most profound. Hope always involves sensitivity, willingness and availability with regard to the future. Where hope exists life broadens its meaning, freedom, enthusiasm and joy. If I can keep my hope alive, my sense of direction tends to remain stable, expansive and meaningful. I nourish a constant source of inspiration and a channel of energy, integration and human fulfillment. Realistic hope implies quality and a fulfilling life that can only be worked out within the needs, demands and aspirations of particular contexts of living.

---

9. Ambrosius Maria Carré, *Hope or Despair* (New York: Kenedy and Sons, 1955), 7.

Conclusion

Hope involves the trustful acceptance of priorities, preferences and norms in the ambiguous world of the individual and human collective. It introduces an assent to life's basic identity, meaningfulness and trustworthiness. One awakens to the experience of interior freedom and life's basic sense of purpose and significance. Because hope is about significant things that are not certain, hoping requires steadfastness by means of which one works for the possible so that it becomes credible. One chooses and commits oneself to a shared history with a centeredness and trust. Hope expresses itself as an outgoingness that persists in uncertainties. It refuses to exist passively in the unexamined social reality. Hope means that one affirms identity despite discord, fate or death. It also means that one affirms meaningfulness despite uncertainty, emptiness, chaos or absurdity. Hope affirms values and norms despite challenges. Sheila Cassidy talks of an example thus:

> The tumor had completely eaten away her nose and one eye and blinded the other so that there was only a foetid gaping hole where her face had been. We longed for her to die to "keep her comfortable" until her nurse came to us and said she was fighting through the haze of the sedation. When we found that she had no desire to lie down peacefully to comfort us, we stopped the drugs and she got up and played the piano, blind and disgusting and disfigured as she was.[10]

As Cassidy also puts it, "the human spirit is a very remarkable thing and not all those we want out of the way want to go."[11]

Petty egotism, bitterness, rash discretion, intolerance and insensitivity cast a dark shadow over life. An overshadowed life diminishes the radiance of hope. It also disregards the inner life of others. Moreover, it makes it difficult for people to truly express who they really are. Furthermore, political repression, economic marginalization, social bigotry and the depredations of human rights diminish the expansive life of hope as they hinder people from going beyond themselves. Under such circumstances, people often feel degraded, lessened, disoriented and unable to realize the wellbeing that embraces others. An unjust context of living cripples human liberty and emancipation; it simply breeds misery, mistrust and fear among people. Only in positively living with others do we reconfigure and unify our pur-

---

10. Sheila Cassidy, *Light from the Dark Valley* (London: Darton, Longman and Todd, 1994), 111.
11. Ibid.

poses, goals and projects. The human spirit flourishes in a communion that exalts and celebrates the identities and welfare of others.

Hope grounds itself in a love of life as an acceptance of the realness of life. This love of life bears little resemblance with the unhealthy taste or the indulgence in immediate enjoyment. Love of life does not merely refer to pleasure, honor, sport, career, money, property or the need to consume. It includes the uncertainty of human praxis and history. Love of life refers to human life in all its warmth, opportunities and successes as well as defeats, disappointments and losses. When we love life, we refuse to be deprived of the aspiration that goodness and beauty sink to naught. A truly human life critiques and refuses to submit to discouragement, cynicism and despair which come with pain and misery.[12]

Every moment of our lives remain incomplete. Our lives always remain unfinished and fragmentary with unfulfilled promises, unsettled justice and unmet goals. We always long for more justice and freedom, love and peace. In other words, in this life we long for heaven as a symbol of transcendence, warm-heartedness and expansive life. We yearn for the continuation of this life in heaven.[13] As a result, hope emboldens and consoles people to live well and do right, be in compassion and solidarity with others and to keep on loving life in spite of everything.

Individuals and communities who symbolize hope believe that love between people can and should be passionate, liberative, enlightening and respectful. They understand that the past is a heritage of encounters, narratives and discourses. They understand the present as a milieu of transcendence and that the future can be exciting. Life can always be lived and experienced with zest, significance and empowerment. That is the promise of hope. When this promise grasps us, it gives life a momentum which moves us ahead despite complexity, controversy and ambiguity.

---

12. Ibid.

13. The heaven of hope is not a supraworld above nor is it an extraworld beyond. Heaven symbolizes fullness of the world and human being in his or her individual and social life. The symbol of heaven completes what remains unsettled and insufficient. Heaven then means that the unambiguous life is future.

Bibliography

Primary Sources

Monographs

Marcel, Gabriel. *Awakenings*. Milwaukee: Marquette University Press, 2003.

———. *Being and Having: An Existential Diary*. New York: Harper and Row Publishers, Inc., 1965.

———. *Creative Fidelity*. New York: The Crossroad Publishing Company, 1982.

———. *The Decline of Wisdom*. London: The Harvill Press, 1954.

———. *The Existential Background of Human Dignity*. Cambridge: Harvard University Press, 1963.

———. *Homo Viator: Introduction to a Metaphysics of Hope*. New York: Harper and Row Publishers, Inc., 1965.

———. *Man Against Mass Society*. Chicago: Henry Regnery Company, 1971.

———. *Metaphysical Journal*. Chicago: Henry Regnery Company, 1952.

———. *The Mystery of Being, Vol. 1: Reflection and Mystery*. Lanham: University Press of America, 1984.

———. *The Mystery of Being, Vol. 2: Faith and Reality*. Lanham: University Press of America, 1984.

———. *The Philosophy of Existentialism*. Secaucus, N.J.: The Citadel Press, 1967.

———. *Philosophical Fragments 1909–1914 and The Philosopher of Peace*. Notre Dame, Indiana: University of Notre Dame Press, 1965.

———. *Presence and Immortality*. Pittsburgh: Duquesne University Press, 1967.

———. *Problematic Man*. New York: Herder and Herder, Inc., 1967.

———. *Searchings*. New York: Newman Press, 1967.

———. *Tragic Wisdom and Beyond*. Evanston: Northwestern University Press, 1973.

Articles

———. "Desire and Hope." In *Readings in Existential Phenomenology*. Lawrence, Nathaniel, and Daniel O'Connor, eds. Englewood Cliffs: Prentice-Hall, Inc., 1967, 277–84.

———. "Introduction." In *Fresh Hope for the World: Moral Rearmament in Action*. Marcel, Gabriel, ed. London: Longmans, 1960.

———. "Reply to Charles Hartshorne." In *The Library of Living Philosophers Vol. XVII: The Philosophy of Gabriel Marcel*. Schilpp, Paul Arthur, and Lewis Edwin Hahn, eds. La Salle, Illinois: Open Court, 1991, 367–70.

———. "Reply to Erwin W. Strauss and Michael A. Machado." In *The Library of Living Philosophers Vol. XVII: The Philosophy of Gabriel Marcel*. Schilpp, Paul Arthur, and Lewis Edwin Hahn, eds. La Salle, Illinois: Open Court, 1991, 156–58.

———. "Reply to Otto Friedrich Bollnow." In *The Library of Living Philosophers Vol. XVII: The Philosophy of Gabriel Marcel*. Schilpp, Paul Arthur, and Lewis Edwin Hahn, eds. La Salle, Illinois: Open Court, 1991, 200–203.

———. "Reply to Gene Reeves." In *The Library of Living Philosophers Vol. XVII: The Philosophy of Gabriel Marcel*. Schilpp, Paul Arthur and Lewis Edwin Hahn eds. La Salle, Illinois: Open Court, 1991, 272–74.

———."Reply to Kenneth T. Gallagher." In *The Library of Living Philosophers Vol. XVII: The Philosophy of Gabriel Marcel*. Schilpp, Paul Arthur, and Lewis Edwin Hahn, eds. La Salle, Illinois: Open Court, 1991, 389–90.

———. "Reply to Paul Ricoeur." In *The Library of Living Philosophers Vol. XVII: The Philosophy of Gabriel Marcel*. Schilpp, Paul Arthur, and Lewis Edwin Hahn, eds. La Salle, Illinois: Open Court, 1991, 495–98.

———. "Reply to Pietro Prini." In *The Library of Living Philosophers Vol. XVII: The Philosophy of Gabriel Marcel*. Schilpp, Paul Arthur, and Lewis Edwin Hahn, eds. La Salle, Illinois: Open Court, 1991, 240–43.

———. "Reply to Richard M. Zaner." In *The Library of Living Philosophers Vol. XVII: The Philosophy of Gabriel Marcel*. Schilpp, Paul Arthur, and Lewis Edwin Hahn, eds. La Salle, Illinois: Open Court, 1991, 334–35.

———."Science and Wisdom." In *Bulletin de la Socéité Américaine de Philosophie de Langue Francaise*, Vol.VII, No.1–2, 1995, trans., Maurice Cranston, 30–48.

———. "Some Reflections on Existentialism." *Philosophy Today*, Vol.8, No.4, 1964, 248–57.

———. "Truth and Freedom." *Philosophy Today*, Vol.9, No.4, 1965, 227–37.

Secondary Sources

Angeles, Peter A. *The Harper Collins Dictionary of Philosophy*. London: Harper Perenial, 1992.

Berman, David. "Pessimism and Optimism." In *The Oxford Companion to Philosophy*. Ted Honberich, ed. Oxford: Oxford University Press, 1995, 656–57.

Boros, Ladislaus. *Living in Hope: Future Prospectives in Christian Thought*. London: Search Press, 1969.

Canhan, E. D. "Christian Science Church of Christ, Scientist." In *The New Catholic Encyclopedia*, Vol.3, 1967, 645–46.

Carré, Ambrosius Maria. *Hope or Despair*. New York: Kenedy and Sons, 1955

Cassidy, Sheila. *Light from the Dark Valley*. London: Darton, Longman and Todd, 1994.

Dube, Musa W. "*Adinkra*! Four Hearts Joined Together: On Becoming Healing-Teachers of African Indigenous Religion/s in HIV/AIDS Prevention." In *African Women, Religion, and Health: Essays in Honor of Mercy Amba Ewudziwa Oduyoye*, Isabel Apawo Phiri and Sarojini Nadar, eds. Maryknoll, New York: Orbis Books, 2006, 131–56.

Dunne, Tadd. *Lonergan and Spirituality: Towards a Spirituality of Integration* Chicago: Loyola University Press, 1985.

Farley, Margaret A. *Personal Commitments: Beginning, Keeping, Changing*. San Francisco: Harper and Row, 1986.

Glanz, Barbara A. *The Creative Communicator: 399 Tools to Communicate Commitment without Boring People to Death*. Homewood, IL.: Business One Irwin, 1993.

Gourevitch, Philip. *We Wish to Inform You That Tomorrow We Will Be Killed With Our Families: Stories from Rwanda*. New York: Picador, 1998.

Bibliography

Haight, Roger. *Dynamics of Theology*. New York: Paulist Press, 1990.
Halverson, William H. *A Concise Introduction to Philosophy*. New York: Random House, 1981.
Haughey, John C. *Should Anyone Say Forever? On Making, Keeping and Breaking Commitments*. Chicago: Loyola University Press, 1975.
Heelan, Patrick A. "The Lifeworld and Scientific Interpretation." In *Handbook of Phenomenology and Medicine*, Philosophy and Medicine Series, Vol.68, Baylor University, Waco, Texas, Kay Tombs, ed. Dordrecht and Boston: Kluwer Academic Publishers, 2002, 47–66.
Hentz, Otto H. *The Hope of the Christian*. Collegeville, Minnesota: The Liturgical Press, 1997.
Hocking, William Ernest. "Marcel and the Ground Issues of Metaphysics." *Philosophy and Phenomenological Research*, Vol. XIV, No.4, 439–69.
Jerome, Bruner. *Actual Minds, Possible Worlds*. Cambridge: Harvard University Press, 1986.
Johns, Sheridan, and R. Hunt Davis, Jr. eds. *Mandela, Tambo and the African National Congress*. New York: Oxford University Press, 1991.
King, Coretta Scott. *The Words of Martin Luther King, Jr*. New York: Newmarket Press, 1983.
Koenig, Thomas R. *Existentialism and Human Existence: An Account of Five Major Philosophers*. Malabar, Florida: Krieger Publishing Company, 1992.
Kuhn, Thomas S. *The Structure of Scientific Revolutions* Chicago: The University of Chicago Press, 1996.
Küng, Hans. *Global Responsibility: In Search of a New World Ethic*. New York: Crossroad, 1991.
Leibniz, Gottfried Wilhelm. *Theodicy*. New York: Bobbs-Merrill Company Inc., 1966.
Loemker, L. E. "Pessimism and Optimism." In *Encyclopedia of Philosophy*, Vol.6, 1967, 114–21.
Lonergan, Bernard. *Insight: A Study of Human Understanding*. New York: Philosophical Library, 1958.
———. *Method in Theology*. New York: Herder and Herder, 1972.
Lynch, William F. *Images of Hope: Imagination as Healer of the Helpless*. Notre Dame: University of Notre Dame Press, 1966.
Macquarrie, John. *Christian Hope*. New York: The Seabury Press, 1978.
Minow, Martha. *Between Vengeance and Forgiveness: Facing History After Genocide and Mass Violence*. Boston: Beacon Press, 1998.
Pannenberg, Wolfhart. *Systematic Theology, Volume 3*. Grand Rapids, Michigan: William B. Eerdmans Publishing Company, 1998.
Schneiders, Sandra. *The Revelatory Text: Interpreting the New Testament as Sacred Scripture*. Collegeville, Minnesota: Liturgical Press, 1990.
Schreiter, Robert J. *The Ministry of Reconciliation: Spirituality and Strategies*. Maryknoll, New York: Orbis Books, 2004.
Thielicke, Helmut. *Nihilism: Its Origin and Nature—with a Christian Answer*. New York: Schoken Books, 1969.
Thompson, Cameron. *Philosophy and Literature: Truth/Beauty/Goodness/Commitment*. New York: Harcourt Brace Jovanovich, 1969.
Trigg, Roger. *Reason and Commitment*. London: Cambridge University Press, 1973.
Vanier, Jean. *Becoming Human*. Toronto: House of Anansi Press Limited, 1998

Subject Index

[Illustrations are indicated by italicized page numbers. The letter *n* following a page number indicates a note on that page. The number of the note on that page follows the *n*.]

A

absurdity, 31–33
    nihilism and, 12
action
    freedom and, 71–74
    love and, 73
admiration, 169–70
ambiguity of life, 6–7
    acceptance of, 25
    hope and, 15–20
    nihilism and, 10–13
    optimism and, 13–14
    pessimism and, 7–10
atomization, bureaucracy and, 48
authority, 3
    community and, 174
    fraternity and, 3, 78
    intrinsic value and, 233
availability, 168–69

B

being, 29
    dignity and, 17
    self-validation and, 30–31
    thought and, 61–62
betrayal
    communion and, 146–47
    guilt and, 147
bureaucratization, 48

C

capitulation, 25
"care paradox," 7
Cassidy, Sheila, 263
choices, selfhood and, 65–66
commitment
    belief and, 248–49
    conformism and, 243–44, 257–58
    constancy and, 241–43, 251, 257–58
    dimensions and, 246–48
    discernment and, 252–53
    ego and, 251–54
    faithfulness and, 241
    fidelity and, 236–37, 240–41, 253–54
    freedom, responsibility and, 254–57
    issue of, 235–38
    metaphysical character of, 244–51
    presence and, 250–51
    relationship and, 248
    subjects of, 239–41
    understanding of, 238–41
    values and, 238–39
communion
    betrayal and, 146–47
    compassion and, 151–53
    joy of living and, 145
    light of being and, 155
    as openness and bonding, 144–46
    otherizing and, 155–56
    possession and, 153–56
    presence and, 147–49
    transcendence and, 143–44

Subject Index

community
  accountability and, 174–75
  authority and, 174
  communion, transcendence and, 171–75
  diversity and, 172
  living tradition and, 173
  multiplicity of perspectives and, 174
conflict, humanity and, 206–7
control and domination, degradation and, 55
Creative Communication, The (Glanz), 236
crisis
  religious faith and, 161–62
  transcendence and, 159–62
  ultimate situations and, 159–60
culture, 117–18, 119
  deception and, 56
  hope and, 261
  language and, 197
  science and, 119
  social exigency and, 213
  society and, 1–2
  values and, 5

D

death
  evil and, 185–86
  finitude and, 177
  freedom and, 74–75
  functional categories and, 49
  grief and, 178–79
  intersubjectivity and, 182–83
  obsession and, 179–81
  piety and, 183–84
  technological conception of life and, 176–77
  trajectory of hope and, 176–86
deception, culture of, 56
degradation, 55

despair
  essence of, 24–25
  hope and, 24–28
  problematic world and, 57–58
detachment, existential, 95, 201
dignity, 6, 29
  being and, 17, 207
  HIV/AIDS and, 84
  moral community and, 136
  propaganda and, 56
  respect for, 2, 35, 102
disponibilité
  hope and, 23
  love and, 167, 169
divinity, 165–67
Duden, Barbara, 120–21

E

Eddy, Mary Baker, 13–14
education, 5
ego, 27, 35
  commitment and, 251–54
encounter, 34, 54
  HIV/AIDS and, 84
  language and, 193, 195
environment, 221 n.135
  degradation of, 52
  social exigency and, 217
evil
  language and, 87
  as lesion, 80, 82
  as maeutically uplifting, 91–92
  meaning and, 84–88
  as mystery, 81
  mystery of, 78–79
  personal character of, 82–84
  reconciliation and, 126
existential insecurity, 27
existentiality, 189–90
extrinsic validation, 24–25, 27, 32
  sense of self and, 88–89

F

"fetus," 120–21
fidelity, 149
  commitment and, 236–37, 240–41
  compassion and, 152
  time and, 184–85
forgiveness
  as an act of freedom, 137
  reconciliation and, 136–38
freedom
  actions and, 71–74
  attention, significance and, 66–67
  authenticity and, 67
  autonomy and, 75–77
  captivity and, 67–69
  context of, 73–74, 75
  death and, 74–75
  as forgiveness, 137
  fraternity and, 67–68
  grace and, 69–71
  liberty of being and, 74–75
  mystery of, 65–78
  openness and, 69
  sacrifice and, 70
  social embeddedness and, 77–78
functional identities, 47–48

G

gender, social exigency and, 216
Glanz, Barbara A.
  The Creative Communication, 236
God
  commitment to, 237–38
  mystery and, 63
goodness (the good), 165
grace
  belief and, 70
  freedom and, 69–71
grief, 134–35. *See also* suffering
guilt, 87, 198
  betrayal and, 83, 147
  innocence and, 147
  mercy and, 125

H

Hartmann, Eduard Von, 8
heritage
  gratitude and, 114–15
  wisdom and, 113–14
HIV/AIDS, 3, 59–60, 79–92
  anguish and, 83
  despair and, 90
  dignity and, 84
  as evil suffered, 81–82
  existential crises and, 87–88
  justice issues and, 81–82
  loneliness and, 85
  nihilism and, 86
  suffering, transcendence and, 91–92
  wakefulness and, 86
hope, 15–20
  agape and, 35
  alternative world and, 16–17
  attitudes of, 262
  awareness and, 36–37
  communion and, 33–36
  as creative advancement, 19–20
  despair and, 23, 24–28
  difficulty of, 16
  disponibilité and, 23
  energy and, 19
  fostering of, 36–39
  freedom, community and, 33–35
  heaven of, 264
  imagination and, 41
  kinship ties and, 37
  language and, 195
  love of life and, 38–39, 264
  Marcel and, 21–24
  meaningfulness and, 31–33
  as *mysterium*, 22
  mystery and, 64
  praxis of, 259–60
  priorities and, 262
  problematic life and, 18
  problematic world and, 57–58

hope *(continued)*
  as realistic response, 19, 20
  resignation and, 15–16
  salvation and, 22
  sense of wellbeing and, 31
  significance of, 39–40
  spontaneity and, 37–38
  temporality and, 261
  time and, 36
  true charity and, 28
  unconditional character of, 28–31
  visible world and, 30–31
  vision of, 259
human rights, grammar of, 135–36

I

innocence, 206
  guilt and, 147
interpretation, 118
  creativity and, 87–88
  knowledge as, 62, 87, 118
  of language, 190
  love and, 189
  mercy and, 125
  science and, 122–23
  of symbols, 193 n. 8
intersubjectivity, 21, 33–34, 208
  death and, 182–83
  despair and, 152–53
  presence and, 148–51
  progress and, 121
  spiritual economy of, 26
  values and, 53
inwardness, 30

K

King, Martin Luther, Jr., 15

L

"labor paradox," 7
language, 190–97
  care in the use of, 194

language *(continued)*
  creative spirit and, 193–95
  experience and, 191
  flexibility of, 196–97
  hope and, 195
  interpretation of, 190
  limits of, 195
  presence, openness and, 195–96
  self-sharing, 192–93
  thought and, 196
Leibniz, Gottfried, 14
lifeworld, 117–18
love
  death and, 33
  freedom and, 189
  generosity and, 3
  of life, hope and, 38–39
  oblative, 182–83

M

Mandela, Nelson, 17–18, 20, 38
Marcel, Gabriel, 20–24
mass atrocity/violence
  amnesty and, 130
  grief and, 134–35
  moral responses to, 126–31
  narrative origins of, 131–32
  retribution and, 127–28
  silence and, 129–30
  vengeance and, 132–33
mass enslavement, 57
medical care, 5–7, 47, 109–10;
  abortion and, 120–21
mercy
  interpretation and, 125
  reconciliation and, 125–26
microworlds, 97–98
  science and the lifeworld, 116–23
mystery, 43 n. 2, 58–64
  defined, 60–63
  God and, 63
  hope and, 64
  as meta-problematic, 58–60

Subject Index

mystery *(continued)*
    over problem, ascendancy of, 102–3
    presence and, 44–46, 59–60, 62–63
    the profound and, 59

N

Nature, 117
nature, nurture and, 119
neo-liberal thinking, 10
Nietzsche, Friedrich, 10–12
nihilism, 10–13
    absurdity and, 12
    disconnectedness and, 13
    futility and, 10–11
    HIV/AIDS and, 86
    meaninglessness and, 11

O

optimism, 13–14
other, the
    technical progress and, 53–54

P

Pannenberg, Wolfhart, 28 n. 31
pessimism, 7–10
    suffering and, 8–9
"poverty paradox," 7
presence, 28–30, 52–54
    charity and, 28
    communion and, 147–49
    encounter and, 34–35
    existential security and, 148
    intersubjectivity and, 148–51
    mystery and, 44–46, 59–60, 62–63
prisons, U.S., 80
privacy, problematic world and, 49–50
problem and mystery, precincts of, 43–44
problematic world, 53–54, 123

problematic world *(continued)*
    degradation, propaganda, techniques and, 55–57
    despair and, 57–58
    hope and, 57–58
    human consciousness and, 52
    individualism, egotism and, 53
    presence, significance and, 52
    primary reflection and, 94–99
    privacy and, 49–50
    techniques and, 58
problems, 43 n. 1
    definitions, 45–55
    techniques and, 46–47
productive exigency, 218
    creation and, 218–20
    material satisfaction and, 223–24
    respect and, 224–25
    sacredness of human life and, 222–23
    work and, 220–22
propaganda, 55, 172–73
    dignity and, 56
psychic exigency, 202–3
    naming and, 204–5
    power of animating and, 207–8
    self-doubt and, 209
    subjectivity and, 203
psychological exigency, 209–10
    attentiveness and, 211
    patience and, 211
    recognition and, 210
    self-definition and, 210–11
    wisdom and, 212

R

Reality, plenary, 61. *See also* social reality
reconciliation
    forgiveness and, 136–38
    mercy and, 125–26
    narrative and, 133–36
    politics, truth and, 138–40
    question of evil and, 126

Subject Index

reconciliation *(continued)*
  spirituality and, 136
reflection, primary, 116
  defined, 94–95
  microworlds and, 97–98
  relational living and, 95–96
  techniques and, 95–97
reflection, secondary, 116–17
  defined, 99–100
  recollection and, 100
  self-intimacy and, 101–2
  transformation and, 100–101
religious faith, crisis and, 161–62
restorative justice, 127–29
retribution, 127–28
Ricoeur, Paul, 23
rural conditions, 5–6

S

sapiential exigency, 125
"scarcity paradox," 7
Schweitzer, Albert, 236
science
  good will and, 107
  knowledge and, 105–10
  medicine and, 109–10
  metaphor and, 120
  ontology of, 122
  popularization of, 105–6
  precincts of, 107–10
  subjective intuition and, 108–9
  symbolism and, 108
  verification and, 109, 122
  wisdom and, 110–11
self-acceptance, 4–5
selfhood, choices and, 65–66
self-perception, 206
self-respect, 50–51
social exigency, 212
  common sense and, 214
  cultural context and, 213–14
  environment and, 217
  gender and, 216
  harmony and, 216–17

social exigency *(continued)*
  respect, affirmation and, 215–16
  rootedness and, 214–15
  social self-understanding and, 213
social reality
  love and, 3
  negative dimensions of, 4–7
  positive dimensions of, 2–4
  technology and, 3–4
society, culture and, 1–2
suffering, 79–92
  despair or hope and, 89–90
  emancipatory wisdom and, 92–94
  joy of living and, 92–93
  relationships and, 93–94
  self-centeredness and, 27–28
  sense of self and, 88–89
suffering and transcendence, 91–92
suicide, 23–24, 26, 34
symbols, 193 n. 8

T

techniques, problematic world and, 58
technology
  inner life impoverishment and, 51–52
  material conditions and, 50
  social reality and, 3–4
thinking versus *thinking of*, 201–2
time, transcending, 184–85
transcendence
  communion and, 143–44
  crisis and, 159–62
  finitude and, 157
  generosity and, 158
  God and, 165–67
  history and, 162–64
  intentionality and, 163
  love and, 164–65
  meaning of, 156–59
  reconciliation and, 158

Truth and Reconciliation
    Commission, 139

U

universe, past and, 200–201

V

values, 161
vengeance, 132–33
violence
    atrocity and, 124–25
    reconciliation, the sapiential
        exigency and, 123–40
vital exigencies, 197–99
    implications of, 227–29
    liberative morality and, 225–27
    responsibilities, rights and,
        229–33
    vulnerability and, 198
    worldly situatedness and, 199–202

W

wisdom, 103, 110–11
    authentic freedom and, 112–13
    common sense and, 112–13
    egalitarianism and, 111
    heritage and, 113–14
    positive relationships and, 113
    suffering and, 92–94
    technical development and, 97
world, problemmatic nature of,
    40–41

www.ingramcontent.com/pod-product-compliance
Lightning Source LLC
Chambersburg PA
CBHW071239230426
43668CB00011B/1512